Transitional Justice in Troubled Societies

STUDIES IN SOCIAL AND GLOBAL JUSTICE

Series Editors:
Ben Holland, Lecturer in International Relations, The University of Nottingham
Tony Burns, Associate Professor, The University of Nottingham

As transnational interactions become more prevalent and complex in our interconnected world, so do the questions of social justice that have often featured in political discourse. From new debates in human rights and global ethics to changing patterns of resistance and precarity in the global economy, via an interrogation of the impact of climate change, *Studies in Social and Global Justice* publishes books that grapple with a broad array of critical issues faced in the world today.

CENTRE FOR THE STUDY OF SOCIAL AND GLOBAL JUSTICE

Labour and Transnational Action in Times of Crisis, edited by Andreas Bieler, Roland Erne, Darragh Golden, Idar Helle, Knut Kjeldstadli, Tiago Matos and Sabina Stan
A Human Right to Culture and Identity: The Ambivalence of Group Rights, by Janne Mende
Exploitation: From Practice to Theory, edited by Monique Deveaux and Vida Panitch
Regulation Theory and Australian Capitalism, by Brett Heino
Transitional Justice in Troubled Societies, edited by Aleksandar Fatić, Klaus Bachmann and Igor Lyubashenko

Transitional Justice in Troubled Societies

Edited by
Aleksandar Fatić, Klaus Bachmann
and Igor Lyubashenko

ROWMAN &
LITTLEFIELD
INTERNATIONAL

Lanham • Boulder • New York • London

Published by Rowman & Littlefield International Ltd.
6 Tinworth Street, London SE11 5AL
www.rowmaninternational.com

Rowman & Littlefield International Ltd. is an affiliate of Rowman & Littlefield
4501 Forbes Boulevard, Suite 200, Lanham, Maryland 20706, USA
With additional offices in Boulder, New York, Toronto (Canada), and Plymouth (UK)
www.rowman.com

British Library Cataloguing in Publication Data
A catalogue record for this book is available from the British Library

ISBN: HB 978-1-78660-588-7

Library of Congress Cataloging-in-Publication Data Available

ISBN: 978-1-78660-588-7 (cloth)
ISBN: 978-1-78660-589-4 (paper)
ISBN: 978-1-78660-590-0 (electronic)

Contents

Introduction

Transitional Justice as Conflict-Resolution

Aleksandar Fatić

The title of this book is *Transitional Justice in Troubled Societies*. One might wonder whether the title is an oxymoron, given that transitional justice is often understood as pertaining, by definition, to difficult and challenging societies. Our view here is different. Transitional justice exists even in the most stable and traditional societies, which do not appear to be undergoing any kind of political, social or value 'transition.' Rather than being some sort of partial, extraordinary, intervening form of justice in irregular social circumstances, as it is sometimes made out to be, transitional justice is a form of justice per se. It is a type of justice which relates the abstract goals of justice (the achievement of proportionality between crime and punishment, the satisfaction of moral intuitions, or expressing a society's attitude to certain values and types of behaviour, for example) to other social ends. Thus it is a sobering type of justice, which tells us something about justice in general, primarily that justice always serves other social goals. On an institutional level, it is always instrumental to something else, and thus also, necessarily, prejudiced by broader social and political considerations. In other words, transitional justice indicates the political nature of justice in general.

This view, which the editors of this volume have espoused in several places so far, may seem unpalatable at first, especially to those who have become accustomed to thinking about justice as a set of values or standards that rule society and thus, in a sense, 'emanate down' to institutions and the political system. This essentialist view of justice is traditional and is built into our thinking that political orders may be more or less just, that dictators ought to be ousted if they rule unjustly, or that penal policies are subject to the requirements of the moral law as their ultimate foundation and testing ground. Indeed, all of these considerations apply to institutional justice, but only because such justice is a political construct, and not because it is an

1

emanation of abstract, pure justice, which is supposed to rule them. This means that political considerations are not as immoral as we are used to thinking of them: they arise from deeply held moral reasons and a difficult, often unpredictable, balancing of various utilitarian, deontic, virtue- and other types of ethics which various stake holders adopt. Political judgements are based on human thought, and human thought is morally laden just as it is subject to emotional and interest-driven views. Justice is thus a construct of the political process, and the way in which this process is governed depends on a complex interplay of the various values which cause social leaders, including the policy makers, to make their decisions.

We have chosen to provide a forum in this book for the discussion of transitional justice in troubled societies not because such justice is specific to such societies, but because troubled societies make the general features of transitional justice more obvious and easier to convey. The same principles of transitional justice apply to war crimes trials at the Hague and to land ownership issues in Zimbabwe, just as they do to the transformations of criminal law in European countries, where, in many jurisdictions, money laundering is now treated as a more serious crime than the very crimes by which the criminal profits were generated in the first place. All of the decisions and changes in institutional justice are dictated by broader social policy. However this does not usually agree with the dominant rhetoric of the institutions of justice and their leaders. Only too often we hear that justice should be 'blind' to who is before it. Justice is never blind; in fact, we would contend that a blind justice is the worst possible form of justice: justice always considers one's position in society, their relative value to the others and the relationship between the person's actions and the prevailing social values. The personhood, or the subjectivity of those who are judged, is as important as the deeds which are being judged. This is the nature of justice in general, and the instrumental dimension of it is the most obvious in transitional justice.

While all the chapters in this book address the various aspects of transitional justice in a postconflict transitional context, they assume, to various extents, that in addition to, or even as opposed to, implementing transitional criminal justice, transitional justice serves the crucial goal of conflict resolution. This extended introduction therefore discusses this underlying thread of the book in some detail.

If indeed transitional justice is instrumental to achieving the goals of political transition, then one of its important dimensions ought to be its ability to act as a conflict-resolution mechanism in its own right. The troubles of political transition manifest themselves as multiple conflicts that often spread deep into society. Conflicts usually, and unpredictably, emerge where they were not expected. The setting in motion of a transition may start a conflict with neighbours, disenchanted constituents, or groups and interests whose power and influence in society is likely to be adversely affected by any particular type of political transition. Thus the feasibility of the transition, and one of the main tasks of transitional justice, ought to be to stabilise social conditions, reduce conflicts and stimulate greater cooperation and collective action. If successful, such a role of transitional justice can both accelerate and strengthen the political process of transition itself, and at the same time minimise the cleavages which the process naturally creates within parts of society.

Transitional justice's conflict-resolution potential depends on how frankly and skilfully its fundamentally political characteristics and facets are accepted and handled. The exercise of this potential within transitional justice processes requires leadership just as it does in politics, and *leadership consists of specific skills and attitudes that make the management of complex processes well structured, relatively predictable and endows them with a relatively broad consensus of the parties concerned.*

In this introduction I propose to make some general observations on conflict in society and comment on the most effective ways to resolve conflict, in their relevance to transitional justice. I particularly focus on the *skills and training* required within the transitional justice *system* to identify the relevant conflicts, understand and interpret their internal dynamics and key structural elements, and address them in the way which is most likely to reduce tensions and lead to an optimally successful resolution. There is vast literature on conflict resolution, ranging at least from the work of John Burton to the more recent research by Johan Galtung and his associates (Burton, 1990; Galtung, 1958). In this introduction, I do not propose to elaborate all the theories of conflict resolution, or even all of the generic concepts employed to interpret conflict, in any great detail. Rather, I approach the topic more modestly, with the intent to merely generalise and use the key concepts and interpretations as complementary, eclectic means to show why leadership skills are largely the same as conflict-resolution skills, and why they are so crucial to successful transitional justice. My work here is thus more an essay than a stringent scholarly chapter, for two main reasons: it is easier to read, and the essay form allows for greater flexibility and experimentation, without having to devote space to arguing the technical details of every idea. Such experimentation is necessary within topics which in themselves are largely experimental at present stage. Although transitional justice is well supported by academic literature, from its very conceptualisation to its particular practical dimensions it remains a highly experimental and innovative theme in social science and social practise alike. As in many other areas of social endeavour, making any serious inroads in the theme probably requires a good deal of risk, and the more liberal form of writing is arguably more suited to such conceptual risk-taking.

LEADERSHIP IN TRANSITION

No structured political transition would be able even to commence without deliberate and motivated leadership. The mission, goals, calculations of costs and benefits, strategy and logistics of any political transition are exceptionally complex, require planning and personal resources, as well as considerable leadership skills of those who lead the transition. One of the first illusions that we must rid ourselves of when interpreting transition is that there are 'spontaneous' transitions or social changes. One or more people may be spontaneously unhappy about the state of their lives or their society, and they even may spontaneously demand something different. However, to pursue a transition, a coherent, qualified group of people must work out a clear *plan* and persuade a large number of others to *follow that plan*. Transition is a political project which, if left to the devices of a few who are spontaneously motivated to protest against the existing social and political arrangements or demand a different kind of society, invariably collapses very quickly, and sometimes with dramatic consequences for those who engage in it 'spontaneously.' Thus the political changes in the Arab countries early in the twenty-first century, which have come to be known as the 'Arab Spring,' were only somewhat cynically described as 'happenings of the people.' The phrase suggested that large crowds had amassed in the squares of Tunis, Cairo, Alexandria or Tripoli through Facebook initiatives or based on information spread around on Twitter. In fact, the fate of the transition processes was decided, in each individual case, on the basis of the geopolitical visions and foreign policy trade-offs. Egypt is a very good example of this. The non-aligned, long-standing Hosney Mubarak government was toppled through popular revolt and, initially, an Islamic regime was installed, led by the Muslim Brotherhood. However, soon the elected president was again toppled through a military coup, the Muslim Brotherhood outlawed, and its leader, elected president, sentenced to death. The military rule ended with the election of the leader of the coup, an army general, to the country's civilian presidency, and Egypt entered a period of stability again. The foreign policy orientation of the new government is pro-Western. The values of that government were not what had motivated the revolt and onset of the transition, however the transition could not end without the values acceptable to the western powers being instituted through an appropriate government structure, so the revolution was repeated until that outcome was eventually reached. That is how most transitions in 'troubled regions' tend to unfold.

The Muslim Brotherhood had been no less skilful in organising the initial revolt than the military and the western powers were in setting in motion a second phase of the revolution and the beseating of the Muslim Brotherhood.

Both political projects, comprised in one process of political transition, required effective and sophisticated leadership in order to have hundreds of thousands of people gather in the same place and demand the same thing in a coordinated and highly publicly articulate way. That is simply not the way in which masses spontaneously act. A complex set of preparations is required for such a public performance: this includes secure communications, control of parts of the media, supply of banners, food, drink, entertainment, speakers, crowd security, and most importantly, charismatic leadership to keep the protesters together, motivated and in sync with all of the other protesters in mood, reactions and perceptions. Only a coordinated, well-led mass can become a politically forceful factor, rather than an amorphous, divergent group which is easily dispersed by police or military action. Political change may not always involve a violent revolution, but it always involves mass movements, planning and precise execution; specific *training* is required for all of these things.

Once a political transition is set in motion, it produces its own social world: those involved in it must be informed, provided with appropriate interpretations of events and allowed to create their own sense of orientation in what goes on. They must be enthused for the cause, controlled in order to stay the course and retain a sense of purpose and meaning throughout their political activism. In other words, they must be led. Transitional justice regulates the leadership of political transition, and at the same time aids it by removing stumbling blocks to the process between those who are led. It is capable of influencing the political agenda of transition (e.g., by targeting and removing nationalist or discriminatory elements, such as the religiously thick political agenda of the Muslim Brotherhood in Egypt). In addition, transitional justice is capable of removing leaders who do not fit in an acceptable agenda (such as the leader of Muslim Brotherhood and elected Egyptian president, Mohammed Morsi). Finally, once an acceptable political agenda of the transition is set and acceptable leaders are in place, the transitional justice process is able to assist them in executing the process of transition by removing 'bumps on the road': uncooperative local leaders, dissenting intellectuals or popular groups, pockets of armed or political resistance and so on. Morsi was not simply removed; he was sentenced to death. Hosni Mubarak, his predecessor, had been tried for various 'crimes against the people.' Saddam Hussein in Iraq was not simply beseated; he was hanged. In Libya, Colonel Gadhafi was shot dead without a trial. In postcommunist Romania, Nicolae Ceausescu and his wife Elena were arrested, 'sentenced' to death by a kangaroo court, and summarily executed within less than an hour of the 'trial,' in which they had not been allowed to speak, present any evidence, did not have a real defence attorney, or right of appeal (see Catalin Constantinescu's chapter in this volume). All of the leaders were capable of presenting serious

Aleksandar Fatić

challenges to the smooth unfolding of the transition; therefore they were removed in the most drastic ways, within what is considered 'transitional justice' processes.

One of the main problems with transitional justice is that, just as it can be draconian in its measures intended to eliminate potentially obstructive leaders, as in the previously mentioned cases, it can also be less than proportional in the punishments that it metes out on more ordinary suspects. As the overall aim of transitional justice is to alleviate conflicts associated with transition, both old and new (any process of social change mends some and creates new conflicts), its repressive arm must be tempered by forward-looking considerations. It is not about 'giving people their dues' for their past wrongs; it is never a purely deontic justice, which seeks to establish a reciprocity between the gravity of the offence and the severity of the punishment. The reason for this is simple. If the 'dues' seen as being deserved by a particular person are exceptionally heavy, and especially if there are many such individuals from the same community, then giving all of them their 'dues' in the court might so antagonise the entire community that many of the broader aims of transition could be jeopardised. In particular, the passing of severe punishments on members of one and the same group, or predominantly on one group, may push the groups formerly in conflict further apart and create conditions for a renewal of the conflict. Furthermore, such deontic justice, if it were adopted by transitional courts and other transitional justice mechanisms, might undermine trust between the postconflict communities and the international institutions which typically help administer transitional justice. This is the case in Bosnia today: the heavy-handed international intervention after the 1991–1995 civil war, including the meandering policy by the International Criminal Tribunal for the Former Yugoslavia (ICTY), which, until the very closure of the tribunal, vacillated between a rhetoric of basically deontic justice and exceptionally pragmatic indictments policy. For example, ICTY did not bring forward any indictments against top Croatian and Bosnian wartime political leaders, and it quite pragmatically acquitted (in the first instance) the wartime Serbian secret police head, Jovica Stanišić and the commander of the Serbian state security turned paramilitary units, Franko Simatović (who, bizarrely, happens to be a Croat). Both accused are now being retried, the acquittal having been quashed on appeal. ICTY has been involved in what could be considered pioneering work for modern transitional justice in Europe; in this relatively uncharted territory, it occasionally wandered around, taking contradictory and confusing directions in its judicial policy. As a partial result of that, as well as the other, equally confusing aspects of the transitional intervention in Bosnia (Office of the High Representative's confusing moves with regard to the status and composition of the armed forces, etc.), the level of trust between the postconflict communities on the one hand, and the international administration of transitional justice, on the other, is extremely low. The reason that Bosnia-Herzegovina today is on the verge of state disintegration, almost at the same level as immediately before the onset of the civil war in 1991, is the poor policy planning of the transitional intervention, including transitional justice. One does not need much empirical data to specifically support this claim other than taking account of the chronology of events. The war ended in 1995, and in 2018, after twenty-three years of continuous international transitional intervention, including the twenty-two years of operation of ICTY, the level of trust between the communities remains defeatingly low (I say more about Bosnia-Herzegovina later on in this introduction).

It is at least doubtful whether the task of transitional justice can possibly be to fulfil metaphysical precepts of a criminal desert meeting its due punishment. This is certainly possible where such a policy coincides with broader considerations, such as the desired shared sentiments and reactions by the relevant communities, in other words, where the seeming 'due deserts' policy coincides with utilitarian policy considerations and is likely to contribute to the achievement of other, nonjustice-related goals of transitional justice. The more uncontroversial goal of transitional justice is to help along the processes of reconciliation and social healing. In doing so, it often must take care not to offend the moral intuitions of most victims (or of those who see themselves as victims) on the one hand, and at the same time not generate too much fear and resentment in the communities of those who are penalised on the other. Transitional justice is a *balancing act*, which takes into account moral principles, social values, the goals of social change and the interests, perceptions and potential future actions of various parts of society: it is an exercise in leadership which seeks to provide sufficient peace and sense of justice to most, while at the same time leaving enough hope for those who are at the receiving end of justice for them to eventually accept change. The aims of transitional justice are thus much more complex and demanding than the aims of an ordinary system of one country's and one society's system of criminal justice. Thus the types of leadership required in transitional justice and in any national system of justice tend to be different: in the former, what is required is essentially political and policy leadership, with a very broad perspective of the aims of peace and reconciliation; in the latter, leadership is confined to sufficient professionalism and ability to run the system legally and efficiently. The former type of leader may or may not be able to serve in the latter type of institutions; however, the latter type of leader, without the additional qualities of policy vision and political sensibility, would almost certainly not be suited to transitional justice institutions. Transitional criminal justice mechanisms depend on various political actors internationally, and transitional criminal courts in particular are not merely criminal courts: they are also, inevitably, political institutions (Bachmann and Fatić, 2014).

Unlike ordinary institutional systems of justice, transitional justice institutions and mechanisms balance various cultural and political concerns emanating from more than just one country and one society. Most transitional processes concern regions and not single countries, and most transitional justice institutions have a mandate which covers the actions of agents from more than one country, even if they are tasked with dealing with events in a single country. Thus the *diplomatic* aspects of transitional justice are pronounced. For example, to be effective, international criminal courts must have workable relations with specific countries' governments, militaries and international decision-making bodies. To secure such cooperation, they must know the ropes of diplomacy. However, diplomacy requires adjustments in all aspects of the work of such courts, including those considered particularly sensitive from a 'strictly legal' point of view: indictments and sentencing policies are the most obvious examples. One cannot indict people on whom one depends to have the accused arrested and transferred, or whose political superiors must continue to fund and politically support one's tribunal. These are obvious and unavoidable realities of operating an international tribunal. At the same time, this is the answer to the often asked questions of the type why a particular tribunal has not indicted military and political leaders of the major powers which support the tribunal. It is a simple answer. In each case, the tribunal did not indict such a person (provided there was real legal reason to indict them) because it could not. Does this automatically mean that this particular tribunal is fundamentally illegitimate and worthless? I don't think so. Justice is always selective, and a circumspect, careful, though selective, transitional justice may be the best one can hope for given the circumstances in which transitional justice operates.

The decisions made by transitional justice instruments, including the tribunals, must satisfy two basic criteria: (1) they must not offend the public sense of morality, and (2) they must not alienate those without whose assistance the tribunal could no longer operate or be effective. This balancing act is basically the same as those required in any kind of high-level leadership: leaders must balance the interests of their organisations (they cannot let their organisations be existentially threatened through their choices) with the integrity and general interest associated with the missions of these organisations. In companies, leaders must fulfil duties to the public and to society, including the socially responsible conduct of business and provision of honest and beneficial services and goods to the customers; however, at the same time, they must do all of these things in a way which preserves the profits of their companies. The various requirements on the leaders' performance are often mutually contradictory, thus the need for leadership skills to balance the right concerns in the right way and take responsibility for such choices. Leading a transitional justice institution is the same: the interests of the institution are balanced against the integrity and vigour in its pursuit of its public mission: to institute an optimum of justice and contribute to the transition process. There is a price to be paid for the balancing act, just as there is a price to be paid for a balanced approach to most human relationships. Institutional justice is no different: it is not a metaphysical or mathematical process devoid of human concerns and practical exigencies. Once we accept the fact that judicial work is fundamentally a social process which takes place in accord with and under the influence of social policy, and that this is even more the case with transitional justice and in particular with the transitional judiciary, it becomes more conceivable to us that diplomatic and political skills are required for running a transition as a political process, and for running the institutions of transitional justice as an element of that process.

VALUES AND CONFLICTS

A starting point in the interpretation of conflict is the realisation that particularly hard or important conflicts are always over the same values that help shape our sense of selves. Our emotions are elicited by our more or less important values being either affirmed, or militated against by particular people or particular situations. If a value we deem highly important is affirmed by our interlocutor and by the treatment we receive from others, this will result in pleasant feelings. If, on the other hand, an important value is threatened, this will elicit very unpleasant feelings. Once the values which we deem vital to our survival or our identity are seriously threatened, we become immersed in a conflict. To show who we are, and to reinforce our sense of self in the face of the opposite values or experiences, we may be prepared to go to quite dramatic lengths. This is the general psychological meaning of the common phrase that we need our enemies in order to know who we are: often members of the same community, who otherwise constantly fight and argue, are suddenly drawn together by the presence of a common enemy. The enemy makes their commonalities, their shared identity, surge to the surface. They start feeling that they are the same 'sort of people,' 'nation' or whatever binds them together and they mobilise to protect themselves and each other. The more important the values one defends, the more extreme one's actions will tend to be. One's having to protect one's house usually makes one prepared to take more extreme steps than if one is defending one's company against a hostile takeover by another; one's defending the safety of one's child, however, will lead one to adopt strategies which in their reach are likely to far surpass those one adopts in defending one's home. Similarly, the more important one's values which others respect and acknowledge, the greater one's willingness to collaborate with others is likely to be. We make friends with people who share or at least respect our important values and who we are; alternatively we feel unpleasant in the presence of those who disparage or openly threaten our important values and sense of self; we try to avoid them, and when we cannot, we enter into open conflict with them. The conflict, just like the friendship, serves to affirm and reinforce our values and sense of identity. This applies to individuals as well as to groups ranging from two friends to entire nations. It is the basic motivational dynamics of conflict and of collaboration alike. Our values and the attitudes others take to our values are the deciding factors in human relationships.

The dynamics of conflict are logically connected to the various strategies to engage in conflict. One way of approaching conflict is increasing the stakes for the antagonised party to lose even more important values if it does not yield. This is a strategy based on intimidation: rather than entering into any kind of discussion over the contested values, it tells the opponent that they will essentially perish if they persist in the conflict. The focus of the intimidation strategy is on the person of the opponent, rather than on the issue or value at stake. The point of the strategy is not to win the issue, but to force the opponent to withdraw from discussing the issue lest she is destroyed. Such are the policies of great powers in the global arena. The most powerful countries do not pacify their antagonists. While they may conduct secret diplomacy and reassure the opponents that their vital values will ultimately be preserved if they yield, publicly they demonstrate their ability to inflict the ultimate damage. A superpower does not compromise with a small antagonist over an arms proliferation, territorial or any other contested issue: it introduces trade sanctions and threatens military action and diplomatic isolation instead. The strategy of intimidation shifts the focus of the conflict from its substance to its actors: it is not important here who is right and who is wrong, but merely who is who. A small country cannot win a key international issue against a superpower; it can only risk its own economic and political degradation, all the way to potential physical destruction. This strategy of approaching conflict in the international arena leads small or medium-sized countries who are determined to resist the global trends to attempt to nuclearise their military (Iran and especially North Korea are good examples in the twenty-first century). The idea behind the nuclearisation policies is that unless one has 'the bomb,' one can never have serious independence in ones policies, even in one's internal affairs.

A good recent example was the confrontation between the United States and North Korea during 2017 over the latter's advancement of its nuclear arms programme and the Korean firing of missiles capable of carrying nuclear warheads. The crisis reached a high point in August 2017 when Kim

Jong-un, the North Korean leader, announced that his country had developed a strategic missile capable of striking the US mainland and announced, in the way of demonstration, that he would fire, during August 2017, a ballistic missile which would fly all the way from North Korea to the American strategic outpost in the island of Guam, in the Pacific, and 'fall in the ocean some 30 kilometres from Guam.' The challenge was meant to send a clear message that North Korea wanted to be considered a nuclear power, with all the prerogatives this brings in the modern geostrategic world, including both the respect of her military capability and, it is to be assumed, the gradual easing and eventual lifting of the long-standing international sanctions against her. The escalation in the nuclear and missile testing during 2016 and 2017 in North Korea was also partly connected with the constant pressure that the United States had been putting on the country for years by holding annual large-scale military exercises with North Korea's antagonist and American ally, South Korea. The threat seemed very real for some weeks and caused disputes over the rhetoric used by American President Donald Trump who, at one stage, promised to visit 'fire and fury' upon North Korea if she decided to fire any kind of missile, armed or unarmed, towards Guam or 'any US allies' (*LA Times*, 2017). This statement was flouted in the public for days as an example of poor statesmanship and a dangerous rhetoric that could do more harm than good.

A nuclear conflict between the United States and North Korea would have devastating consequences for South Korea and Japan, and the immediate nuclear fallout and refugee influx, across the borders, into China and Russia (both major nuclear powers) would destabilise relations between the world's leading powers. Such a conflict could have happened not only by intent, but also by accident and misinterpretation of the words or actions of the other side. English is not the native language of the North Korean leader, and words such as 'fire and fury' may not be easy to correctly understand in the midst of an escalating relationship with a traditional arch-enemy. Despite all of these elements of danger, the United States did not seek to address the values of the North Korean leadership that stood behind their part in the conflict. Doing so would be a constructive and rational way to approach conflict resolution. However, to maintain its status as a superpower, the United States had to use a different strategy: it decided to send a message to Pyongyang that, whatever the values which made North Korea threaten the United States with nuclear missiles, the United States was determined to inflict the ultimate damage on North Korea should it persist with the conflict. In other words, the strategy of conflict resolution was not based on identifying the threatened values and reassuring the other side that they would in fact be preserved. Instead, it was showing disregard for whatever values might have caused the conflict to escalate, and threatening even more vital values of the adversary, namely the very existence of the North Korean nation.

American officials intermittently sent mixed bellicose and conciliatory messages. On the one hand, they said that North Korea risked the 'annihilation of its entire people' (which was a direct threat with nuclear holocaust). On the other hand, other American officials publicly played down the gravity of the situation and declared that they saw 'no imminent threat of conflict.' Eventually, Kim Jong-un backed down on 15 August 2017, issuing a statement that he would 'delay the firing of the missiles towards Guam and watch the foolish actions by the Yankees for a while longer.' The insulting rhetoric was there to help save the face of the Pyongyang regime, however the backing down was real: the strategy used by great powers is effective because it is supported by a *real capacity* to inflict the ultimate damage on the opponent without suffering the same themselves. In the case of a nuclear war, the United States would likely be able to destroy the North Korean missiles at launch phase (in North Korea, or on its vessels in the sea), halfway through their flight, or close to their destination. The likelihood of any North Korean missiles actually hitting the US mainland would be very low. On the other hand, it is virtually certain that almost all US nuclear missiles fired at North Korea would hit their target, because North Korea does not have the technology to intercept high-speed missiles in mid-flight. With such overwhelming superiority of one side in the conflict, intimidation is an effective way of ending conflicts, at least temporarily.

One of the problems with this approach to resolving conflicts is that most of us individual people, and most countries, too, do not have the strength of the great powers. Most of us in our human relationships, and most countries in their international relations, do not have an actual capacity to inflict the ultimate damage on their opponents without suffering the same fate. The mutual differences in power between most sides in most conflicts are not as dramatic as between the great powers and small countries. In most ordinary conflicts, including most relatively low-level civil conflicts or regional crises, parties are capable of inflicting considerable (but not the ultimate) damage on one another, they share similar values, similar concerns over identity and the long-term sustainability of their communities. These are the most common conflicts that call for transitional justice, including the international adjudication of crimes. In such situations, the approach of threatening the most vital values in the opponent is a suicidal strategy. A different and more moderate approach is required to diffuse and eventually resolve conflicts. This approach must draw on leadership skills and must consider the values of the opposing side which make the opponent ready to fight. To prevent or win a confrontation without serious fallout, the *identification and handling* of the opponent's values must be accurate and effective.

All behaviour is driven by values, and so is all conflict. Thus, conflict-resolution must be driven by the recognition and acknowledgement of values. When this principle is applied to transitional justice, it becomes clear that justice is inevitably a matter of perspective: it is shaped by the values of those who judge and by those who are judged. The two perspectives are frequently different, even mutually incompatible, but unlike in standard criminal justice, where it is the perspective of society and institutions that counts the most (more than the perspective of the accused), in transitional justice *both perspectives* are roughly *equally important*.

Most suspects indicted for war crimes at ICTY, for example, have been middle-aged men with no criminal record, many considered upstanding, law-abiding members of their respective communities. During the civil wars in the former Yugoslavia, they had played various leadership roles in the military and civilian establishments of their ethnic groups. Few had any history of violence, and many refused to even identify with the crimes committed under their formal leadership, because they saw those crimes simply as 'by-products' of the war which no sane person could condone. They themselves had assumed a psychological distance to the crimes committed by their subordinates; this puts them apart from ordinary criminals. It should be noted that in civil wars, especially ones like the one in the former Yugoslavia, formal subordination often meant very little in terms of real power and ability to control the forces on the ground. Most civilian local government figures, by the mere declaration of war, automatically assumed military or paramilitary 'commanding' roles: these people, local mayors, for example, usually knew little about the military and had no real authority to command forces on the ground. Many were formally responsible for actions that they personally considered unacceptable, but had no real way of preventing. Their perspective, and that of their respective ethnic group, is thus very different from the perspective of the outside observers, prosecutors or the media. This does not necessarily make them innocent of the crimes, but it makes any reconciliation impossible if their perspective is not acknowledged and taken into account in the legal process. For transitional justice to effect reconciliation it is equally important whether the victim community sees someone as guilty of a crime and whether the community of the accused sees the accused as guilty. Ideally, some kind of a negotiated agreement should be reached on this. The perpetrator of murder in ordinary circumstances generally knows that she is guilty, though she may consider herself a victim of circumstance; the same is the case with the direct perpetrator of a mass execution in civil war. However, a local mayor in whose municipality a war crime occurred may not see himself as guilty, nor may his constituents, if he knows that, realistically, he had no viable options to influence the events, even though he was formally 'in charge.' It is important for transitional justice to understand this. During the wars in the former Yugoslavia, the infamous criminal Željko Ražnatović, known as Arkan, routinely committed murders in parts of the country that had still a semblance of law and order and were now directly engulfed in warfare. He and his gang were able to kill, rob and intimidate virtually anyone under the protection of the former Serbian government under Slobodan Milošević and his family. Subsequently the same criminals formed their own military units (a group of thugs who preposterously named themselves 'the Tigers'). Under the direct protection of Serbian Security Service (headed by Jovica Stanišić), they ventured into Bosnia and Croatia to incite bloodshed, intimidate local people into joining the local 'territorial defence units,' and then steal and plunder with no control. The notion that a local Bosnian mayor who found himself 'in charge' of such a territorial defence unit, created overnight and sent, for example, to burn a Muslim village and kill the inhabitants, could really do anything to prevent the crime is totally unrealistic. In most cases, the only outcome of such interference would be a dead mayor and, most likely, his entire family. The same applied to Bosnian Serb and Croatian Serb military officers. The situation was likely very similar on the Croat and Muslim sides in the conflict. In civil war, hierarchic responsibility has a very different reach and meaning than in ordinary wars, with well-organised militaries and clear chains of command. Thus penalising a local politician for war crimes, where the community knows that this person was an exemplary community member who intimately deplored the war and the bloodshed it brought, but had to cooperate at the time, is likely to stifle reconciliation. It is also doubtful whether such penalisation is even in line with moral justice, by any feasible standards.

In an ethnic conflict, many people become entangled in it completely independently of their will. There are communal pressures to join the fighting forces, voluntarily or de facto by force. Once in the army, an individual has very little choice in taking or not taking part in virtually everything that army does: if the unit burns a village, or murders villagers, or shells a city, or holds civilians prisoner, even executes some of them, the individual has no real, feasible choice but to take part in all of this and do what she is told to do. The alternative is heroic and realistically accessible only for very few people: sacrificing one's own life and, sometimes, the lives, or at least the livelihoods, of one's family and friends. Ethnic groups at war with each other are neither understanding, nor tolerant of disobedience or different opinion, especially by men in uniform in the midst of what they see as the ultimate battle for the survival of their communities. Thus the judgement of one's actions in civil war after the heat of battle has passed, in calm and rational legal procedures, in value terms, is a process very removed from the realities of the circumstances in which the crimes were committed.

Most perpetrators in civil war were pressured to commit crimes; they had no real criminal intent, and had demonstrated this by their prior lives; it was primarily the circumstances, the peer pressure and the threat to their own security that had driven them to tacitly, or even explicitly, agree to the commission of crimes or to participate in them through their own action or inaction.

It is difficult, of course, to take an unequivocal view on this matter. From the perspective of a community whose children were mercilessly butchered by the militias, the mayor represents that militia and bears the responsibility for the blood of the innocent. It is very hard for an international tribunal to acquit her; such actions would most likely increase the hostility and detract from the prospect of reconciliation between the two communities. However, judging the mayor too harshly, even regardless of the traditional legal considerations such as a prior criminal record, is likely to send the wrong message to the community of the perpetrators. The perpetrator community rarely really see themselves as having freely chosen to commit the crimes of which they stand accused. This is where the difference between transitional trials and standard criminal justice comes to the fore. In the latter context, whether the perpetrator sees herself as responsible or not is almost irrelevant, as long as certain legally established 'objective' and 'subjective' criteria of culpability are established (*mens rea*, or 'guilty mind,' as defined by the criminal law). The reason for this is that the goal of standard criminal justice is general prevention and the institution of a sense of responsibility for crimes: seeing someone being punished should (it is mistakenly assumed) cause other potential perpetrators to think twice. However, in transitional justice there is an additional goal, and that is reconciliation and collaboration within a transitional process; for this reason the perspective of the perpetrator community cannot be so easily bracketed out of the legal process. There is a higher standard of realistic judgement that transitional justice is held to than standard criminal justice.

Reconciliation is intimately connected with forgiveness, and forgiveness is possible only where another's motives are understood. Ideally the victim community may understand that many perpetrators of crimes against their loved ones had no criminal intent to commit the crimes and were led by inertia, cowardice or pressure of circumstances. This may not make the perpetrator innocent in the eyes of the victim community, but it may make her less guilty. In civil wars, which are often driven by a 'hatred of small differences,' the local communities tend to share very similar values. Serbs, Croats and Muslims of the former Yugoslavia are so similar in their values, lifestyles, habits and language that for an uninitiated outsider it is virtually impossible to distinguish who belongs to which community, either by their language or by their way of life. Surely there is potential in such small differences for greater mutual understanding and reconciliation if adequate communication is facilitated through transitional justice.

The role of transitional justice is not only to present the communities with the value perspective of another, but also to encourage the making of *practical gestures* and introduction of local policies that aim to facilitate the actual reconciliation processes. Such gestures involve the explicit *recognition* of the values and *grievances* of one community by members of the other. Again, traditional criminal law recognises similar gestures: if an accused who has caused someone's death, say by reckless driving, shows concern, visits the victim's relatives, offers compensation, and shows a willingness to endure the discomfort and reprimand that accompany such visits, they are often judged less harshly in the court itself, especially if they don't have a prior criminal history. The very criminal sentencing routinely involves a judge's invocation of the convicted person's 'remorse' or 'remorselessness' during the proceedings.

In war crime trials the situation is more difficult, for several reasons. First, the perpetrators are physically more removed from the victim community. They are entrenched in their own, antagonistic community. In such circumstances it is neither easy, nor particularly popular with one's own peers to go to the other community and express remorse. Second, most suspects of war crimes are immediately arrested. Third, the reactions by the victims' communities are often extremely violent; thus any reconciliatory gestures must be well prepared and, often, moderated by a third party. Such 'face-ups' between the perpetrators and the victims, with the perpetrators' expression of a sense of guilt for what had happened, are at the very heart of South Africa's 'truth commissions.' The truth commissions are not 'objective,' sterile legal mechanisms geared to establishing responsibility. What is at stake in truth commissions is not just an admission of responsibility; it is the expression of a subjectively felt guilt, which helps the victim community achieve closure. The truth commissions have been highly effective in advancing interracial reconciliation after the apartheid. The tribal tradition of alternative dispute resolution is rich in Africa and is often used by modern African societies to solve contemporary conflicts. For example, during the 2015–2016 conflict at South Africa's universities (with a focus in the Johannesburg-based University of the Witstwatersrand) over access to education for the poor (and the wealth divide in South Africa largely coincides with race, with poverty being heavily concentrated among the black people), university management resorted to tribal reconciliation procedures with students when using the police and the courts proved futile (*The Guardian*, 2016a). The two student movements, 'Fees must fall' and 'Rhodes must fall,' the latter referring to the statue of Cecil Rhodes at the University of Cape Town, challenged the level of fees payable at South African universities, which were unattainable for poor black families, and the alleged persistently colonial profile of university management and administration. Cecil Rhodes was one of the key figures of British colonialism in South Africa, who had called for the creation of a secret society which would promote British colonial interests (*The Guardian*, 2016b). The protests turned violent in parts of Johannesburg, with the universities closing for a part of the academic year, a massive police and security forces involvement, clashes with students and a high level of social anxiety in various South African communities.

It is interesting that in South Africa today the official policy is one of reverse discrimination: the government favours black South Africans in employment policy and through various social policies; however the aftershocks of the apartheid era continue to manifest themselves through low-level interracial conflicts, such as those over education. It is, of course, doubtful whether reverse discrimination is either morally or practically desirable with a view of reconciliation and prosperity: any kind of discrimination reduces the efficiency of transactions in society. Appointing someone to a government position because of the colour of their skin, whether it is white or black, is not economically efficient (*Mail&Guardian*, 2016). In addition, any type of discrimination may engender resentment in the side that is discriminated against (this is the case among many whites in South Africa today, who exclaim: 'We are South Africans, too') (*BBC*, 2013). Finally, such discrimination may induce a triumphalist sense of domination in the community which discriminates against the other: there is already a highly exclusionary atmosphere in parts of Africa where 'being African' is perceived as being black (Roets, 2017). This is a very similar view to that of European nationalism, and we know something about the potential consequences of collective arrogance arising from that nationalism. There is thus every reason to be reserved about the newly arising sense of 'Africanism,' which is far more sinister that traditional Pan-Africanism (Henry, 1959). This phenomenon is a sign that something is likely wrong with the African transitions, and the manifestations of such problems show themselves in various areas (election fraud in Kenya in 2017, the individual African countries' withdrawal from the International Criminal Court, etc.) (*BBC*, 2017; *The Economist*, 2017). There is a tangible absence of transitional justice in Africa, and this may be the cause of questionable transitions in a number of African countries. This is the case despite the rich local tradition of alternative dispute resolution. That tradition cannot be put to effective use because of a lack of highly skilled leadership focused on values, rather than on identity politics, which prevails in most of the continent, including its most economically developed country, South Africa.

RESTORATIVE JUSTICE

Conflict resolution is closely associated with the so-called restorative justice. Unlike standard justice, which seeks to establish and expressively emphasise a relationship between *the offence and the treatment* the offender receives, restorative justice is forward-looking. It is based on the idea that an underlying relationship between the *offender and society*, or *the offender and the victim* of the offence, ought to be 'restored.' The aim of the treatment the offender receives in the justice process is thus instrumental to reconciliation and conflict resolution between the offender (or the offender's community) and the victim, victim's community and society at large. Restorative justice is thus methodologically very different from any kind of punitive justice, whether it is retributive or utilitarian. This is its most important distinctive feature. It would be mistaken to assume that restorative justice would always be less restrictive on the offender than punitive justice; however it ought to be assumed that in its intent and the manner of treatment of the offender it will not be punitive: it will not deliberately seek to inflict pain on the offender; quite the contrary. While long-term detention is consistent with restorative justice (in particularly unforgiving communities), such detention must never be deliberately depriving or degrading: it ought to resemble normal living circumstances for the detainees as much as practically possible. There is no assumption in restorative justice that the offender is being 'punished' for something: detention is there merely to facilitate the simmering down of the tensions in society and allow the offender an eventual re-acceptance and restoration into the community (Fatić, 1995).

Restorative justice is naturally more forgiving and more conciliatory than the justice based on legal punishments. Its most interesting features lies in the identification and strategies of repairing the relationships which the offence has damaged. It is a model of justice which deplores the use of pain as a means of social regulation. In 1981, Norwegian social theorist Nils Christie wrote a brief but programmatic book for restorative justice, *Limits to Pain* (Christie, 1981). He argues that societies that use pain in fact *encourage* the use of pain and violence by their members, and contrariwise, that societies which avoid the use of pain help create a more tolerant and worthwhile living environment for everyone. One of the arguments to be drawn from this basic insight is that any control measures implemented by society, if they are to be humane and maximise the quality of life in society, must be nonpunitive in character and intent.

According to restorative philosophy, even imprisonment, including life imprisonment (which is conceivable only in the most extreme of cases), should be nonpunitive by intent. It is one thing to keep someone apart from society because their relationship with society is deeply damaged, and it is quite another thing to mistreat that person while imprisoned, subject them to forced labour, impose on them austere regimes of rest and waking time and structure their day contrary to their needs or wishes. Imprisonment as it is practised is not a measure of detainment: it is a measure of active punishment. Prisoners are not merely 'deprived of liberty.' They are subjected to overcrowded rooms, forced to wake up at 5 a.m., forced to go to bed at 9 p.m., disciplined, forced to work, forced to wear prison uniforms, deprived of entertainment; in other words, they are actively punished. There is a difference between imprisonment and house arrest that pictures the difference between punitive and nonpunitive detainment: under house arrest, a convict has limited freedom of movement, but she is not actively punished and lives a relatively normal life. In prison, the convict is a victim of the system; imprisonment is a measure of legal victimisation as 'pay back' for the crime. Restorative justice is incompatible with this latter idea of institutional victimisation of anyone, including the perpetrators of criminal offences. For this reason, restorative justice holds promise for the conceptualisation of future transitional justice with its conciliatory goals and inevitable balancing imperatives between offenders and victims. At present imprisonment is waved in front of the eyes of all 'potential offenders' (in fact all citizens) as a threat. This is a form of psychological violence by the state over all citizens. The message is: 'Life in prison is hell, and if you commit a crime, you will be subjected to it.' This is a violent, imposing way of thinking and relating to citizens that characterises a forceful, domineering state, even if it is formally democratic. It is a form of governance based on the use of pain and threats by it. No wonder, then, that, contrary to the 'general deterrence' philosophy, it has proven counterproductive in so many cases. Christie is most likely entirely correct in suggesting that the way in which control power in society is exercised is mimicked by those who are controlled. Thus the use of violence and pain by the state in fact encourages, rather than deterring, the use of pain by ordinary people in society (Fatić, 1995).

These described ideas have been voiced twenty or thirty years ago, and they remain highly experimental and unorthodox today: that is because there is insufficient will by policy makers, and even by the present academia, to work with these world-changing concepts seriously. As a result, justice systems continue to fail in their controlling role, and exceptional amounts of pain are inflicted on people throughout the world, whatever the political system and the prevailing understanding of 'punishment.' Likewise, the threat of global violence, including the ultimate damage which might arise from a nuclear conflict or major mishandling of environmental policy (such as those leading to a reduced availability of water, or fuels) continues to increase. The reason behind these increased threats of ultimate violence, threatening the human society as a whole, is in the minds and not in any 'objective' circumstances. We continue to think about violence and the infliction of pain on others as legitimate, or the only, ways of resolving our differences and conflicts. While restorative justice has grown and developed considerably over the past couple of decades, it has remained largely technical and microscopic in its perspective. It has focused on various 'organic' mechanisms of social control which may be noninstitutional and predominantly culturally shaped (e.g., encouraging a sense of social shame). Such research is valuable and relevant, however, restorative justice cannot change the world of social control without adopting a macro perspective on institutional and cultural change. This is where the key difference between restorative justice as a criminological theory and restorative justice as a philosophy lies. The former *describes* what restorative procedures may achieve. The latter *envisions* how our way of thinking about crime and our institutions may change in order to achieve a greater human good, reduction of pain and violence. Restorative justice as a philosophy and a comprehensive social theory has remained fairly underdeveloped and quiet in the face of a liberal social discourse based on 'rights,' 'entitlements,' and a fundamentally punitive 'justice,' which is 'proportional' either to the gravity of the crime, or to some kind of consequentialist expectations.

The most important thing about restorative justice to understand is that it is not a particular ethical methodology of thinking about justice: it is reconcilable with any of the major methodologies, whether they are deontic or consequentialist. The deontic philosophy is based on an overarching principle, such as duty: it implies that an action is justified if it is in line with a particular duty or value. On the other hand, the consequentialist philosophy judges actions based on their expected consequences: if these consequences are desirable by a preset standard (e.g., increasing the welfare of most people concerned), then they are morally sound. Restorative justice plays well with both types of moral thinking: its key value is reduction of pain. This implies that a restorative philosophy takes the deliberate infliction of pain as an evil; violence, whether physical or psychological, is morally unacceptable, whether it is committed by an individual person, or by a legal state institution, whether it is an illegal action (such as mugging someone in the street) or a legal one (such as imprisoning or executing someone). Further, the restorative philosophy suggests that nonpunitive ways of mending community ties and broken relationships are the task of social policy, including criminal policy, rather than instituting any kind of abstract 'justice.' For restorative philosophy, concepts such as 'guilt' and 'responsibility' are primarily psychological, and not legal. They are important insofar as they allow the mending of the broken ties and help shape a sense of personal relationship to one's crime, the crime's victims and one's own future actions. Such concepts are not to be used, within a restorative philosophy, as an excuse to subject someone to institutional mistreatment other than that required to remove them from the community if and insofar as the mending of the broken social ties is unsuccessful. In extreme cases, the practise of restorative justice and that of punitive justice may superficially seem similar: people are detained for long periods. However, in essence, in intent and in the substance of how people are treated by the state, restorative justice is fundamentally different from the current punitive justice.

Transitional justice is particularly well suited to advance restorative justice, because it is less susceptible to illusions about any detached and 'blind' goals of justice. It is closer to the realities of conflict resolution and collective values and interests that manifest themselves in local politics and in international relations generally. Its significance for a reconceptualisation of institutional justice as a whole lies in its greater proclivity to achieve practical reconciliation. Every type of institutional justice should strive to achieve reconciliation, but transitional justice, in a sense, must do so, and failure to do so is always obvious, often threatening to the very existence of transitional justice institutions. Again a good example is the ICC, whose foundations are being shaken by the withdrawal of support by African countries, because of the ICC's indictments policies which were seen by African government as undermining reconciliation and African cooperation. I am not suggesting, of course, that African governments are justified or unjustified in leaving the ICC, or that the ICC does or does not in fact undermine reconciliation. The substance of that issue is a separate topic. I am merely pointing it out that the ICC, as a largely transitional court (most of its cases fall within the realm of transitional and postconflict justice), depends on its ability to effect reconciliation, among other goals, and that it is existentially vulnerable to its own failure to do so. This particular vulnerability of transitional justice institutions to any failure to help reconcile the parties to conflict makes transitional justice a stark example on which to test the role of reconciliation in any system of justice more generally.

There are several important considerations that I must address here.

First, it could be argued that people have a natural inclination to see repressive justice done, and that it is the implementation of repressive, rather than nonrepressive justice, that contributes the most to reconciliation.

Second, one could note that an entirely nonrepressive approach to institutional justice might encourage crime, because for some perpetrators life in a nonpunitive prison might be better than the lives they have at present.

Third, it might be argued that, while punitive penalties may not be particularly effective in reducing the current rates of crime, there is no real way for us to be sure that their abolition would not lead to dramatic increases in crime, including war crimes. For example, it could be argued that an overly conciliatory treatment of war criminals might lead to a more lax kind of behaviour by belligerents in armed conflict, with greater tolerance of civilian casualties and less concern over the consequences of reckless military operations.

All three potential objections, and many others like them, are both coherent and have rational merit; I do not propose here to 'refute' them. However, the three arguments are interesting to me because they tell us something about the values on which the dominant social control discourse in our societies hinges. I consider the values of the public discourse to be the most important in understanding any room for innovation which transitional justice might broach in the general understanding of criminal justice.

The assumption of all three arguments is a conservative one. Currently we inflict pain on offenders and subject them to suffering deliberately. Although we don't have enough evidence to actually believe that this practise is improving our social situation, we should be afraid of dropping pain and suffering from our agenda because it is (theoretically) possible that without such means our security would deteriorate still more rapidly. On the other hand, it is theoretically equally (or more) possible that our situation would improve immensely. Most things are theoretically possible and the attitude of fear, which has been culturally ingrained in many of us and in our policy makers, makes especially some of those possibilities particularly repugnant to us. What is at work here is what psychologists call 'fixed action patterns,' namely reactions to certain stimuli that we have learned so well that we find it virtually impossible to move past them.

In his book on influence and persuasion psychologist Robert Cialdini illustrates the fixed action patterns by the example of turkey mothers, who only respond to and care for their young if the offspring produce the unique 'cheep cheep' sound: if the chick remains silent the mother will either ignore or, sometimes, kill it (Cialdini, 2005: 15–20). The fixed action response has been developed because most healthy turkey chicks constantly produce the 'cheep cheep' sound: thus, within the limited cognitive abilities of turkeys, it is the most reliable stimulus to which the mother turkeys can possibly associate their caring response for the young. Turkeys are unable to move past this fixed action pattern even if they are deliberately manipulated into obviously bizarre behaviour. Stuffed chicks with hidden recorders that produce 'cheep cheep' will be cared for, while real chicks that do not make the sound will be ignored by their mothers. Fixed action patterns are almost unchangeable in animals. Are they changeable in humans, and to what extent? We do, of course, have more significant cognitive abilities than turkeys, but our abilities are also limited. We cannot grasp the complexity of all situations which demand action, and thus rely on simplified 'principles' which translate complexity into simpler environments for decision making.

Looking back at the three objections to my earlier argument, is there anything inherently wrong in offenders having a 'better life' behind walls than they might have had in society, if their lives had been so depraved before they committed the offence? Maybe indeed some people who live utterly unbearable lives in society might consider committing a crime in order to be imprisoned. However, in a forgiving and caring society the meaning of this would be completely different from that which is suggested by the first objection to my argument. In a caring society, if someone commits a crime in order to go to prison because that is a better life for her than her life in society, this is an urgent call to address the depravity in society, rather than a call to make the conditions in prisons even more degrading for the person. When looked upon from a humane and constructive point of view, the latter way of thinking is not only wrong; it undermines the very moral legitimacy of a society which adopts such thinking about its members and their social situations.

The second argument posits that we don't know whether without punitive punishments the crime rates would suddenly soar (and again it bases its appeal on a solely theoretical possibility, equivalent to the opposite possibility that the crime rates might as well plummet). The third argument suggests that, without a threat of severe sanctions, countries and their leaders might entertain a more permitting way of warfare, where the innocents would be even less protected from military violence. The last argument is close to the famous 'impunity' argument: if the perpetrators of war crimes, especially those who hold high political office, are not efficiently prosecuted by international criminal courts, that would create a sense of their inaccessibility to the institutions of justice, their de facto 'immunity' to prosecution, and motivate them to commit even more grievous crimes.

By my lights, the last argument does not substantially differ from the second one: it is an argument based on a fear of what (theoretically) might or might not happen. For example, releasing people on bail might encourage other people to commit crimes, or allow those released to commit crimes. Is that a reason not to release anyone on bail? If a convicted murderer lives in my neighbourhood, I can easily imagine that if I had a parking spot dispute with that neighbour she might murder me. A violent person likely presents a greater risk of violence than a nonviolent one. I would by no means be irrational in harbouring such concern, but there is a matter of wider proportions at play here. Nobody can be considered infinitely guilty of something they had done in the past. At some stage we must be prepared to *take a risk* in continuing to live with them. I can reasonably fear my neighbour; the question is whether I should learn not to fear him. This decision depends on me, but it also depends on what my society tells me.

The same principle of fear versus risk-taking applies to social innovations, including restorative justice. If a radical, restorative policy innovation is to be pursued by eliminating the punitive dimension of criminal penalties, then of course there are some theoretical and even practical risks. The relevant question here is not whether or not there are risks, but what *importance* we will attach to them. That last decision depends on our personal values and, equally, on the values of our society. If I am a particularly tolerant person and try to behave to my former convict neighbour in a friendly way, and all of the other neighbours shun and alienate him, then my experience with him is likely to be different than if everybody accepted him. He will likely be more suspicious of me, it will be harder for me to get through to him, and when I do, he is likely to become very attached to me as to a sole friend in a hostile environment. I may lose other friends and neighbours. The social values determine our experience as much as our personal values do.

If our values are based on a general belief that others will tend to reciprocate kindness and avoid trouble, then a restorative policy innovation will come to us more easily. If we are a phobic, distrustful community, taught to believe that people will only behave if they fear penalties for misbehaviour, then, just like Cialdini's turkeys, we remain prisoners to our fixed action patterns. The three objections only emphasise a value choice which we must make in the face of any major reform of social policy, including criminal policy. They highlight the limiting beliefs which cause us to stick to the current policies despite the numerous indications of their ineffectiveness and their detracting from the quality of life of both offenders and nonoffenders in society. Sticking to limiting fixed action patterns is an obstacle to social innovation generally. This does not mean that any innovation is desirable or useful, but it means that fixed action patterns are only practical devices to reduce complexity that ought to be reexamined and changed from time to time. We are limited in our cognitive abilities, but even our fixed action patterns should be able to do more than the repetitive 'cheep cheep' of punitive deterrence.

PUTTING FIXED ACTION PATTERNS TO WORK FOR RECONCILIATION

One of the principles close to fixed action behaviour is the principle of reciprocation in interpersonal relationships. In modern cultures, most of us have all been tirelessly taught to adopt reciprocity as a measure of fairness in our mutual interactions. Acting reciprocally makes us feel morally well integrated. It instils a sense of being within our rights in morally and otherwise practically challenging situations. 'Act towards others the way you would wish them to act towards you' is the more philosophical formulation of the principle, which is considered as one of the most universal and practically useful guides for decision making, even in morally nontransparent circumstances. The use of this principle can do much to facilitate a restoration of good mutual relations between communities caught up in transitional conflict.

In civil conflicts, rarely anyone in positions of authority is entirely 'innocent' of faults towards the opponent side. In such situations, civil institutions assume military and paramilitary roles and responsibilities overnight, states of emergency are declared quickly, and the social climate changes to one that is permissive of extreme violence and nonpermissive of differences in opinion. Most people in positions of military authority understand the positions of those on the other side much better than ordinary folks, because they face the same experience. A military officer of one party to the conflict will often sympathise with the fate of a military officer of the opponent army more than a politician or a judge. Soldiers know the theatre of operations and the circumstances in the field. They know what kind of pressure the army is under from a community in conflict. People who run municipalities and 'command' civil defence forces during ethnic strife understand the challenges to integrity and personal sense of security of those in the same positions on the other side. The parties to such conflict usually share the same culture, history and geography. They understand the psychology of each other; in fact, often they share the same psychology. Not everybody is able to behave perfectly morally in challenging circumstances. Local people can understand this if the situation of the significant others is related to their own experience. They should be encouraged to talk to each other through their representatives who were *in similar positions* during the war. Judges and prosecutors are usually not the best people to encourage reconciliation. A judge thinks primarily of herself in the legal proceedings: she acts with a view of the appeals process and attempts to reach a legally sustainable verdict. No judges wish for their verdicts to be overturned on appeal. This does not mean that they don't care about reconciliation, but they certainly care more about their careers than about reconciliation. It is a fact of life in modern society. A prosecutor thinks first of all about securing a conviction: that is a success for him, not reconciliation. Again, this does not make the prosecutor an insensitive or 'bad' person: it is a fact of life in the prosecutorial profession. Thus, for completely practical reasons, prosecution and criminal trial are not necessarily the best ways to restore confidence and peace. A prosecutor might be a good interlocutor for the prosecutor of a community in conflict; a judge might be the ideal counterpart for a local community's judge; military commanders, politicians and ordinary soldiers will most productively communicate with their respective counterparts in the other community. It is a kind of intercommunal diplomacy that makes up the essence of an effective restorative process.

This principle is often seen in public shows about a variety of professional issues. When policy issues in the railway are discussed in open forum, the often repeated comment is that 'railway men will easily agree with other railway men, it's persuading the governments that is a problem.' The same is the case with doctors, nurses, police officers or soldiers. The reciprocity in positions is a powerful factor of agreement because of a shared experience and knowledge. This is witnessed in the tribunals' detention units. In the ICTY detention unit, the late Slobodan Milošević was closest friends with one of Croatian leaders, and Serbian nationalist radical Vojislav Šešelj (now acquitted of all crimes) was the most intimate friend of one of the nationalist Croat paramilitary commanders. Known for his hateful nationalist speech, upon his release from detention, Šešelj publicly spoke about the former opponent in the fondest of terms. The reciprocal experience creates a sense of shared identity that is capable of bridging even the most severe political antagonisms. It is this social capital of personally shared experience that must be used for reconciliation in the restorative transitional justice process, rather than the classic criminal adjudication.

There are two problems here for modern democratic decision making.

First, if the people who should 'do the talking' between the postconflict communities are those with shared experience, then the intercommunal relations are not necessarily articulated between their 'democratically elected' representatives. This is formally and procedurally a problem for democracy.

Second, the trust established between those in reciprocal positions, with shared experience of the conflict, does not necessarily, or automatically, translate into trust between the communities at-large. More importantly, trust does not necessarily satisfy 'justice': if some, or most community members start trusting the former adversary community, there could still be a few whose grievances and a yearning for justice persist, and such justice may not be done in light of the new spirit of trust and collaboration between the two communities.

I am not entirely sure how to respond to the first query, simply because I think that democratic legitimacy is more about dominion in the psychological sense than about mere procedure; if the goal of transitional justice is to balance justice with reconciliation, and negotiations and talks between those in reciprocal positions in the postconflict communities help reconciliation, that is a positive result. Reconciliation is not primarily a political process; it is a social process first of all. Thus the fact that elected representatives do not coordinate parts of it is of no consequence: political representatives are neither the supreme authority in the social sense, nor are they necessarily the best or the most appropriate individuals to conduct the society's affairs that are not predominantly political. War is only partly a political affair; it is also a social, military and security affair. Security professionals have as much legitimacy to be at the decision-making table about war and postwar affairs as do politicians. Hence, I do not see the problem of democratic legitimacy in reciprocal negotiations as sufficiently acute or of sufficiently commanding relevance.

The second question about pockets of injustice or sense of injustice despite reconciliation is more serious and theoretically more challenging. If the majority of a community reconcile with another, formerly adversarial community, and a sufficient number of those grieving from violence and injustices of the war do not, what does that do for justice? Is such as reconciliation morally acceptable?

I think the answer to these questions depends on two key concepts: the prevalent conceptualisation of 'justice' and the relevant sense of 'community.' If 'justice' is giving everyone their moral dues, or if justice primarily caters to the feelings and needs of the victims, then the described reconciliation would, to some extent, be unjust. However, if justice is seen as a more complex process, which does not mean that the victims are necessarily satisfied, but that some kind of resolution of the past injustices is reached on the level of the community, such reconciliation would be justice. There is no implication in the concept of justice that, whatever kind of 'justice' is performed in society, some people would not sense this as insufficient justice or as an open injustice. The current model of punitive justice in all modern societies also leaves some people (this author included) with a sense of profound injustice, because for them, justice cannot possibly be based on the infliction of harm on someone. Similarly, the adoption of a restorative model would inevitably leave some people longing for a different type of 'justice.' Obviously, when these people experience crime or their family members and friends are the victims of crime, then their feelings have a greater moral weight than a situation in which a philosopher feels the injustice of a dominant punitive model of corrections. However, in principle, little can be done to change the fact that people have their own sense of justice and it takes time for the minority to adopt any change in the prevalent model of justice. This is a cultural process. In some organic communities (later on I will speak about restorative justice among the Australian Aborigines) grieving does not include a sense of punishment, or includes only very symbolic acts of 'punishment,' not really meant to harm the perpetrator. In the modern, industrialised, alienated societies grieving tends to be connected with a desire for the perpetrators to die on an electric chair or be routinely raped while serving life imprisonment. It is a cultural difference, and it is a matter for our aesthetic appreciation to judge which one is more agreeable and desirable.

This argument is connected with the concept of 'community.' In liberal societies, the community is a political group whose most important virtue is its normative respect for the individualities of its members. In such a community the normative influence on individual vengeful feelings after being victimised by a crime is negligible. A person is entitled to their own values and views, and if these views are to seek to see the perpetrator 'fry on the chair' or 'die a thousand deaths,' as is sometimes heard in statements by victims' families, then the community respects such views, and, in some cases, goes a long way to meeting them (the death penalty). As with every other social practise, ultimately it is a matter of aesthetic appreciation or approbation. In nonliberal, more tightly knit and more caring communities, the normative pressures to uphold shared substantive values might be stronger. In such communities a vengeful or distrustful person is considered morally suspect; there is every reason for members to shape their moral views in conciliatory and constructive ways. In such a community, seeking vengeance may be seen as socially deviant in the victims and their families themselves. Again a number of organic communities which survive today, such as the Aboriginal ones in Australia, potently illustrate this point. Different concepts of community and of justice are associated with different fixed action patterns in people: these patterns can change when social values and social policies change accordingly.

MIMICKING AND MUTUAL RECOGNITION

Another fixed action pattern in human relationships which is relatively well known is that of mimicking. People mimic the values and actions by their social elites and governments. Individual people mimic the reactions by the groups they belong to. Mimicking is one of the most prevalent ways of social learning. It starts with a child's mimicking of her parents and ends with adult citizens mimicking the political views and sentiments of their leaders. One of the well-recognised ways of conducting effective communication is to deliberately mimic the body language of the interlocutor: this strategy creates a sense of commonality and eases the conversation closer to agreement on important issues. While seemingly a superficial and fleeting strategy to gain a handle on others in communication, mimicking is merely a sign of a deeper human need which drives all of our behaviour, namely the need for *acknowledgement and recognition*.

I have already mentioned that the former adversaries in postconflict communities usually understand the values of each other very well; much more so than do the outsiders, including the international intervenors. What they need to do is to *explicitly acknowledge* those values and *pay respect* to them. For example, the loss of life of dear ones by members of the other community should be acknowledged in no uncertain terms. This should be done by expressing the same emotions and making the grieving gestures as for one's own lost relatives. Although there is a natural human propensity to show sympathy for such losses by the adversary, the social pressures in postconflict societies often stifle the expression of these emotions, instead of encouraging them. A physically traumatised body clenches its fists and contracts its muscles, causing itself more pain, instead of relaxing and letting others assist and carry the victim to safety. One of the greatest challenges for lifeguards near the water is to avoid being drowned by the drowning victims themselves. Entire protocols have been developed to approach the drowning victim from behind and have them hold on to a floater, which is then dragged considerably behind the lifeguard, who swims to the shore. Drowning victims, instead of letting the lifeguard save them, reflexively try to climb on top of him or to pull him underwater underneath them. Likewise, postconflict communities, reeling from the stress of combat and destruction, keep their members on a tight leash; they watch for any signs of empathy for the antagonist community as a sign of weakness or treason, even after the violence is over. In this case, like with the victims of physical assault or drowning victims, a methodology must exist to encourage collaborative actions in the interests of the community itself. It is a form of collective psychotherapy that resembles the post-trauma counselling given to victims of terrorist attacks or natural disasters. People have trouble getting a hold of their lives after trauma; they need third-party help to regain judgement, motivation and orientation in life.

Showing recognition for the feelings of others by sincerely mimicking their expressions of grief at a loss is a life skill that needs to be coached to postconflict communities as part of the restorative process. Just as the skilful salespeople have no problem telling their customers 'I like you' or sending birthday cards every year, showing empathy with a former adversary goes a long way to establishing trust. Even if the other side is suspicious about the sincerity of the expressions of solidarity and empathy, such experiences are still far more pleasant than those of indifference or mocking. With time, they will bring about collaboration. At first it might be shy, but gradually both parties will be emboldened to put their past behind almost fully. It is difficult to insist on a full range of institutional, 'eye for an eye' justice with regard to someone who grieves with you and shows remorse. The fixed action pattern of reciprocation makes it very difficult to ignore someone's solidarity, even if it is the adversarial community. There is a sense of indecency which most of us would feel if we asked for the death penalty or severe prison sentence for a perpetrator who grieves with us for our victims. We are taught to reciprocate acknowledgement; accordingly, once we face a full recognition of our grief, our own dignity moves us in the direction of forgiveness and reconciliation, rather than retribution. In the absence of immediate ideas how best to acknowledge another's feelings, mimicking is the simplest and most persuasive way available, especially in the high-stress environments of post–civil war violence.

Obviously, I am not suggesting here a direct and obviously manipulative mimicking of another person's actions; this could increase, rather than decreasing the animosities, because it can be seen as mocking the victims. What I am suggesting is that any kind of triumphalist behaviour by the 'winning' community should be avoided at any cost. Homage should be paid to others' victims in the media and in public discourse. Minute's silences should be observed on important dates commemorating traumatic events for the other community. Condolences and emissaries should be sent to funerals. Temples of religious worship destroyed during the violence should be restored by the perpetrator community. Members of the adversarial community who return to their homes after being expelled should be given careful and special protection and recognition. Any cultural, artistic or spiritual legacy of the other community should be carefully preserved and publicly appreciated. All of these actions acknowledge the other community, mimic their own actions related to their losses, and make up the toolbox of restorative justice itself.

ORGANICISM IN 'JUSTICE'

Unlike modern institutional justice, restorative justice is organic and ancient. Organic societies are those where interpersonal and intergroup relationships are immediate, unmediated by institutions. In such societies institutions serve specific purposes, but they do not replace or overarch the human dimension of people's interactions as they do in modern societies. In an organic society, communities such as the family, neighbourhood or guild remain vital elements of social organisation. This has consequences for the way in which people interact. It is more spontaneous, more direct and sincere, and more encouraging for the expression of and reactions to others' emotions. Such directness and spontaneity allow for a greater quality of the experience of shared values and shared social existence; overall, this manifests itself as a higher quality of life from an individual perspective (Fatić, 2016). Organicism in social organisation directs people's attention to one another, rather than to institutions and policies. People have less of a need for the media to be informed about things that immediately matter to them, because they are surrounded by other people whose identities and values are familiar to them, and who make up their social world. In some cases, this makes organic societies parochial, with limited interest for events outside the people's immediate circle of social contacts. Again it is a matter of aesthetic appreciation whether this aspect of organicism is to be seen as necessarily detracting in any way from the moral soundness of organic social life. In such unmediated human relationships recourse to restorative justice is almost a natural reflex, the most immediate response to a crisis in the community's sense of security and trust generated by crime.

There is much we can learn in the way of restorative justice from the organic communities of the past. In Aboriginal villages in Australia, criminal justice with a punitive dimension was virtually unknown. Aborigines were not violent people; they were gatherers and hunters with a pantheist religion, so they never waged wars and rarely ever fought between themselves. Still, killings happened, if only by accident while hunting, or with the occasional brawl unintentionally going too far. The Aboriginal treatment of the perpetrators of killings was highly exemplary for restorative justice. The offender would first be detained briefly until the passions stirred by the killing have simmered down and the grieving process was underway. She would then be tied to a pole in the middle of the village. Relatives and friends of the murder victim were given a spear. They would face the perpetrator, shout their anger and rage out, demand remorse and apology, some would hit the offender or spit at her. At the extreme, with particularly recalcitrant offenders, the grievers were allowed to stab the offender with a spear to the calf. Such stabs occurred very rarely: in most cases the drama of the situation was sufficient to defuse the enmity. Most offenders genuinely felt remorse and were culturally encouraged to fully express it. Before long the offender would be readmitted into the community even by those whose family member was killed. It was left to those who 'owned' the conflict, the offender and the affected family of the victim, to determine the time required for reconciliation. There was limited but tangible social pressure on the victim's family to reconcile; it was a cultural expectation. Modern punitive systems of justice consider themselves more advanced than the aboriginal, restorative systems of the past. One can wonder instead if today's punitive sanctions are in fact dramatically less culturally advanced than those of the organic societies.

The work of the principle of *reciprocation* is obvious in aboriginal restorative justice: the offender is encouraged to express grief and remorse over her actions, and the victim's family are expected to respond, reciprocally, by gradually easing their animosity to the offender and, ultimately, forgiving her. Organic communities relied on reciprocation as much as we do today; in fact, reciprocation is one of the organic behaviours to which modern cultures have retained access to date. Despite all the differences between organic and modern societies, today, as in the past, not to reciprocate an understanding, or a favour, is not only an expression of bad taste, but also of *social inadequacy*. Not living up to cultural expectations of reciprocation diminishes a person's and, equally, a group's self-respect. Most communities involved in transitional justice already have problems with self-respect and collective identity.

This makes them particularly sensitive to any further damages to their self-respect and sense of social adequacy.

Obviously, there are communities, just as there are people, who are not sensitive to reciprocity and who have a damaged sense of self-respect, which does not respond to moral or cultural expectations. Such people are psychopaths, insensitive to the norms and expectations of all those around them, although they may have exceptional skills of disguise and 'blending in' with the mainstream. Similarly, there are groups and communities that are so deviant in their approach to wider-held, universal human values that it is impossible to influence them through any appeals to morality or sense of self-worth. It may well be that such individuals and groups respond only to the direct and open exercise of power and punishment, but they are deviants. A policy of transitional justice, just like any other policy, must not be led by what characterises deviance, but rather by what characterises most normal situations. Deviants are exceptions, and policy might allow for certain punitive exceptions when dealing with such cases. However, most people with whom transitional justice deals are not deviants; they are often otherwise exemplary members of their respective communities or decorated military leaders. In most cases, they can be influenced through reciprocity and other fixed action responses in order to avoid the unnecessary infliction of pain. Such an approach broadly characterises and defines restorative justice. It has potential to contribute to conflict resolution between the former adversaries substantially, on a functional, everyday level, thus promising a more peaceful and satisfying relationship in the future. That is exactly the overarching goal of transitional justice.

ENHANCEMENT OF COMMUNITIES

In their insightful essay on technology, Branden Allenby and Daniel Sarewitz say that the most widely grown culture on this Earth are human beings ourselves: ultimately all technology is aimed at enhancing us and our ability to respond to life's challenges, thus supposedly increasing the quality of our lives (Allenby and Sarewitz, 2011). While it is dubious whether any kind of enhancement necessarily increases the quality of life, especially the enhancements brought on by technology, the desire to enhance is overwhelming in most communities. The rise of expectations of individual performance by the human group goes hand-in-hand with the expectation for individuals to constantly enhance themselves. Several decades ago it was almost unthinkable that somebody would undergo plastic surgery in order to improve one's odds of getting a promotion at work; today this is almost normal. Millions of Americans take Prozac, not so much as an antidepressant (its effectiveness in this regard has been proven extremely dubious), but essentially as an enhancement drug: either through the actual chemical effects of Fluoxetine (Prozac), or merely as a placebo effect of mere self-suggestion, people tend to find it easier to smile and show a friendly face when they are on the drug. Smiling and being friendly is both an expectation in the work-place in America, and a recommendation for someone to be accepted and advance in one's social and business circles (*The Guardian*, 2008).

The same applies to the enhancement of human groups, especially when they feel that their collective identities are threatened and sense that they are insufficiently recognised by significant other groups. Strategies that promise to enhance a group's identity or ability to deal with challenges provide the group with a sense of empowerment and a new self-confidence, thus making it less likely for them to seek violent means of resolving conflicts. The more a group is confident, the less likely it is to rush into violence. Obviously, with most postconflict communities and regions, by the time institutional transi-tional justice sets in, these communities have already rushed into numerous ill-conceived mutual confrontations (over policy, if not over territory). This then creates additional mutual grievances and puts more distance between them, so that transitional justice must seek to build the skills and opportun-ities for the groups to regain confidence in each other. Such confidence is helped by a sense of empowerment and the consequent downplaying of a sense of vulnerability. Empowering postconflict groups to venture to trust each other again and to pay less attention to their own overemphasised vul-nerabilities allows them to focus on promoting their vital interests in peace-time despite the fallout of the conflicts. Almost invariably, such interests (trade, mobility, regional integration, etc.) enhance cooperative and stifle confrontational values and strategies, thus solidifying optimistic prospects between the former adversaries. Self-empowerment is a form of enhancement (and perhaps the most important enhancement of all) at least in the social and political life. Part of that process is building adequate self-awareness, namely the awareness of one's (or a community's) actual feelings and perceptions, even when they are quite disempowering in themselves. Once the ineffective self-perceptions are identified, the process proceeds to noting and evaluating the same self-disempowering tendencies and self-perceptions in the other, adversarial community. Transitional justice should follow the well-tried model of deescalation of a sense of vulnerability: a community (and a person alike) will feel less vulnerable once they identify the same or similar vulner-abilities in those by whom they feel vulnerable in the first place. This seems simple and obvious, but it is usually hidden from the view of members of the communities affected by conflict.

A sense of another's vulnerabilities helps people deal with their own vulnerabilities, not by removing those vulnerabilities — groups remain vulnerable to the same things whatever their perception of the vulnerabilities of others — but by reducing their focus on the vulnerabilities. Grievances from the past will not simply go away once a group understands that the other group suffers from the same 'baggage' of the past; however such recognition will empower the group to move beyond their grievances and it will be more capable of engaging the other group despite and against their own sense of grievance. In other words, the recognition of another's existential situation which is equivalent to our own tends to reduce the importance of our own situation in our own eyes, and this is what empowers us to move on. This is the value of communication between group representatives with equivalent experience, and at the same time the value of the whole set of communication skills and formats which transitional justice ought to be able to bring to the communities. Of course, this means that transitional justice is more about skills of togetherness and clarification of the perceptions of collective selves in postconflict situations than about implementing justice itself. In this sense, transitional justice is more a policy, and less a judicial practise; the policy includes a judicial practise, but only as a minor part. Thus transitional 'justice' is somewhat of a misnomer: it is not really 'justice,' or at least it is not primarily about 'justice.' Transitional justice is about society and about its enhancement in the aftermath of a conflict.[1]

The main practical challenge in enhancing postconflict communities is at least twofold. On the one hand, these communities often seem very cohesive in the aftermath of warfare: they close ranks in the face of common adversity, and transitional justice may be seen as an adversary if it insists on examining their conduct during war. On the other hand, the apparent cohesion is superficial. It is based on fear and not on affirmative adoption of values. The ranks are closed in fear of what might be found out to have happened during the war, not because members of the community believe that their ways are correct and productive for the future. This makes it necessary for transitional justice to both relax the fears and implement some kind of justice at the same time. Obviously, restorative justice is more useful and more acceptable here than retributive justice. Second, the postconflict communities gather around values which need to be substantively changed. In this latter role, transitional justice must focus not on 'justice' itself, but rather on enhancing the communities' political and social and policy structures and skills alike. In other words, transitional justice is as much a source of social expertise as it is a source of 'justice' in the transitional sense of the word.

BOSNIA

One of perhaps the best examples of ill-advised international intervention in terms of enhancing the communities is that of the postconflict Bosnia-Herzegovina. The 1991–1995 civil war saw massive movements of the population, which amounted to the so-called ethnic cleansing (people being expelled en masse from their homes in order to establish a particular ethnic composition of towns and villages). After the Dayton Peace Accords in 1995, the international community initially maintained a heavy international military presence throughout Bosnia. An Office of the High Representative of the International Community was introduced to oversee the transition and the work of all of the local institutions of government. This particular international office was headed by various former diplomats (and, in one case, a former British political party leader, Lord Paddy Ashdown), who had sweeping powers to change legislation and remove elected politicians, including the heads of state. The High Representatives have lived in Bosnia ever since Dayton (1995), and have received what is by local standards considered an insultingly high salary (the net salary of €25,000 per month at base level, before benefits, in a country where the average salary is about €300). Overall, they have been seen as a hindrance to the country's democratic development and establishment of the rule of law. The use of the High Representative's special authorisations to interfere in domestic institutional decisions, or to blatantly overturn them by decree, often made a mockery of the country's parliament and governments of the two constitutive 'entities' created by Dayton: the Federation of Bosnia-Herzegovina and Republika Srpska. The High Representatives have the authority to literally rule the country in an undemocratic, imposing way. They can influence every institution from the local government to the central bank. These are dictatorial prerogatives, and obviously not all High Representatives have been equally willing to use them routinely: this depended very much on their personalities, political views, perceptions of the Bosnian political, ethnic and existential situation and the like. Hence, at some stages the country functioned almost as a normal democratic state, while at others it resembled an occupied territory under foreign administration. Any attempts by the local political structures to rid Bosnia of the Office of the High Representative have been portrayed in the international public arena as concealed attempts to reignite conflict. In this atmosphere, transitional justice has had a difficult task enhancing the Bosnian communities, and it is probably fair to say that its failure is largely attributable to the distrust by the international interveners of the capacity of the local institutions (which those same interveners had helped establish) to carry the burden of reconciliation and postconflict normalisation.

Obviously the very institution of the High Representative is fraught with controversy in principle. On the one hand, the Office of the High Representative is envisaged as a corrective influence on potentially divisive decisions by the various ethnic communities and the institutions which they control. Thus, prima facie, some kind of international authority with overarching powers seems justified, at least in the initial years of a postconflict process. On the other hand, the Office makes sense only if it 'dies away' gradually, namely if it has a clear mission to gradually hand over the country's decision making to its government. In addition, the sweeping powers make the personality and judgement of the High Representative extraordinarily important. With the ability to interfere in democratic processes, the High Representative must be extremely conservative in using his prerogatives and must be very careful never to be seen as crude or insensitive to the particular concerns of the individual communities. The High Representative is in fact a *mediator* in conflict: any mediator who appears as a sword-wielding authority immediately loses all credibility among the parties and can no longer do their job effectively. It is probably fair to say that among the High Representatives in Bosnia, most were not in possession of the leadership and mediation skills which were necessary for this position. Thus the two entities, in 2018, are so far apart politically that one of them (Republika Srpska) keeps hinting at a referendum on splitting up from Bosnia and creating a separate country. The former Yugoslavia was broken up exactly by secession referenda held in the constituent republics, and this is precisely how the civil war in Bosnia started, with the three ethnicities flocking to their ethnic political parties and holding referenda. Crudely put, the current rhetoric about yet another secession referendum summarises the overall failure of the approach taken by the international community in Bosnia. Part of the reason for the mistakes and wrong strategies taken by the High Representatives has been the ill-conceived mission of transitional justice: most High Representatives simply saw Bosnia as a community that needed to be stabilised and institutionally solidified through a firm imposition of standards the High Representatives were familiar with from their own countries. They saw transitional justice in the same way as they saw criminal justice. These were grave misconceptions, as transitional justice, or international postconflict intervention, are by no means equivalent to national criminal justice: they are complex missions of enhancing and strengthening communities first, and only afterwards of strengthening the institutions and the rule of law. Likewise, developing democracy in a postconflict area is nothing like 'installing' it, although this is precisely the rhetoric which is sometimes used. One does not install a democracy one has brought from one's own country; rather, one allows a local democracy to develop. Understanding and implementing these general principles is the main challenge of transitional justice overall.

One of the goals of the entire oversight of Bosnia's transition was to void the effects of ethnic cleansing by allowing all those expelled from their homes to return. The failure of this effort illustrates the poor conceptualisation of how communities should be enhanced, as well as the pitfalls of a heavy-handed, repressive conceptualisation of transitional justice in Bosnia.

The assumption that in Bosnia all of the mass movements of the population were the result of expulsions fitted nicely with the prevailing international opinion which was created after the 1993 Srebrenica massacre of Muslim men and boys of military age by the besieging Serbian forces. However, the subsequent developments proved the assumption largely false, and have thus, naturally, falsified all of the conclusions. The result was that attempts to get the people to return to their villages have been unsuccessful overall. While in Bosnia expulsions have happened, most movements of the population were the result of people seeking more secure and prosperous lives in the midst of war by emigrating to other countries: Bosnia had been a country of emigrant workers for decades before the war. It had a relatively highly qualified workforce, and when the warfare started, even in places that saw only low intensity conflict, many people simply emigrated and stayed away, regardless of their ethnicity.

Many ethnic Croats and Serbs went to Croatia and Serbia, they were given citizenship and established themselves in a way that made their return to Bosnia unlikely. Many Bosnians, especially the younger generations (now middle aged) started new lives in Australia, the United States, Canada or Europe, and whatever they may be offered in Bosnia as an incentive to return (refurbishment of houses, preferential treatment when seeking a job or enrolling their children in kindergartens and schools) is insufficient motivation to come back. The most obvious example is that of the Croatian population in what is now the Serbian 'entity' within Bosnia-Herzegovina: despite the policies of ethnic tolerance and return of those who have left, only the Muslim former residents of Republika Srpska have returned; the Croat villages remain empty because Croatia had a policy of granting citizenship to all ethnic Croats from Bosnia. Croatia is an EU member and a more economically prosperous country than Bosnia, which means that few young or middle-aged people would consider returning to Bosnia. Looking back at their lives during the war, they see the move they have made as a strategically justified long-term decision. The failing policy of 'return' causes the abandoned settlements to draw on even more resources from the government because only the elderly return; they can't do much agricultural work and require all kinds of medical and social services. In fact one of the growth industries across Bosnia is the establishment of *nursing homes for senior citizens.* The Bosnians who live and work abroad pay for their elderly relatives to live in the nursing homes, while the rural parts of Bosnia get increasingly deserted.

Thus the social situation resulting from the international conceptualisation and policies of community enhancement is *exactly the opposite* of what was desired: the communities are ageing, taxing the limited state resources, and the human potential of Bosnia continues to decrease relative to other countries of the region.

DERVENTA

Close to the Bosnian town of Derventa, which is now a part of Republika Srpska, and was one of the most devastated places in Bosnia during the 1991–1995 conflict, there is an ethnic Croat village of Kulina. The village had been notorious throughout the post–World War II period for the particular architectural design of its Catholic Church: the roof of the church was designed, very precisely, as the military hat of the World War II fascist 'Ustasha' forces. During the former Yugoslav times legal action was attempted to make the village change the shape of the roof because it was seen as offensive to the local Serbian population, who had suffered under the Ustashas during their Nazi-puppet 'Independent State of Croatia,' just twenty or so miles away and fifty or so years ago. Nothing worked at the time, and the roof remained as it was. When the Bosnian civil conflict erupted in 1991, severe fighting engulfed the region of Kulina and Derventa. The town first fell to Croat soldiers, and then to Serbs. Kulina and the neighbouring Croat villages were destroyed, Croat houses dynamited after the residents had left, and surely enough, the controversial church was levelled. Most residents of Kulina had left the picturesque village for good: today, few houses in the village are inhabited. However, the church has been restored to its former glory, all with the roof precisely as it was.

This particular roof makes no contribution to the Catholic faith of Kulina's villagers, nor is it required for regular service. It is no more practical than a more ordinary church roof might be. The roof is there as a statement; it serves to maintain the old antagonisms and uphold a collective identity that does not correspond to the modern Croatian nationality. The roof is there to say: 'we have not been defeated,' but the identity which the roof symbolises has been both defeated and rejected by the modern Croatian state. It is an anachronistic 'finger in the eye' of the Bosnian transition that bellows: everything is the same, hatred will not change. There is nothing either Christian, or particularly politically useful for the community of Kulina in this church roof.

Within the town of Derventa itself the old Orthodox church, which had been placed modestly in a lower part of the town, had been destroyed by the Muslim fighters during the war, and a new, grand church has since been built in the very centre of town. It is said to be the biggest Christian church in

Bosnia. The church is on slightly lower ground than the old Roman Catholic church, which has survived the fighting, however it towers so high that, when looked at from a distance, it is a little higher than the Catholic Church.

The Muslim population of Derventa has declined: some Muslim residents have returned, but many younger people have stayed away. However, where there was once just one mosque in Derventa, with many more Muslim inhabitants, there are now nine and they are multiplying. Most are empty. So in the end, in a Serbian-dominated town, there is one large congregational Christian Orthodox Church and one small Christian Orthodox Monastery outside the town, however there are nine mosques instead of the prewar two mosques, with Derventa now being home to about one-quarter of the Muslim residents it used to have before the war. Pubs and restaurants are increasingly segregated: various ethnic communities, while still civil to each other, patronise different establishments. There is a growing sense of segregation on an ethnic basis.

Derventa is a good example of the typical postconflict community in Bosnia where the constituent ethnic groups have neither been trained, nor encouraged, to communicate effectively. All three communities have been victimised in different, but not entirely dissimilar ways. It has now been more than twenty years since the end of the war, and the communities' progress towards a greater mutual understanding appears completely thwarted. The destruction of Kulina has not brought home any lessons whatever: if the circumstances were to reoccur in the same way as in the early 1990s, the same events would most likely unfold in much the same way. The church roof is standing there again, as a statement that nothing has changed, although there are few people left to attend that church. Mosques are built with funds from the Middle Eastern donors, and while they have imams and perform their service, few people attend them. It is almost as if differences which, after being inflated to the point of explosion, had led up to the war, are now being cultivated again.

The described situation is perhaps the most symbolically powerful in Bosnia's capital, Sarajevo. Once a liberal, multicultural city proud of its ethnic tolerance, its particular music and artistic scene and home to many influential intellectuals, today's Sarajevo is a city that looks as though it has been transplanted onto the Bosnian landscape from somewhere in the Middle East. Where once young people from all over the former Yugoslavia preferred to serve their compulsory army terms, because the city was so friendly and inclusive, today the main streets bear names such as 'the Mujahedin Street,' or 'the Green Berets Street' (Green Berets were the special forces of the Bosnian government during the civil war). The Green Berets street is where the main Christian Orthodox cathedral is located, which makes for quite a contrast in meanings. The city's once picturesque, small white mosques with pointy minarets that had used to dot the landscape have now given room to enormous, imposing Saudi-style glass-and-concrete mosques. It has taken the local Muslim people some time to even realise that these are mosques and not residential buildings, they are so foreign to the architectural heritage of Bosnia.

Young men in Sarajevo are said to be paid by the Middle Eastern promoters of a particular type of Islam to wear the 'goatees' — the peculiar trimmed beards indicating their religious affiliation. Equally, women are widely believed to be paid to wear hijabs, though those same young women can on other occasions be seen smoking or drinking alcohol. The whole mannerism of the city's life has changed. The street names are written on green plates, indicating an Islamic identity of the city. The one street in the city centre has retained its old name — 'Marshal Tito' — (the former communist leader of nonaligned Yugoslavia). However, this street name looks really awkward on a new green plate among the Islamic names of most other streets.

The situation is similarly strange in other parts of Bosnia. The country claims to be a 'maritime' country because it has access to the Adriatic sea at just one narrow point where it 'breaks through' the Croatian coast, in the Bosnian coastal town of Neum. However, although it is part of Bosnia, Neum is populated mainly by ethnic Croats. Its main street, which stretches right along the coastline, is now named 'Franjo Tudjman Street.' Franjo Tudjman was the nationalist leader of Croatia during its war of secession from Yugoslavia and is credited with securing independence for Croatia. He is not a Bosnian at all; in fact, his forces fought against the Bosnian forces on a number of occasions. Yet, the main street in a Bosnian town bears his name.

In the capital of the Serb entity, the city of Banja Luka, one of the main streets is named 'Nemanjina Street.' Stefan Nemanja was a medieval ruler of Serbia. He had nothing to do with Bosnia whatsoever.

These selective facts illustrate the current political and psychological situation between the Bosnian communities. It is as bad and as dangerous as it ever was, despite two decades of transitional justice, international intervention, billions of dollars of aid and changes in the legal system and institutional structures. With all the resources and effort, one thing has been consistently lacking: an intelligent, constructive and skilful conduct of transitional justice and the transitional process as a whole. The main aim of these processes should have been community building and community enhancement. Instead, the processes putatively aiming to advance the Bosnian transition have degraded the Bosnian communities and even detracted from their ability to work together in the face of their differences.

The town of Derventa is paradigmatic for the fate of Bosnia. It is working hard to pull itself out of the disadvantages brought on by the war, and economically it is succeeding. Derventa is now a prosperous town with some industry (private manufacturing plants, mainly) and relatively dynamic trade. It has been thoroughly renovated, partially restored to its prewar image and partially modernised, and it has its fair share of young people with children who see a future for their families in the town. Thus it is a town with both current substance and a potentially rewarding future ahead of it. However it remains dogged by political and ethnic instincts which no town, and no local community, can deal with by themselves. This is why transitional justice was invented, and this is why international intervention exists: to address those reflexes which essentially have little to do with local circumstances, and everything to do with generalised prejudice, fear and trauma of the war. The workings of transitional justice for Bosnia have not helped create opportunities for the development of new skills and communal capacities which would make the likelihood of another ethnic war in the future lower. The transitional justice, and the international intervention overall, have not enhanced the Bosnian communities, although this should have been their main task. But what does it really mean for a community of Derventa, or any community in Bosnia, to be 'enhanced' in the described circumstances? The answer is well illustrated by the example of a charismatic if simple Muslim man from Derventa.

'BARBA MEHO'

The Institute for War and Peace Reporting has produced a video report on a Muslim man from Derventa known to locals as 'Barba Meho' ('Boatman Meho' in rough translation). Meho was and, interestingly, remains a symbol of Derventa. A poor, virtually homeless labourer in a socialist shoe factory during the former Yugoslavia, Meho developed a love of boats and started renting small rowing boats on the beautiful Ukrina River, flowing through Derventa. His boats were right at the bank next to his 'house' — a shack made of a loosely connected brick foundation and wooden boards on top. Meho has been a friend everybody cherishes. He is an interesting character. For example, he keeps chickens which nest in low tree crowns and behave almost like flying birds, though they are otherwise completely normal chickens. His shack has often been the scene of music and artistic performances, intellectual gatherings and debates between the local people of all three faiths and from all three ethnic communities.

When the civil war erupted in 1991, naturally, the situation of the ethnically mixed communities on the ground got out of control. As soon as it was heard that Serbian forces advancing from outside Bosnia, which had joined the effort to take the city from the Croat army, had threatened Barba Meho, local Serbs evacuated him to a Muslim-controlled part of Bosnia. Having survived the war, Meho returned to Derventa. With the help of a German aid agency, he resumed his boat 'business,' rebuilt his 'house' and returned to the life he used to know. Today, Barba Meho is close to ninety years old. He wears a white beard, a ship captain's hat with an anchor on it and commands his river fleet in a life with his neighbours that is completely unchanged by either war or transition (IWPR, 2010).

This man, poor and uneducated, but rich at heart, is in possession of skills typical of leadership. Barba Meho is a Muslim man in an ethnically divided country. He was saved by Serbs at the time of the fiercest fighting between his ethnic community and the Serb one, and was then reaccepted in a divided community in a way so complete that he is now able to see the war as a bad dream which has since dispersed. After waking up, the same dear people were there around him again. Meho, an almost illiterate man, makes people around him tolerant almost automatically. To join his social circle is at once easy and difficult. It is easy because Meho never says 'no' to anyone; it is difficult because the expectations of groups gathering around Meho are high: one must know how to play a guitar, tell a good story, paint, act, write poetry or, if having none of these skills, be a good listener and communicator. Meho is a leader in the sense that to become a member of his community one must enhance oneself. It is impossible to participate in his circle and harbour feelings or attitudes of animosity, intolerance or impatience. He doesn't know the names for these dispositions, so he tells his visitors just to 'love everybody else at the table.'

One of the problems with the Bosnian conflict is that the fears and concerns of the three ethnic communities are not irrational. They are not some kind of nationalist, paranoid confabulations about the other which lead one to resort to violence in their presence. Each of the communities has suffered either violence or some kind, or a serious letting down by the other communities. Some of these abuses included genocide, mass murder, levelling of villages, rape, torture and plunder. It was sufficient for the warlords of the early 1990s to revamp the memories and psychologically, the situation was ripe for an ethnic conflict.

The example of Barba Meho shows one important aspect of community enhancement which is identical to individual moral enhancement: it is the improvement and change in one's sensibilities. There is reason to believe that the decisions we make as individuals, just as those we make as groups of individuals, do not primarily arise from our rational 'faculties' or logical reasoning, but from our emotional, instinctual, subconscious preferences and desires, which are only expressed and subsequently justified by our appeals to logic or by our use of rational arguments. At least this is what modern neuroscience suggests, with all the consequences of this insight for our traditional notions of personal autonomy and free will (Damasio, 1994). This is why our moral enhancement depends more on what we learn to desire, what values command our subconscious existence, than what kind of reasoning we adopt rationally. Becoming a better person requires a change in our sensibility and spontaneous preferences. That is only possible through a thorough internalisation of values which are constructive, empathetic, understanding and collaborative. Moral education turns out to be the root of personal moral improvement, because it is through education that we both accept and adopt values which, in time, spontaneously determine and direct our sensibility and inclinations. In this sense, a perfectly morally educated person would not desire to act immorally and would not need to restrain themselves based on a recognition of duty or propriety, because they would not find pleasure or satisfaction acting immorally in the first place. The idea is built deeply into at least some of the Christian concepts of human enhancement (Fatić and Dentsoras 2014).

Barba Meho is an exemplary human being in the social sense, with a benevolent and outgoing sensibility, welcoming of others and easily perceived as such. This causes reciprocal attitudes of acceptance and respect. Thus his character is a blueprint for what it means in practise to enhance transitional postconflict communities. Such improvement would require a certain sensitisation of the communities to the feelings and concerns of others in ways which allow them to relate the concerns and the life situations of others to their own. This kind of sensitisation allows persons to actually feel, or at least reach out emotionally to, the concerns and fears of others. Empathy is a crucial disposition here because it causes people to spontaneously dislike causing discomfort to others, and conversely, to find pleasure in helping others feel good. The quality of life in empathetic communities is higher than in confrontational ones mainly because empathy causes people to actually enjoy assisting others. This, then, leads to aggregate outcomes of satisfaction that far exceed those in confrontational or indifferent communities. In nonempathetic communities the principle of pleasure does not lead people to come to the aid of others; to the contrary, it often leads them to compete with others for the scarce pleasures that they feel will bring them satisfaction (the liberal paradigm). Because of his sensibilities and his social success, Barba Meho's overall satisfaction in life far surpasses the material facts of his life: he used to work in a factory, has barely been able to make ends meet all his life, and lives in a shack at the end of a mud road on a river bank. With these facts of life, most people would consider themselves desolate. Barba Meho, however, is a true community leader.

TRUST

How can institutions of transitional justice encourage the described type of enhancement of communal sensibilities in postconflict societies? They are obviously not able to do that by meting out harsh penalties, promoting a discourse of responsibility, insisting on labelling individuals as perpetrators and victims, respectively. My point is not that we should obscure the concepts of perpetrator and victim; it is rather that these concepts, while they must be acknowledged, do nothing to *enhance* communities. They are neither the *most important*, nor the *most effective* way to foster a postconflict transition, and Bosnia is a very powerful example of that ineffectiveness, just as Barba Meho is a powerful example of what personal and community enhancement might actually look like. He operates on a level above victimhood and perpetratorship, although he is surely not unaware of the fact that crimes have occurred and that some people have committed those crimes against other people. The way in which transitional justice works must emphasise the values that it wants to advance, and these are not confrontational, deontic and absolutist concepts such as proportional justice. Rather the values, and the corresponding sensibilities, which must be promoted are connected with solidarity, a focus on mutual similarities rather than differences, and a specific focus on the universal human condition that the perpetrator- and the victim-communities (if they can be divided in this way at all) share. A focus must be placed on the experiences and emotions, such as fear or desperation, which during civil wars each member of each community knows pervade the lives of the other community as well. It is such focus that encourages collaboration rather than confrontation; retaliative 'justice' and punishments do the opposite.

The way in which we treat communities, or individuals for that matter, is not only expressive of our own values, identities or attitudes; it is *formative of attitudes* in our interlocutors or counterparts, as well. Those who face divisive language, who get classified into perpetrators or victims (all of which has been the case with postconflict Bosnia) actually start to identify themselves, as individuals, with perpetrator- or victim-communities. Both tend to become defensive, for various reasons, and their mutual relationships sour rather than healing. As Barbara Hudson argued back in the 1990s, the discourse of 'justice' has a way of doing incredible damage to the quality of community identity and to intercommunal relations. In fact, Hudson was the first to principally point it out that punishment can never lead to justice (Hudson, 1987).

Eric Uslaner has made an important distinction in his discussion of one of the most important emotions of solidarity, namely of trust, between the so-called moralistic and strategic trust (Uslaner, 2002). This distinction is directly relevant to the way in which the dominant discourse and treatment of individuals generates community identity and impacts the community's self-perceptions and sensibilities. According to Uslaner, strategic trust is present in most communities; it is the trust which needs to be earned or guaranteed by a third party. A person who falls ill while on vacation in a foreign country and is taken to a hospital will generally trust that the person with a stethoscope who examines her is actually a doctor, although they know nothing about this person. The trust is strategic because the very presence of a person who claims to be a doctor in a medical system with its institutional checks generally guarantees that this person must be a doctor, or else she would not be allowed to examine patients. Essentially the same type of trust is extended to people we know, who have proven themselves to us as being loyal, competent, reliable and the like. People whom we have known for a long time tend to command our trust: this is strategic trust because it arises from a long experience which gives us lots of *reasons* to trust.

On the other hand, Uslaner points to situations, and communities, where people are trusted morally, a priori, with no prior knowledge of the person, no specific reason or guarantee to 'corroborate' that person and facilitate trust. In such communities people are trusted because of the belief that people are *generally trustworthy*, exceptions granted. It is a normative view which is directly opposed to the underlying normative view of strategic trust. Importantly, in moralistically trusting communities it is considered *a sign of good character to extend trust* to strangers; conversely, a distrustful attitude is a sign of problematic moral personality of the distruster. Uslaner describes parts of suburban Maryland, United States, where people erect unmanned food stalls along the road where passersby help themselves to the fruit and pay for the quantity they take, all completely unsupervised. Apparently theft is a rare occurrence and the practise is a long-standing one. While people occasionally take the fruit without paying for it, the fruit stall owners do not withdraw their trust in the general trustworthiness of the humanity (Uslaner, 2002: 14–23).

The most important aspect of moralistically trusting communities for my discussion of postconflict community enhancement is the way in which a moralistically trusting attitude *sets in*. It is introduced in a community by a *moral education* of its members into acquiring a *particular moral sensibility*, which presents morally trusting people as nice and pleasant, as persons to respect and associate with. Contrariwise, suspicious, distrustful persons are presented as problematic, unpleasant, and to be avoided. This normative approach, which probably begins with children watching how the adults behave and how the community labels individuals, then becomes the collective moral sentiment of the entire community. Moralistic trust becomes a defining part of the community's identity and the dominant way in which it thinks about human relationships. Uslaner correctly refrains from claiming that either moralistic or strategic trust is rational or irrational, justified or unjustified. Either may or may not be justified or unjustified in particular circumstances; the choice, however, arises from a moralistically trusting culture or from one which is not a priori trusting. The choice itself is neither rational, nor irrational; it is a value choice which is based on a particular moral sentiment that, in each individual, is acquired from one's culture. On one level, a priori trust allows more efficient transactions between individuals (both material and nonmaterial), without the usual safeguards that are typically required in a distrustful culture (contracts, lawyers, institutional mediation and adjudication, etc.). On another, more personal level, a trusting culture allows a greater sense of inclusion and acceptance, and this, existentially, increases people's quality or experience of life. Life in a morally trusting community is simpler and more manageable than life in an overly cautious, distrustful, litigious community.

To understand the way in which communities fall into backward and antagonistic models of thinking one needs to consider that in most postconflict societies the true social elite, the most advanced and most enlightened members of the community, leave the community first. One of the reasons is that they are the ablest ones to anticipate the developments, secure alternatives for themselves, and find a new country in which to pursue a new life. Those who stay are left to their own devices and to leadership by individuals who often see the conflict, and the postconflict situation, as the only circumstances in which they can flourish socially and politically. Instead of teaching the community new skills and reaching beyond the limiting circumstances, the local leaders see the isolation, animosities and mutual fears as safeguards against potential challenges to their authority and positions within the community. Gradually, instead of being dissipated and discredited, fear, discrimination and protectionist feelings gain strength. One can see this in many transitional communities, including the postcommunist communities of Eastern Europe. The initial political change is that from an authoritarian, communist leadership to a neoliberal one. With time, however, if the community does not advance and become internationally integrated fairly rapidly, the old instincts awaken, and the old faces, with their old political habits, repopulate the political scene, albeit under a different party name. The result is often the old form of authoritarianism and backwardness combined with the mostly negative aspects of neoliberal governance (reduction in workers' rights, corporatisation of the institutions, etc.). The most advanced and creative people leave the country, and those who were once discarded politically as representatives of a dysfunctional regime return, and establish new, or reinforce old, atavisms of fear and exclusion which keep them safe in their positions. Such a situation is the sign of a fundamentally failed transition.

THE POWER OF FIXED ACTION PATTERNS
IN LEADING COMMUNITIES

Fixed action responses are those reactions which, over time, have proven the simplest and most productive ways of acting in typical, challenging situations for a person or a community. The 'cheep cheep' response, while bizarre when the typical circumstances are deliberately altered, is in fact a highly effective way for turkeys to cater for their young in ordinary circumstances. The same is the case with automatic submission to legitimate leadership: it is a fixed action response in human society.

In the highly irregular circumstances of war, especially of civil war, a fixed action response, which is effective in times of peace, might cause incredible atrocities to be committed by otherwise completely ordinary and decent people. Consider an ordinary example. By far the most people, if approached by a uniformed person and asked for personal documents, will automatically obey. The reaction will come almost without a thought, although the presence of a uniformed person might be unpleasant, or even seen as unjustified. We are taught, and have deeply *ingrained* it in our psyche, that a uniformed person is legitimate in asking for our papers and that it is our civil duty to provide them. This general obligation holds even in situations when we see no realistic need to identify ourselves or to be questioned by anyone. Where this example becomes interesting is in its implications *once we have conformed* with the initial request and shown our documents. Having given our identification papers to a uniformed person, we have effectively said 'yes' to the request. If they now *proceed* to question the authenticity of our papers, the purpose of our travel or the truthfulness of our answers, we will, in most cases, become entangled in either answering the questions or arguing, because we are drawn into an interaction by the initial 'yes': by showing our papers. Even if the officer who questions us, on closer inspection, turns out to have no real authority to do so, it is very difficult to fight our fixed action pattern from the outset: a uniformed person approaches, asks for our papers, and we comply. Having once entered into a discussion about our papers, we have implicitly recognised the person's right or authority to inspect them, and we feel a further obligation to continue the discussion. If, on the other hand, the questioning person was a real police office, but, for some reason, wore sandals, a t-shirt and shorts, we might stop for a moment, ask them for their own identification, or even ignore them completely. The fixed action response is ingrained by social practise, which fosters a close mental association between uniform and compliance, authority and following.

Consider a related example. Imagine that you receive a telephone call in your house from a government minister's secretary, asking you to come to see the minister at a certain time. You are a private citizen, have no connection with the relevant ministry, vote for a different political party from that represented by the minister, and have a highly critical view of the minister herself. The minister has no direct authority over you. You don't work for her ministry and have no legal obligation to see her. Principally, you would be entirely within your rights to respond that, if the minister wishes to see you, she should call at your house at a time convenient for you. However, very few people would not comply, because of the fixed action pattern: the minister represents the government, and the government represents legitimate authority for the entire community. Even if we dislike that particular government, when we are called upon by the minister we tend to comply, because it is a fixed action pattern to respond to legitimate authority. It would be odd not to show up, because we assume that the reason the minister calls us as a private citizen is important.

This model of human behaviour is generally not easily changeable on a case-to-case basis: it is a general pattern which can be modified only by *sustained influence* over a long time. This behavioural pattern explains why ordinary people, suddenly caught in a civil conflict, obey the orders of political authority and uniformed persons whose legitimacy, intentions, morality, and even intelligence are highly questionable. It explains why people follow nothing short of murderous political structures and fail to raise their voice about the authorities' actions which violate their basic personal sense of humanity and decency. When the Allied Forces in the occupied post–World War II Germany became desperately frustrated over the seeming imperviousness of the German civilians to suggestions of their responsibility for the atrocities committed by the Nazis against the Jews, they decided, in desperation, to march the German civilians through the concentration camp of Buchenwald, and make them see the decaying corpses, gas chambers and the crematoria. The civilians were most likely overwhelmed by the experience, however it is questionable whether this caused any change in their self-ascriptions of guilt. What the Allies failed to understand was that the mechanism behind compliance was a fixed action response, which few people in any community would ever be able to 'short-circuit' and defect from. The Nazis were the authority, and people obeyed, considering the authorities primarily, or even exclusively, responsible for whatever transpired, including the mass murder in concentration camps. On one level, this is intuitively morally unacceptable; on another, functional level, it is largely inevitable. Overcoming a fixed action pattern is exceptionally difficult for anyone. A considerable reason for the failure of punitive transitional justice to effect any reconciliation lies in the failure of the international criminal tribunals to recognise the limitations to personal criminal responsibility for war crimes. This limitation of responsibility arises from fixed action patterns for ordinary soldiers and mobilised civilians. Those soldiers are unrealistically expected to be able to fight those patterns effect-ively in situations where they are revolted by what they are told to do, but numerous others conform with the orders. The soldiers go 'cheep cheep' and pull the triggers. Personal autonomy and free will, while a 'transcendental assumption' of all human action, tend to be a very distant possibility in spe-cific life situations of mass obedience.

Instead of assuming, quite mistakenly, that fixed action patterns can be defeated by individuals acting out of their free will or conscience, transi-tional justice institutions should use fixed action patterns to facilitate political and social transition. The same model of automatic obedience of authority suggests that local authority figures can act as allies in inducing new skills and value change in the community within a transition process.

Transitional justice should recognise the potential benefits of alliances with local leaders, whose responsibility for war crimes is limited to their formal participation in wartime decision-making hierarchies (leaders who did not commit crimes themselves). In addition, institutions of transitional justice need to appreciate the fact that people value the communities they belong to, especially if they have sustained victimisation or undergone sacrifice because of their membership. The more one community is seen to be the victim of a war, the greater the value its members will tend to place on their member-ship in the community. Thus, the more the international community assigns victimhood to a particular community, the more homogenous that commu-nity will tend to become. Many Muslim intellectuals who, before the war in Bosnia, used to be 'cosmopolitans' and anti-nationalists, have since embraced a primary identity as members of the Bosnian community. This general prin-ciple is well illustrated by initiation rituals of most communities, ranging from the military to special groups at universities. Some of these rituals are quite cruel; consequently, the new members perceive their joining the group as an achievement for which they have paid a price and which is therefore to be cherished.

Before the 1991–1995 civil war, Bosnia had an exceptionally high rate of interreligious and interethnic marriages, was an example of tolerance and of a progressive, civil society. However, as the conflict started to emerge, people flocked to their respective ethnic communities. Belonging meant having an identity; falling out was equal to being nationless. At first, though people homogenised within their ethnic groups, there was palpable hesitation between them; however, as soon as the international discourse started to label the parties to the conflict in various ways, and national elites emerged which claimed various types of victimhood for each group, even those who were hesitant became full-fledged supporters of their national cause. *The labels made groups more coherent.* The stage for a proper war was thus set, and the international community inadvertently helped this happen. The described process illustrates how ethnic homogenisation could occur in an exceptionally tolerant, multiethnic society such as the pre-1991 Bosnia.

Once the confrontational events were set in motion, the logic of the conflict itself radicalised the respective national causes of the groups. The natural tendency *to be consistent*, which is well known in social psychology, made sure that those who had once made a decision that 'Serbs needed to finally protect themselves in Bosnia' (although just a year or two earlier they had despised any kind of nationalism and considered themselves 'Bosnians') followed up by developing increasingly nationalist views and attitudes. The process was applauded by all three groups of national leaders, who thus had the stage set for a de facto carving up of Bosnia along ethnic lines. *Trying to be consistent is a fixed action pattern*: once we make a decision, we can be easily manipulated into following up with larger decisions that we see as 'consistent' with the initial decision, however small it might have been. Thus, having once joined a national party (all three ethnic groups in Bosnia immediately established their national political parties: initially the Muslims established the SDA — Party of Democratic Action, the Serbs; the SDS — Serbian Democratic Party; and the Croats the HDZ — the Croatian Democratic Union), it was a natural next step for an individual to become an activist, assume some kind of political responsibility, or join the army. It is much less difficult to say 'no' at the beginning than later, once a person has already made a decision in a certain direction. A progressive national homogenisation was a process to be expected as the next step after the initial flocking of people to the national political parties.

One way to counter fixed action responses and their solidification with time is to use *other fixed action patterns*, which will reverse the effects of the initial ones. One such approach might be to get people to join *other identity groups*, which are cross-ethnic and multiethnic, and which focus not on ethnic identities, but on other values. If Barba Meho could do it, surely the international community could, too. Bosnian people are obsessed with building houses. Everybody wants to have a nice house, regardless of whether they need it or not. Most Bosnian towns are full of luxury villas that are empty most of the time, because their owners live and work abroad, and they actually pay someone to look after their real estate while they are away. It would have been fairly easy to forge various transethnic associations of homeowners, builders, or professional associations of building industry craftsmen, which would be given some kind of leadership role, meet at different parts of Bosnia, and draw people together on nonethnic, yet highly attractive value grounds. The relatively massive renovation effort, funded through international donations, of rebuilding the homes destroyed during the war, could have been entrusted to such a multiethnic association of builders, where, for example, Muslim builders would work in Republika Srpska, Serb builders in the Muslim-dominated Sarajevo, and Croat builders everywhere but in the Croat-held Herzeg-Bosnia. The next step could have been to establish a professional management system for the builders' association. People who are involved in management would likely soon become advocates of 'impartial' professionalism. Having once joined on professional, rather than ethnic grounds, by following the principle of consistency they would likely start arguing *against* an ethnic logic and for the interests of the profession.

The role of fixed action patterns is such a major element of our behaviour that decisions initially taken within these patterns can change our self-perception and our functional identities. A nationalist builder or musician who once makes a decision to join a professional 'guild' that is transethnic and multicultural will likely start to see himself as a progressive, tolerant and pragmatic person. Giving a person an identity and a 'reputation' of tolerance and an enlightened inclusiveness to live up to may well cause that person to adopt the reputation as their true identity. Countering fixed action patterns once they are triggered is extremely difficult; however they can be used as antidotes to their own toxic effects: this requires a critical and psychologically informed approach to transitional processes, including that of transitional justice.

The proverbial 'message of disallowing impunity,' on which so much retributive transitional justice seems to rely, is a plainly wrong one. Rather than discouraging future crimes, retribution raises the threshold of 'loyal' ethnic community membership and adds a dimension of victimhood to fighting for the national cause, even if the war is lost. This makes ethnic community membership even more praiseworthy and triggers new and enhanced fixed action patterns which set the stage for a new war in the future. Just look at Bosnia in 2017, twenty-two years since the Dayton Peace Accords. The leader of Republika Srpska, Milorad Dodik (who, by the way, had opposed the war in the early 1990s and had led a Social Democratic Party, which was antinationalist) has understood the fixed action patterns, and now advances from a position of a nationalist leader. During the writing of this introduction, in August 2017, he just called for another referendum in his entity, this time on Bosnia's (already ongoing) NATO membership candidacy, because 'NATO was interfering in the domestic affairs of Bosnia-Herzegovina.' Now, NATO has undoubtedly interfered in Bosnia's domestic matters, simply because it is part of the international intervention mechanism and had de facto occupied Bosnia. On the other hand, in 2017, Bosnia-Herzegovina already had a fully negotiated MAP (individual Membership Action Plan, leading to NATO membership), and was thus, institutionally and politically speaking, already firmly on the road to NATO membership and committed to it. However, the failure by the international interveners to enlist the help of local leaders leads to trends of reversing political decisions which have already been made, such as NATO accession. If transitional justice does not contribute to reconciliation through community enhancement by the use of leadership techniques such as that relying on fixed action patterns, and its putative message of 'preventing impunity' is failing so obviously, then what exactly is the point of transitional justice, given all the financial, social and political costs that are attached to it?

FEAR VERSUS HOPE

The dynamics of group motivation lies in shared emotions, not in a group's or its leaders' rational judgement. All emotions are so-called intentional states of mind: they are states of mind which reach out to something, to an object; they concern something other than themselves. Emotions concern either other people, events or experiences which the person encounters, or the person who is the subject of the emotion herself. It is crucial whether the emotions the group feels towards the other group, as well as the emotions it has for itself and its own members, are positive, constructive, or fundamentally couched in fear. The commonplace reasoning found in ideas such as 'fighting impunity' and 'sending a message of responsibility for crimes' is character- istic of conservative, traditional criminal justice and criminal law: it is the sort of thinking based on the idea of 'general deterrence.' 'Special deter- rence' assumes the punishment's role in 'scaring the perpetrator' away from re-offending in the future through the hardships endured as part of the punish- ment. 'General deterrence,' on the other hand, is supposed to frighten other, potential offenders (all of us, in fact, for all citizens are 'potential offenders') away from committing any kind of crime by our witnessing the suffering inflicted on the actual perpetrators through the punitive legal sanctions. The effectiveness of this logic is highly dubious, to say the least (Fatić, 1995). Most importantly for my present argument, the whole reasoning behind punitiveness focuses squarely on one emotion: *fear*, which is likely the most destructive of all emotions.

There are two fundamental weaknesses of all reasoning about social control which is based on fear. First, almost invariably, societies which are controlled by fear (by particularly harsh legal punishments and administrative sanctions) are more brutal and cruel in their interpersonal dealings and group dynamics than societies that are ruled in less intrusive and punitive ways. In the United States today, the relatively high crime rates are controlled, among other strat- egies, by the use of extreme penalties. Executions in the United States over the past several decades have included the use of gas chambers (reminiscent of some of the darkest periods in the humanity's modern history), lethal injections (the European manufacturers have since stopped delivering their anaesthetics to the US criminal justice institutions because they are used for chemical executions), and electrocutions, to name but a few brutalities. These horrendous methods of killing people were supposed to send a *message of fear*. The effects of the message appear to be exactly *the opposite* to what was intended: crime rates in the United States remain among the highest in the world, so much so that in certain periods the security situation in the streets of Washington, for example, was statistically a comparable risk to life and limb as was life in wartime Sarajevo during the Bosnian war in the early 1990s. Murders, kidnappings and drug-related crimes are an hourly occurrence. One of the growth industries in the United States is that of self-defence training, including the use of firearms, blades, and unarmed 'urban combatives.' An atmosphere of fear imposed by the American criminal justice system degrades the quality of life with a view of reducing violent crime. However it does not reduce violence at all, because, fundamentally, violence *arises from* fear rather than being controlled by fear. The most horrendous violence arises from desperation in the face of fear and powerlessness; this is the way in which human beings are 'hardwired.' This is well illustrated in cases of the so-called family violence: persons who commit the gravest act of such vio-lence, for example, killing one's children or spouses, are almost invariably driven to the crimes by what they see as desperate circumstances in which they find themselves: an inability to maintain contact with their children, a legal process or institutional intervention having gone wrong or corrupt, or an absence of any institutional assistance to address their grievances. Very often, the perpetrators of such crimes take their own lives. Most have no his-tory of violence and many, in hindsight, are found to have exhausted all legal methods of recourse with no results. Almost all such crimes could have been prevented, not by imprisoning the offender, but by facilitating the optimal satisfaction of the offender's needs and family contacts, thus preventing des-peration. In most cases of family violence, the responsibility lies not with the killers, but with the social services, prosecution or the courts, who have failed to address the numerous appeals to act impartially and justly on behalf of an increasingly desperate person. In all cases, however, criminal responsibility is squarely assigned to the perpetrator, while all the other, indirect perpetrators of the tragedy go unpunished and even continue in their jobs. Institutions whose job is to prevent fear and desperation as triggers of violence, when they fail in their work, powerfully illustrate the causal relationship between fear and desperation on the one hand, and violence on the other.

In transitional conflicts, fear drives people in formerly tolerant ethnic communities to turn against their neighbours of different ethnic origin. Most campaigns of ethnic homogenisation are based on fanning fears in the popu-lation: the message is usually that unless people put aside their differences and personal values and join their ethnic brethren, they, their children and their communities risk destruction. This simple message is so powerful that it almost invariably succeeds in drawing people to join the national cause or movement, and the fixed action patterns which favour consistency take care of their subsequent actions and make sure that they become radicalised.

Once ordinary people have been led to fire the first bullets in the direction of their former neighbours, that helps change their self-perceptions and the fixed action pattern of consistency takes over. The 'mindscape' of war is different from that of peacetime, and the psychological and normative circumstances in which one makes one's decisions cannot be compared to, or measured by, the circumstances of decision-making in peacetime. Life in wartime is fraught with fear. This dimension of everyday existence systematically influences the mental well-being and actual decision-making capacity, as well as the values against which decisions are made, in everybody involved. Fear changes the chemistry of our brains and our bodies; by doing so, it changes who we are. If the responses of most people who have committed violent acts, especially those in civil conflicts, were analysed statistically, it would be quite clear that a large majority identify the primary driver behind their actions as fear. Taking this into account, fear must be considered the primary risk for violence; its use as a control mechanism for violence is thus entirely misplaced and bound to be counterproductive in any case. In light of this way of thinking, 'deterrence from committing violence' is a contradiction in terms. The way to reduce violence would, then, be to create a situation which *reduces fear* and emancipates potential perpetrators from it, rather than generating and 'sending a message' of fear through the society. A person who does not feel threatened is less likely to resort to violence. However it is a real challenge to create social circumstances in which most people will not feel threatened in their everyday lives, especially in the impoverished postconflict societies, devoid of immediate existential and economic prospects and marred by the trauma of war.

One of the experiential, existential aspects of fear in situations of conflict is that is easily solidifies into anger: the combination is potentially lethal for intercommunal reconciliation and collaboration. Anger results from a sense of disempowerment. A community which is frightened and feels disempowered, just like an anxious person driven to desperation by a lack of feeling of control, is prepared to do almost anything, without thinking of the consequences. Such a community might resort to an extreme closing of the ranks before transitional justice; it might isolate itself politically, and even wage localised warfare in volatile regions, thus undermining any progress which might have been achieved up to that point. Conversely, anger is best controlled by *empowerment* and a *sense of control*: giving a person some kind of institutional reassurance or access to legal resort might prevent tragic family violence. Similarly, providing a community with a way out of the seeming impasse might prevent it from obstructing the transition process. Again, threats, 'messages' which are punitive in nature, and half-baked international interventions, without a serious understanding of the dynamics of leadership and the sources of motivation to enhance communities, are counterproductive to the very goals of postconflict transitions.

A particularly damaging feature of combined fear and anger is that they stifle hope and forward-looking considerations about the community and its future life. Both emotions obscure the view of the future: they focus on the present (anger) and a threat from the immediate, undesirable likely future events (fear). Both emotions call for defensive action and degrade the quality of the community's experience in the here-and-now. With such a convulsed, bad experience of the present moment, it is virtually impossible for the community, or for an individual person, to anticipate a bright future and hope. Imagine a frightened and angry person talking to a professional counsellor who, instead of reassurance and comfort, issued threats and invoked punitive responsibility for the person's past wrongdoings. That is what the international criminal tribunals for postconflict societies in effect do.

I am not suggesting here that those who have committed crimes should simply be let go. Some leaders must encounter punishment, but some, whose guilt arises from circumstances which they had no proper control of, ought to be treated leniently and encouraged to redeem themselves by acting as agents of change in their communities. This principle of redeeming oneself through constructive future action is at the heart of the restorative philosophy of justice, and it is, to my mind, the only appropriate philosophy for transitional justice.

NOTE

1. Transitional justice belongs to that group of new concepts in social theory which derive from older concepts, but signify new and ground-breaking ideas and social practises, which inevitably makes them misnomers to some extent. Another example which comes to mind is the concept of 'human security,' also a new generation concept which includes all kinds of rights and entitlements in society (environmental security, security of workplace, right to, or security of, income, etc.), many of which have very little or nothing to do with the traditional concept of security. It is helpful to bear this in mind in the discussion of transitional justice, as it is a vastly expanded notion of 'justice' on a par with that of 'security' in the conceptualisation of 'human security.'

REFERENCES

Allenby, Branden, and Sarewitz, Daniel. (2011). *The Techno-Human Condition.* Cambridge, MA: MIT Press.

Bachmann, Klaus, and Fatić, Aleksandar. (2014). *The UN International War Crimes Tribunals: Transition without Justice?* London: Routledge.

BBC (2013). 'Do White People Have a Future in South Africa?' 20 May. http://www.bbc.com/news/magazine-22554709.

BBC. (2017). 'African Union Backs Mass Withdrawal from ICC.' 1 February. http://www.bbc.com/news/world-africa-38826073.

Burton, John. (1990). *Conflict Resolution and Prevention.* London: St. Martin's Press.

Christie, Nils. (1981). *Limits to Pain.* Oslo: Norwegian University Press.

Cialdini, Robert. (2007). *Influence: The Psychology of Persuasion* (Rev. Ed.). New York: HarperCollins.

Damasio, Antonio. (1994). *Descartes' Error: Emotion, Reason, and the Human Brain.* New York: Avon Books.

Fatić, Aleksandar. (1995). *Punishment and Restorative Crime-Handling: Towards a Social Theory of Trust.* Aldershot: Ashgate.

Fatić, Aleksandar, and Dentsoras, Dimitrios. (2014). 'Pleasure in Epicurean and Christian Orthodox Conceptions of Happiness.' *South African Journal of Philosophy* 33, 4: 523–536.

Galtung, Johan. (1958). *Theories of Conflict.* New York: Columbia University Press.

Henry, Paul-Marc. (1959). 'Pan-Africanism: A Dream Come True.' *Foreign Affairs*, April Issue. https://www.foreignaffairs.com/articles/africa/1959-04-01/pan-africanism-dream-come-true.

Hudson, Barbara. (1987). *Justice through Punishment: A Critique of the Justice Model of Corrections.* London: Palgrave Macmillan.

IWPR (Institute for War and Peace Reporting). (2010). 'Čežnja za domom' ('Longing for home'). 28 September. https://iwpr.net/sr/global-voices/čežnja-za-domom.

LA Times. (2017). 'Trump Warns North Korea of "Fire and Fury."' 8 August. https://www.theguardian.com/uk-news/2016/mar/16/the-real-meaning-of-rhodes-must-fall.

Mail&Guardian. (2016). 'The Rise of a New Black Racism in South Africa.' 16 May. https://mg.co.za/article/2016-05-16-00-the-rise-of-a-new-black-racism-in-south-africa.

Roets, Ernest. (2017).'Anti-White Racism in South Africa.' *Politicsweb*: 14 September 2017. http://www.politicsweb.co.za/opinion/antiwhite-racism-in-south-africa.

The Economist. (2017). 'Kenya's Presidential Election Has Been Overturned. What Next?' 9 September. https://www.economist.com/news/middle-east-and-africa/21728660-it-was-triumph-rule-lawbut-country-now-edge-kenyas.

The Guardian. (2008). 'Prozac, Used by 40m People, Does Not Work Say Scientists.' 26 February. https://www.theguardian.com/society/2008/feb/26/mentalhealth.medicalresearch.

The Guardian. (2016a). 'South Africa: Students Attack Police as Protests over Tuition Fees Escalate.' 4 October. https://www.theguardian.com/world/2016/oct/04/south-africa-students-attack-police-protests-tuition-fees-escalate.

The Guardian. (2016b). 'The Real Meaning of Rhodes Must Fall.' 16 March. https://www.theguardian.com/uk-news/2016/mar/16/the-real-meaning-of-rhodes-must-fall.

Uslaner, Eric. (2002). *The Moral Foundations of Trust.* Cambridge: Cambridge University Press.

Chapter 1

Transitional Justice and Injustice in Transition

Assessing the Penalisation of Wartime Violence in Light of the ICTY Legacy

Axelle Reiter

STANDARDS OF EFFECTIVENESS: MANDATE AND AIMS OF THE ICTY

International law relies on the principles of criminal law to deal with wartime violence and past human rights abuses in postconflict societies. The appropriateness of this approach is presumed, rather than grounded in any actual assessment of its benefits, and alternative means of conflict management are sidelined. The need to test this uncritical assumption calls for an examination of the effectiveness of international criminal justice in meeting the aspirations of the international community (i.e., the international political community that has presided over the creation of international criminal tribunals) and generating the outcomes it is meant to bring about; here, focusing on the penalisation of violence in the Socialist Federal Republic of Yugoslavia (SFRY) before the International Criminal Tribunal for the former Yugoslavia (ICTY). Criminal law aims at determining the individual accountability of the accused for past offences. It is punitive and, although it also aspires to reach preventive and expressive or symbolic goals, its main object is retributive. Besides, the ICTY, which has just been closed having 'fulfilled' its stated mission, purported to fulfil various functions, some of which were associated with transitional justice mechanisms and human rights law, namely rehabilitation, deterrence, the protection of society, public reprobation and stigmatisation, the fight against impunity, redress for the victims, reconciliation and contribution to the peace process. The questionable methods adopted in order to achieve these objectives have resulted in severe violations of the rights of the accused and denial of victims' claims, as well as in undermining reconciliation in the region. These consequences can be traced back to the hybrid nature of international criminal justice and a lack of insights into the causes of wartime criminality. Whereas penal law traditionally rejects collective responsibility, criminological studies demonstrate that international crimes are group offences and manifest systemic violence.

This chapter analyses the causes of wartime criminality, the specificities of this form of violence, the adverse consequences of penalisation of violence by the ICTY, and the social reactions to international trials in the SFRY successor states and entities. It is divided into four sections. The first clarifies the ambitions of the ICTY and discusses the question of how they can be realistically circumscribed in order to provide standards against which to judge its usefulness and determine an operational benchmark for its success. It argues that the mandate and functions of the ICTY should have been cut down to the fulfilment of three main purposes: retribution, redress for the victims, and the restoration and maintenance of peace in the region. The second section examines the roots and distinctiveness of wartime criminality, the challenges posed by the penalisation of acts of systemic violence and the inadequacy of ordinary criminal law mechanisms to establish responsibility for mass atrocities. The remaining sections gauge the ICTY's effectiveness in delivering its three core aims and investigate the reasons for its failure to attain any of these objectives, a failure echoed in the local population's scepticism towards the institution. Finally, this chapter scrutinizes alternative options and advocates a switch of emphasis from penal responses to transitional justice mechanisms like truth commissions and compensatory solutions.

An assessment of the success of international criminal justice calls for an inquiry into its aims. One must then investigate what the prosecution of individuals in supranational fora effectively achieves, in order to determine whether they fulfil (or, as it turns out, do not fulfil) their explicit mandate and the broader expectations that the international community bestows upon them.

The famed statement by the International Military Tribunal at Nuremberg, that 'crimes against international law are committed by men, not by abstract entities, and only by punishing individuals who commit such crimes can the provisions of international law be enforced,' lies at the core of international criminal law.[1] Hence, international criminal law basically regulates the international responsibility of individual actors. Security Council Resolution 827 purported to establish the ICTY 'for the sole purpose of prosecuting persons responsible for serious violations of international humanitarian law committed in the territory of the former Yugoslavia' (§ 2). This allegedly unique function of the tribunal could not be divorced from underlying strategic goals. The Security Council adopted Resolution 827 in the frame of its 'primary responsibility for the maintenance of international peace and security' under Article 24 § 1 and Chapter VII of the UN Charter. After determining that the situation in the former Yugoslavia constituted 'a threat to international peace and security,' it put it forward that the prosecution of international crimes committed on its territory 'would contribute to the restoration and maintenance of peace' (Article 24, Preamble). Accordingly, the main criterion to appraise its adequacy from a teleological perspective was its effectiveness in contributing to the restoration of peace, deterrence of additional violence and the cessation of military hostilities, on the one hand, and the maintenance and consolidation of peace and security in the postconflict era, on the other (Futamura, 2008: 3–4; Kerr, 2000: 17). Thus ICTY aimed to support a lasting peace and long-term stability in the region through the reconciliation of erstwhile enemies. Yet, penalisation tends to be counterproductive on both counts: the indictment and prosecution of civil and military leaders reduce the realistic prospects of a negotiated ceasefire and prompt settlement of the conflict (D'Amato, 1994: 500–501), while the adversarial nature of criminal trials undermines the reconciliation process. In a nutshell, 'peace through justice' often leaves way for 'peace *versus* justice.'

ICTY considered its mandate to be 'threefold: to do justice, to deter further crimes and to contribute to the restoration and maintenance of peace.' It identified itself 'as one of the measures designed gradually to promote the end of armed hostilities and a return to normality' (ICTY, 1994: §§ 11–14). A supplementary purpose was eventually endorsed, that of rendering justice to the victims of international crimes (ICTY, 2002: § 328). ICTY also tried to clarify the 'purposes and objectives' of sentencing. In a misguided attempt at exhaustiveness, it lumped together 'retribution, protection of society, rehabilitation and deterrence' of the accused (special deterrence) and other persons alike (general deterrence). Retribution had been renamed 'just deserts,' while deterrence was sometimes mentioned under the label of 'prevention.' In a competing account, the tribunal emphasised 'public reprobation and stigmatization by the international community'; which partook more to the classical symbolic vision of penalisation. It recurrently brought up the fight against impunity, the end of infractions to humanitarian rules, enhancing public information about the crimes and the establishment of 'truth,' redress, 'appeasement' for the victims and their relatives, reconciliation and contribution to the peace process.[2] The goals enumerated varied from one judgement to the next and none referred to this list in its entirety. The exaggerated ambition, mutual irreconcilability and lack of ranking of the professed objectives were striking.

Interestingly, ICTY appeared to be aware of the mutually exclusive character of some of its self-appointed missions. Retribution clashes with reconciliatory objectives because it originates in revenge and retaliation. As a result, sentences handed out mostly on retributive premises risk to disrupt the peace process.[3] Moreover, invoking classical justifications for the prosecution of ordinary crimes in times of peace hardly makes sense in the context of wartime violence. In particular, the deterrent power of international criminal justice is doubtful. ICTY was created before the Dayton Peace Agreement and was already operational at the time of some of the most serious breaches of the *ius in bello* during the Yugoslav civil wars, including Operations Flash and Storm and the Srebrenica bloodbath. ICTY acknowledged that deterrence, social defence and rehabilitation were problematic targets of sentencing. The tribunal admitted that the improbability of opportunities for recidivism in war crimes rendered the consideration of special prevention 'unreasonable and unfair,' while reliance on general deterrence ignored that 'a sentence should in principle be imposed on an offender for his culpable conduct.' Social protection and the 'incapacitation of the dangerous' cannot justify the removal from society (and preventive detention) of first-time offenders without criminal records. The very nature of international crimes means that they 'can be committed only in certain contexts which may not arise again in the society where the convicted person, once released, may eventually settle,' while the 'rehabilitative effect' of imprisonment is controversial at best.[4] This signifies that international justice cannot (nor should it attempt to) promote the traditional rationales for penalisation other than retribution.

Subsequently, the success of international criminal tribunals essentially depends on their ability to respect the standards of conventional deontic justice, grounded in retributivism, together with their capacity to answer the broader societal concerns that presided over their creation; namely, to deliver redress to the victims and secure peace. Whereas restorative justice facilitates reconciliation by focusing on remedies to the injustice committed and reparation of the wrong done to the victims rather than on punishment, retributivism hinders both. The adversarial character of criminal trials calls attention to the prosecution of the offenders and the defence of the accused, minimising the position of the victims in the proceedings, and leads to the perpetuation of resentments and antagonism between the warring factions. Besides, effective justice cannot be attained if it is marred by unfairness or if it breaches the substantive and procedural rights of the accused. Thus, ICTY was not only meant to be concerned with the punishment of the atrocities committed in SFRY. It was supposed to be equally anxious to try the defendants in conformity with international human rights law.[5] Proceedings before ICTY have unfortunately failed spectacularly in all three respects, by seriously infringing the basic rights of individual participants in the trials (be it accused, victims or witnesses), by denying adequate remedies to the victims of international crimes and by destabilising the process of peace and reconciliation. They most usefully serve as a catalogue of judicial *worst* practises, to illustrate the hazards of tempering with the rule of law through adjudication. As such, they militate for a complete reform (*voire* the abolition) of the international criminal justice system and the adoption of higher standards or alternative solutions, which would satisfy the requirements of effective justice and fulfil the wider aspirations of the international community.

ORDINARY CRIMINAL NORMS AND MECHANISMS FOR EXTRAORDINARY CRIMES

International crimes are intrinsically tied to the specific circumstances of armed conflicts or situations of widespread societal violence. They differ radically from common crimes committed in times of peace. The negation of their specificity creates deep tensions and irresolvable problems, when common (or harmonized) national rules for the prosecution and punishment of ordinary crimes are transplanted onto international tribunals.

From a liberal (rights-based) perspective, the sole claim to the legitimacy of prosecution and penalisation is to be found in deontological or desert-based considerations (Hart, 1958: 448–55). Indeed, 'one clear implication of Kant's prohibition against treating human beings as means to an end is the rejection of deterrence as a sufficient rationale for punishment.' Since 'punishment must respect the offender as an end in himself, as a respon- sible agent called to account for his wrongdoing' (Fletcher, 1998: 43), the reproached offence results from an intentional autonomous act of the accused, whose wrongfulness demands (according to Kant) society's retaliation and encroachment upon her personal rights. This conception of the object of penal justice, entrenched in the general principle of personal culpability, is widely recognised by national systems of criminal law. Unlike civil liability, criminal responsibility requires an element of *mens rea*, the intention to commit the imputed infraction. The notion of *mens rea* comes from the Latin adage *actus facit reum nisi mens sit rea*, which means that the deed itself cannot be deter- minative of guilt in the absence of a blameworthy intent. Penal courts 'should not find a man guilty of an offence against the criminal law unless he has a guilty mind' and the imputation of said crime requires proof of both the crim- inal act and intent of its perpetrator.[6] To satisfy this condition, the offender must have known that what she was doing was wrong (the cognitive element) and must have been able to act otherwise (the volitional element). If one of these two elements is not met, she has not acted of her own free will and can therefore not be held criminally responsible. This exculpates perpetrators who have acted under compulsion and could thus not have acted otherwise, since they do not possess the volitional element of *mens rea*. In addition, it casts serious doubts on the adequacy of penalising individuals who believe that the commission of the imputed offence was not wrong but right (or that it was their duty), because they align their personal judgements to those of the community to which they belong, since their crimes do not satisfy the cognitive element of *mens rea*. The vast majority of national legal systems have adopted the concept of *mens rea* with the result that it most likely qualifies as a general principle of law under Article 38 of the Statute of the International Court of Justice (Pradel, 1995: 251–53; Schabas, 2003: 1015).

Individual criminal responsibility targets transgression or deviance from established social and legal norms. Retributivism and associated expressive goals are grounded in the idea that punishment is not meted solely to penalise specific breaches of the law but also to sanction a perceived moral wrong. The penal system of prosecution and punishment of ordinary crimes is structurally disconnected from the realities of wartime violence and the roots of international criminality. Far from being deviant or in conflict with the prevailing values, the perpetrators of international crimes are usually well-adjusted individuals with good (*voire* high) social skills, characterised by a lack of criminal identity, who neither need reinsertion into society nor jeopardise the society from which they originate. After the cessation of the hostilities, they can easily integrate (and conform to) a new set of social norms and live as ordinary citizens and members of their communities for the rest of their lives. During armed conflicts, individuals commit atrocious crimes out of survival instinct or patriotism, sometimes under the perception that they are defending their own people from ethnic cleansing and possible extermination (Gaynor and Harmon, 2007: 693–95; ICTY, 2006). They do not consider the offences morally wrong, but acceptable or good. While particular actors might act out of different motives (including sadism, opportunism, ambition or an innate tendency to commit crimes) and merely use their violent environment for personal purposes, most culprits are moved by loyalty to a group or a cause, trust in authority, obedience, or pure conformism. Others do not even act out of their own accord and only cooperate reluctantly under pressure, intimidation, force or other forms of coercion. Their crimes cannot be comprehended if divorced from the context of collective violence in which they emerged (Smeulers, 2008a: 240–60).

'The object of warfare is murder' (Tolstoy, 1869: part X, ch. 25). The brutal and fierce conditions of warfare, coupled with the usual sociopsychological mechanisms at work in such conditions, transform many hitherto undisturbed people into willing executors or accomplices of mass scale heinous offences. The limits of sanity are radically redefined; and so are social and moral norms and imperatives. Acts normally perceived as wrongdoings (and sometimes even as evil wrongdoings) in time of peace are considered acceptable, if not commendable, in wartime. This has a double effect on individual members of affected societies, combatants and bystanders alike. First, they get progressively and incrementally desensitised to human suffering and eventually to horrendous cruelties. Second, they often feel compelled to participate in the spiral of violence that engulfs them and to take sides. They frequently lose the rational capacity to tell right from wrong or they end up believing in the rightness of crimes (Arendt, 1963; Smeulers, 2008a: 238–40, 263–64). The international rules that regulate the conduct of hostilities sanction some weighting of humanitarian concerns against military necessity. This aggravates people's perception that anything will do if it serves the general war effort or belligerent imperatives. This situation is further exacerbated in civil wars and internal conflicts, characterised by a higher level of savagery, due to the proximity of the adversary. Civil wars are 'designed to be criminal' and are often accompanied by propaganda campaigns aimed at dehumanising and demonising antagonist groups before the actual start of ethnic cleansing operations (Fatić, 2000: 21, 71–73). The entire opponent population becomes the enemy and no atrocity against this newly fabricated enemy is considered barbaric enough.

International law accepts that violations of the *ius ad bellum* and acts of aggression are not attributable to individuals who have been coerced into taking part in the hostilities. Whereas volunteers and mercenaries could potentially be held liable for such breaches of international law (which might explain why, under Article 47 of the First Additional Protocol to the Geneva Conventions, the latter are not automatically granted the status of prisoners of war), conscripted soldiers would never qualify for full culpability because they would benefit from an excuse of duress. In contrast, international criminal law takes no notice of the challenges that collective responsibility raises for the prosecution and punishment of individuals for grave breaches of the *ius in bello* or other international crimes. However, even if the lack of personal *mens rea* might at first sight seem less striking for war crimes, crimes against humanity or genocidal acts, the question of the actual guilt of individual perpetrators poses itself equally acutely for all international crimes.

Typically, international 'crimes are manifestations of collective violence and are described by lawyers as structural or system criminality.' They mostly purport to obtain or keep political power by the state and the states' apparatus usually sanctions, if it does not encourage, the perpetration of international crimes. This casts the particular offenders as simple executioners of professed 'crimes of obedience' (Drumbl, 2007: 33; Smeulers, 2008b: 971, 973–80). History shows us that individual free will often leads the way wide open to blind submission to authority under totalitarianism and in times of war or general upheaval (Milgram, 1974; Zimbardo, 2007: 324–79). Because of the banality of the evils committed under extreme circumstances (Arendt, 1963; Smeulers and Werner, 2010) and the collective dimension of international crimes, the attribution of responsibility for these offences to specific individuals is not easily reconciled with the retributive and symbolic or expressive purposes traditionally associated with criminal justice. Collective penalisation inherently contradicts any remotely liberal understanding of criminal justice and the core premises of human rights; namely, free will and individual responsibility for one's own *personal* actions. This leads to the wider philosophical question of how to ascribe individual accountability in totalitarian settings or even in ordinary democracies, where national residents did not choose nor necessarily agree with the actions and policies adopted by the government supposed to represent them. Unhappily, the challenge is not adequately met by any penal alternative.

Picking a few scapegoats to bear responsibility for the actions of an entire regime similarly contradicts the ethical underpinnings of deontic justice. On the one hand, 'it fails to hold accountable the full array of people who individually are responsible for the collectivization of atrocity' and contradicts allegations to the effect that it will end impunity (Drumbl, 2007: 37). On the other hand, the arbitrariness of such an indictment process vitiates the most basic conditions of fairness, giving rise to justified charges of partiality and undermining of the legitimacy of the trials: 'the need to select challenges the very concept of fair justice and retribution' (Smeulers, 2008b: 982). The selection process entails these corollaries independently of its focus on the physical perpetrators who actually pulled the triggers, their commanders or hierarchical superiors, people who held certain positions of power on the basis of some sort of functional (presumed or vicarious) liability, or the masterminds who effectively planned and orchestrated the commission of the crimes under judgement. Part of the academic doctrine has tried to establish grades of 'moral blameworthiness' and attach legal consequences to it; for example, placing all individuals belonging to the responsible group or society on a descending scale, extending from the main entrepreneurs of the conflict to simple bystanders who merely failed to intervene, passing by various types of leaders, lower level perpetrators, accomplices and beneficiaries of the atrocities (Drumbl, 2007: 25). Yet, each of these options presents some problems. In particular, most of the rank and file might not possess the required *mens rea* to be held personally culpable, while individuals who occupy higher social positions do not necessarily get involved in the design and preparation of the offences. Furthermore, responsibility is never to be assumed or presumed in penal matters, which nullifies attempts at making people strictly liable or accountable for international crimes on a purely functional, vicarious or other objective basis.

In effect, 'international crimes can only be totally captured as state crimes' or 'organisational crimes' (Chouliarias, 2010: 548–49). International crimes are considered crimes of states in three respects. Primarily, they are committed or provoked by states. Second, they affect other states' interests and interstate relations because of their interconnection with international peace and security and their negative impact on the consolidation of the international legal order. Third, the international organisations meant to represent the international community of states are responsible for their definition and the modalities of their penalisation (Alvarez, 1999: 367–68). This calls for an interstate mechanism to ascertain liability for the wrongdoings, focusing both on states and international organisations directly responsible for the atrocities committed and on those causally responsible for the outbreak of the hostilities of which wartime (criminal) violence is an expected feature. Such a solution would strike straight at the roots of international crimes, take due account of their distinctiveness and ultimately help dispel the main concern by the international community, namely the effect of international crimes on international peace and security, by tackling the whole phenomenon of wartime violence rather than a few breaches of its rules of conduct. The prosecution and punishment of discrete individual crimes by the international criminal tribunals does not provide a remedy to the broader situation of collective violence and faces international lawyers with the difficult task of squaring the accountability circle in relation to individual offences that essentially constitute acts of states. Ignoring the causal link between war and unspeakable crimes hinders any realistic possibility to curb the risks of their resurgence and bring about effective justice. Regrettably, international responses to wartime criminality completely overlook its causes and underplay its distinctiveness.

DOING INJUSTICE: UNFAIR TRIALS AND HUMAN RIGHTS VIOLATIONS

Supranational courts adhere to policy considerations of a teleological nature and extra-legal goals of a political or ideological kind, at the cost of negating peremptory legal rules, in the fashion of authoritarian models of criminal justice (Fichtelberg, 2008; Robinson, 2008; 2010). This is largely due to a lack of insights into international criminology and the inadequacy of ordinary criminal law mechanisms to establish responsibility for mass atrocities. Due to the collective (societal) character of the crimes on trial, international prosecutors and courts have relied heavily on alternative, unorthodox doctrines to attribute personal responsibility for these offences to actors other than their direct physical perpetrators. These new modes of liability have as their main purpose the goal to lower the *mens rea* threshold required as evidence of the criminal intent. They allow the imputation of crimes to people who neither committed nor intended them, on grounds of mere negligence or even solely on account of the predictability of the crimes. Such broadened liability greatly facilitates the work of the prosecutor's office. In fact, it serves as the central charge for many indictments, thus posing serious legitimacy problems for the ensuing trials and casting doubts on many of the resulting convictions.

The shortcomings of the broadened liability used in the trials for international crimes lie in the absence of fair labelling, expanding definitions of crimes, sweeping modes of liability, and reticence towards traditional means of defence and causes of exoneration. The blunt denial of the possibility to invoke duress in relation to war crimes and crimes against humanity exemplifies this last point most compellingly.[7] Traditional modes of liability have been construed in an extravagantly extensive fashion and some of their customary constitutive elements ignored, like the specific direction requirement for complicity;[8] which conditions responsibility to a determination that the acts of the accused were specifically directed to assist the commission of crimes. The mere provision of logistic and personnel support to allied armies has led to convictions for aiding and abetting all crimes committed by these armies. Equating assistance to the overall war effort with aiding and abetting the offences committed during the war criminalises the waging of war per se, creating a brand new crime beside those listed in the ICTY Statute.[9] The expansive interpretation of the doctrines of command responsibility and co-perpetratorship promotes a conception of criminal imputation more akin to absolute liability.

Command responsibility requires some correlation between the actions of the accused superior and the crimes committed by his underlings. ICTY interpreted this link in a much broader fashion than customarily accepted. The resulting offence combines an *actus reus* of omission with a *mens rea* of negligence or lack of diligence, on the basis of a 'had reason to know' standard. It permitted the tribunal to condemn someone for genocide solely 'as a result of his failure to carry out his duty as a superior to exercise control over his or her subordinates,'[10] even though he did not share with them the specific intent to commit such a wrong; this completely sets aside the *dolus specialis* traditionally required as an integral part of the crime of genocide. It does not demand a causal relation between the conduct of the commander and the actual crimes, be it in cases of failure to prevent the culpable acts or punish their authors.[11] A clear cut example of abusive use of the theory, 'the responsibility of a superior for acts which were committed before he became the superior of the persons who committed them,' was seriously considered with mixed results.[12] The accused have been convicted of murder for aiding and abetting by omission and for superior responsibility for their failure to protect prisoners and prevent their transfer to the custody of the perpetrator in principal.[13] This has confused the notions of 'substantial effect on the crime' and failure 'to act in order to render those crimes substantially less likely.'[14] The high rank of the accused, substantial support to allied armies and the payment of salaries and other benefits to re-subordinated military personnel (seconded to a different army than that commanded by the accused) were deemed suffi-cient evidence of the accused's operational control over them,[15] although this finding was quashed in appeals on grounds of 'reasonable doubt.'[16] These wild hypothetical extrapolations hint at a collective responsibility cast on randomly selected suspects. Thus the ICTY definition of command responsi-bility effectively boiled down to strict vicarious liability.

The concept of joint criminal enterprise, invented by the Appeals Chamber[17] and tellingly nicknamed 'just convict everyone' (Badar, 2006; Schabas, 2006: 429), provided an extreme example of guilt by association. Conjuring up the specificity and collective character of international crimes, the ICTY had simply created the doctrine by means of a purposive inter-pretation of several dispositions of its statute, contradicting the principle of legality and the obligation to strictly construe penal statutes. The notion of joint criminal enterprise was an over-inclusive catch-all concept, in the literal sense of the term. It permitted the tribunal to convict the author of a negligible and insignificant contribution to a single offence of all the crimes potentially connected to that offence, through the prosecutor's invocation of a common plan. The accused might have neither committed the *actus reus*, nor possessed the *mens rea* required for the infractions. She might even have had no know-ledge of their occurrence. Here again, it has led to discarding the *dolus specialis* required for the commission of genocide, in several instances.[18] The theory knows of no geographical, structural or temporal limitations. It can apply to an entire region (*voire* a country) and to organisations comprised of thousands of participants.[19] All accused participants in the so-called enter-prise are deemed to have committed the crime and considered to be 'equally guilty of the crime regardless of the part each played in its commission.'[20] At the limits, any member of an army or civilian institution could conceivably be held accountable for the whole range of offences perpetuated by this organisa-tion nationwide; a result which verges on absurd. As a mode of liability, joint criminal enterprise clearly falls short of the slimmest pretence of respect for the principle of personal culpability. Moreover, it proves equally wrong from a teleological perspective. It necessarily resulted in discounted convictions, which trivialised the guilt of the accused and did not vindicate the claims of the victims, and it risked generating further violence in the region: a fact the tribunal was, incidentally, well aware of (ICTY, 1994: § 16).[21]

Besides, the ICTY violated basic human rights of the accused to unpre-cedented extent. It claimed a form of international exceptionalism to bypass a stringent construing of the principle of legality and the ban on retroactive penalisation. It heavily resorted to *ex post facto* creation or specification of penal offences and modes of liability, as well as to reasoning by analogy, in violation of the *nullum crimen sine lege* principle. It imposed heavier sentences than allowed under domestic law, and possibly under general international law, in breach of the *nulla poena sine lege* rule. Clashing decisions concerning international customs and the constant modification and updating of the rules of procedure and evidence of the tribunal generated further legal uncertainty, at the substantive and procedural levels (Reiter, 2013). The accused were deprived of their right to appeal in certain circumstances. In a case where a conviction for additional crimes was entered at the appellate level, the Appeals Chamber substituted its own verdict to the first instance decision and substantially increased the prison sentence, instead of sending the case back to a lower level chamber for retrial and sentencing purposes.[22] Likewise, it ratified the introduction of alternate modes of liability for the first time during the appeals proceedings.[23] In addition, one must deplore the striking inequality of arms between the parties to the proceedings (Bachmann and Fatić, 2015: 55–75); the admission of written summaries of witness statements drafted by prosecution investigators and adjudicated facts from previous trials;[24] the erosion of the right to remain silent and the presumption of innocence by the introduction of a condition of reciprocal disclosure of the parties' files and documents (Rules of Procedure and Evidence, Nos. 66 B and 67); the endorsement of judgements taken on the basis of a single uncorroborated testimony;[25] the exclusion of some accused from the courtroom and the denial of their right to self-representation;[26] the unusual length of the trials, the unacceptably long periods of detention on remand, and the possibility of balancing humane conditions of imprisonment against the imperatives of security and order.[27] This complete denial of the defendants' rights to personal liberty, fair trial and even physical integrity irremediably frustrated any pretention of the tribunal to deliver effective justice.

HYBRID NATURE OF THE ICTY: ABSENCE OF REDRESS AND RECONCILIATION

Criminal law looks backwards and largely ignores reconciliatory considerations. It is centred on the parties to the criminal trial (namely, the prosecutor and the accused or the defence) and typically downsizes the role of victims to that of third parties in the proceedings. Since victims want to be heard and claim some ownership of the process, international criminal law endorses the aims of transitional justice mechanisms and human rights law. The ICTY Statute and its rules of procedure and evidence created a hybrid regime, which was partly punitive and partly compensatory.

The rights of victims could be divided into two categories. The first group facilitated the victims' participation in the proceedings and made possible for them to receive some form of satisfaction or reparation. Victims could not claim any compensation by the ICTY or the United Nations, aside from the restitution of their property, and the tribunal has never ordered the restitution of forfeited property. If the accused was found guilty, they might bring an action before national courts or other competent bodies, in order to obtain reparation for the damages, pursuant to relevant national legislation (Rules of Procedure and Evidence, Nos. 105–106). The second group of rights provided support to victims, through the creation of a victims and witnesses unit within the ICTY registry (Rules of Procedure and Evidence, No. 34), and protected them against intimidation or aggravation of their traumas (Rules of Procedure and Evidence, Nos. 69, 75, 79, 81–81 *bis*, 90, 92 *bis-quinquies* and 96). International criminal tribunals encountered serious difficulties in securing the attendance of witnesses, because of their inability to control any given territory and the risks involved for the personal safety of those willing to testify; these dangers were increased by the highly political context of the crimes and their close relation to unresolved ethnic tensions. International judges regularly discarded the legitimate claims, motivations, allegiances and dramatic or traumatic experiences of the victims, when supervising the examination or cross-examination of the victims by the parties to the trial. Aside from the serious mishandling, harsh questioning and further victimisation of vulnerable persons, during what has been described as 'silencing hearings' (Dembour and Haslam, 2004), they treated abjectly people unwilling to testify under certain conditions, be it because of threats or out of personal loyalty and patriotism.[28] Witnesses were meagrely reimbursed for their expenses and time spent testifying and completely abandoned post-trial (Stover, 2005: 96).

In drafting its rules of procedure and evidence, the tribunal had balanced two sets of objectives: the respect of the rights of the defence and the protection of victims and witnesses, in order to enable them to testify and facilitate the trial (ICTY Statute, Articles 15: 21–22). The power to examine prosecution witnesses and the publicity of the trial were limited when they conflicted with the safety or the rights of victims and witnesses. Specific additional provisions were aimed at averting the worsening of the sufferings experienced by victims of sexual assaults and took into account their vulnerability when confronted with their aggressor or the memory of the attack. Unhappily, the measures adopted did not protect victims and witnesses from reprisals or further victimisation. Numerous witnesses had been killed before reaching the court, to prevent them from giving their testimony, or after they had testified, to take revenge on them. In addition, the media sometimes exercised pressure to dissuade witnesses from testifying against 'what the prevailing state of mind considers proper.' A solution might have been to grant political asylum to endangered persons and their families, but relocation and settlement in a third country was done only in rare instances and witnesses might refuse this protection (Humanitarian Law Centre, 2000: 58–63, 69, 134; Stover, 2005: 113–14). The ICTY and the office of the prosecutor had actively contributed on several occasions to a serious aggravation of the already dire situation of insecurity facing victims and witnesses. The trial of leaders of the Kosovo Liberation Army, where the climate of intimidation and terrorisation was so pervasive that a retrial was ordered,[29] provided an emblematic illustration of the dangers raised by the prevailing unawareness of the various complicating factors by the international actors involved. The Trial Chamber disclosed sensitive confidential information to the general public, in breach of protective measures previously adopted,[30] and initiated contempt proceedings against a witness for the prosecution who had refused to answer questions out of fear.[31]

The current fixation by the international community on personal accountability and the fight against impunity hardly masks the confession of its powerlessness to stop the commission of mass violence and atrocities and hints at a greater concern for their punishment than their prevention. The consolidation of peace and the stabilisation of the security situation in postconflict regions require a comprehensive process of catharsis, mutual forgiveness and rapprochement by the warring groups. International criminal trials do not serve reconciliatory objectives but partake in a vicious cycle of war and penalisation. Their adversarial nature contributes to a widening of discords and divisiveness in the recipient societies and a continuation of the conflicts by legal means: 'lawfare' merely substituting warfare. This predicament also affects interstate trials attributing liability for wartime violence, like the genocide cases introduced before the International Court of Justice. The selectivity and formalism of international criminal proceedings endanger the expressive capacity of punishment. Due process requirements may distort historical records (Damaška, 2008: 336) and international tribunals can only establish a judicial or legal truth — not *the* (historical) truth; which is (and should remain) the task for historians.

Individuation of responsibility masks the more structural and systematic causal responsibility for wartime violence. This might explain why the international community eagerly embraces international criminal justice. Reducing justice to the penalisation of a few individuals permits the tribunals to hide discomforting realities. It shields international organisations and foreign states that intervene in civil wars from accountability for their role in the commission of international crimes. However, the reconciliatory potential (if any) of penalisation can only be achieved by bringing *all* responsible agents to answer for their culpable actions, independent of their nationality. By opposition, selecting the accused on the basis of their belonging to a given ethnic group or faction intensifies grievances and hinders reconciliation in the region, especially if the selection process denotes bias or partiality towards one side in the armed conflict. Likewise, obscuring the faults of the international actors destroys the credibility of the judicial process and any positive impact it might have in the affected societies. The ICTY record is particularly grim in this respect (Bachmann and Fatić, 2015: 36–44, 120–21, 236–37; Fatić, 2000: 1–3, 9–19, 26–29, 45–56, 81–87, 103–105). The unwillingness of the prosecutor to investigate war crimes committed by NATO officials during the bombing of the Federal Republic of Yugoslavia provides the most egregious illustration of the prosecutor's lack of independence and impartiality and her inability to resist political pressures.[32] It corroborates accusations that the ICTY dispensed victor's justice (Benvenuti, 2001; Colangelo, 2003: 1425–36; Darcy, 2007: 393) and has been severely condemned by the International Committee of the Red Cross, in a report that stigmatises a noticeable bias in favour of NATO member states and reliance on double standards (see, for large extracts of the ICRC confidential report, Hazan, 2000: 219–25). The flagrant disparity of treatment between the different warring factions at the level of indictment, conviction and sentencing confirms this want of integrity (Bachmann and Fatić, 2015: 80–92; Scharf, 1997: 310–11).

The picture of the tribunal as an instrument of realpolitik at the service of imperial powers widens the gap between the ICTY and the expectations of the population of the former Yugoslav countries and entities, since sincerity matters immensely for people to accept (if not identify themselves with) charges brought against their own leadership and national heroes (Fatić, 2000: 28, 81). By opposition, victor's justice usually creates cynicism or reactionary nationalistic attitudes in the targeted population. The social perception of the tribunal has been abysmal. According to public opinion surveys, only an extremely small percentage (less than a quarter and, in some areas, less than 10 percent) of the population expressed a modest level of trust in the institution, with the exception of Kosovo* and the Bosnian Federation (where it barely amounted to half of the respondents). The majority of the population in most areas overwhelmingly distrusted the tribunal and saw it as politically motivated, partial and unfair. Local judges and prosecutors viewed it as a political court that was 'biased and incapable of providing fair trials' and they rejected its factual findings and record of the war. Far from improving over time, the confidence in the appropriateness of the institution substantially decreased after it had become fully operational and started to issue convictions. Victims' surveys reveal that they questioned its legitimacy, neutrality, procedural fairness and substantive fairness (i.e., the fairness of its decisions). In contrast, confidence in the national courts has largely increased over the years and most victims indicate it as the preferred jurisdiction for the remaining cases (Hagan and Kutnjak Ivković, 2011: 6–8, 50, 144, 150–52; Stover, 2005: 38).

BREAKING THE VICIOUS CIRCLE OF
WAR AND PENALISATION

In summary, the ICTY failed spectacularly in fulfilling any of its three main functions. First, its ignorance of the nature of international criminality, negation of general principles of criminal law and violation of the rights of the accused prevented it from realising effective justice in any meaningful sense of the term. Second, the punitive character of penal law and its focus on prosecution totally sidestepped the rights of the victims and witnesses. Their participation in the proceedings in front of the ICTY was purely ancillary to the interests of the prosecution and fell short of the slimmest pretence to address their concerns. Third, the tribunal fared extremely badly with respect to the peace process. This tainted legacy militates for the abandonment of international criminal justice and the adoption of alternative adjudication strategies. In addition to the possibility of prosecution and punishment before national courts, addressing the various concerns mentioned previously might involve abandoning the criminal justice approach or developing parallel strategies. The specificities of wartime violence and reconciliatory imperatives argue for the endorsement of transitional justice mechanisms like truth commissions and restorative justice instruments. The transitional and restorative frameworks focus on shared values in the community and reparation of the harm done to promote reconciliation. Victims' narratives have a central role in this inclusive process. Truth commissions investigate the wider patterns of crimes and address impunity at the collective level. Usually, they have quasi-judicial functions, including the possibility to make recommendations concerning reparations (McGonigle Leyh, 2011: 51–52, 62). Besides, local civil courts and tribunals can order restitution or compensation.

Victims of international crimes have followed two promising approaches to obtain compensation in front of domestic or hybrid courts. First, internationally wrongful acts trigger state responsibility (International Law Commission, 2001). In two cases brought up by the relatives of people killed in Srebrenica, a national court judged the Netherlands liable for the fate of several individuals whom Dutchbat soldiers had evicted from their compound after the fall of the enclave.[33] The Human Rights Chamber for Bosnia and Herzegovina condemned Republika Srpska and ordered reparations on account of the fact that its 'failure to make accessible and disclose information requested by the applicants about their missing loved ones constitutes a violation of its positive obligations to secure respect for their rights.'[34] A second solution is to be found in more individuated compensatory and restorative mechanisms, grounded in tort law, contract and restitution (Drumbl, 2007: 195–96). In this frame, a French tribunal found Radovan Karadžić and Biljana Plavšić guilty of wartime abuses against a Bosnian family who had fled to France after a 1992 attack on their home in Foča, and awarded some monetary compensation to the plaintiffs.[35] Proceedings have also been introduced against Radovan Karadžić under the US Alien Torts Claims Act, which permits trials before American civil courts for compensatory and punitive damages.[36] State responsibility, civil liability and corrective justice offer avenues for the bypassing of the insurmountable challenges raised by the ascription of personal responsibility for structural crimes and for adequately compensating the victims. In addition, truth commissions and compensatory solutions, inherited from civil liability adjudication, might give victims a more important place in the process and the possibility to voice their concerns and grievances in a more appropriate forum than a penal trial. Finally, civil processes and remedies like restitution or compensation would foster reconciliation and contribute positively to the consolidation of peace and security.

The sinister legacy of ICTY and its inability to effectively fulfil any of its core functions commands scepticism towards the international prosecution and punishment of individuals for wartime violence. While local courts are more legitimate and better equipped to deliver effective criminal justice, the intrinsic connection between international criminality and wartime violence supports reliance on a combination of judicial and quasi-judicial avenues to help in preventing the resurgence of violence by breaking the vicious circle of war and penalisation.

NOTES

1. Nuremberg International Military Tribunal, *Trial of the Major War Criminals*, Part 22.

2. ICTY, *Tadić (Prijedor)*, IT-94-1-T*bis*-R117, *Sentencing Judgement*, 11 Nov. 1999, §§ 7–9. ICTY, *Karadžić (Bosnia and Herzegovina)*, IT-95-5/18-AR73.4, *Decision on Karadžić's Appeal of Trial Chamber's Decision on Alleged Holbrooke Agreement*, 12 Oct. 2009, § 52. ICTY, *Jelisić (Brčko)*, IT-95-10-T, *Judgement*, 14 Dec. 1999, §§ 116–117. ICTY, *Blaškić (Lašva Valley)*, IT-95-14-T, *Judgement*, 3 Mar. 2000, §§ 761–764. ICTY, *Aleksovski (Lašva Valley)*, IT-95-14/1-A, *Judgement*, 24 Mar. 2000, § 185. ICTY, *Furundžija (Lašva Valley)*, IT-95-17/1-T, *Judgement*, 10 Dec. 1998, §§ 288–291. ICTY, *Delalić et al. (Čelebići Camp)*, IT-96-21-T, *Judgement*, 16 Nov. 1998, §§ 1231–1234. ICTY, *Erdemović (Pilica Farm)*, IT-96-22-T, *Sentencing Judgement*, 29 Nov. 1996, §§ 58–60 and 64–66. ICTY, *Kunarac et al. (Foča)*, IT-96-23&23/1-T, *Judgement*, 22 Feb. 2001, §§ 836–842. ICTY, *Plavšić (Bosnia and Herzegovina)*, IT-00-39&40/1-S, *Sentencing Judgement*, 27 Feb. 2003, §§ 79–81.

3. ICTY, *Delalić et al. (Čelebići Camp)*, IT-96-21-T, *Judgement*, 16 Nov. 1998, § 1231.

76   *Axelle Reiter*

4. ICTY, *Kunarac et al. (Foča)*, IT-96-23&23/1-T, *Judgement*, 22 Feb. 2001, §§ 840 and 843–844.

5. ICTY, *Tadić (Prijedor)*, IT-94-1-AR72, *Decision on the Defence Motion for Interlocutory Appeal on Jurisdiction*, 2 Oct. 1995, §§ 4 and 46. ICTY, *Delalić et al. (Čelebići)*, IT-96-21-T, *Decision on Zdravko Mucić's Motion for the Exclusion of Evidence*, 2 Sept. 1997, § 60.

6. *Fowler v. Padget*, 1798, 101 E.R. 1103. *R v. Tolson*, 1889, 23 Q.B.D. 168. *Sherras v. de Rutzen*, 1895, 72 L.T.R. 839. *Brend v. Wood*, 1946, 175 L.T.R. 306. *Harding v. Price*, 1948, 1 All E.R. 283.

7. ICTY, *Erdemović (Pilica Farm)*, IT-96-22-A, *Judgement*, 7 Oct. 1997, § 19. ICTY, *Kvočka et al. (Omarska, Keraterm, Trnopolje)*, IT-98-30/1-T, *Judgement*, 2 Nov. 2001, § 403.

8. ICTY, *Mrkšić et al. (Vukovar Hospital)*, IT-95-13/1-A, *Judgement*, 5 May 2009, § 159. ICTY, *Milan Lukić and Sredoje Lukić (Višegrad)*, IT-98-32/1-T, *Judgement*, 20 July 2009, § 424. ICTY, *Stanišić and Simatović*, IT-03-69-A, *Judgement*, 15 Dec. 2015, §§ 104–107. ICTY, *Perišić*, IT-04-81-T, *Judgement*, 6 Sept. 2011, §§ 1580–1648. ICTY, *Šainović et al (Kosovo)*, IT-05-87-A, *Judgement*, 23 Jan. 2014, §§ 1617–1651. ICTY, *Popović et al. (Srebrenica)*, IT-05-88-A, *Judgement*, 30 Jan. 2015, § 1758. Contra: ICTY, *Perišić*, IT-04-81-A, *Judgement*, 28 Feb. 2013, §§ 13–74.

9. ICTY, *Perišić*, IT-04-81-T, *Judgement*, 6 Sept. 2011, B. Moloto, Dissenting Opinion Counts 1–4 and 9–12, § 3.

10. ICTY, *Brđanin (Krajina)*, IT-99-36-T, *Judgement*, 1 Sept. 2004, §§ 711 and 717–721.

11. ICTY, *Kordić and Čerkez (Lašva Valley)*, IT-95-14/2-T, *Judgement*, 26 Feb. 2001, § 447. ICTY, *Delalić et al. (Čelebići)*, IT-96-21-T, *Judgement*, 16 Nov. 1998, §§ 398–400. ICTY, *Perišić*, IT-04-81-T, *Judgement*, 6 Sept. 2011, §§ 138–140 and 1653.

12. While this dangerous extension of the traditional customary norms was accepted by trial chambers, the majority of the Appeals Chamber ruled it out in an authoritative decision. Compare: ICTY, *Kordić and Čerkez (Lašva Valley)*, IT-95-14/2-T, *Judgement*, 26 Feb. 2001, § 446. ICTY, *Hadžihasanović and Kubura (Central Bosnia)*, IT-01-47-PT, *Decision on Joint Challenge to Jurisdiction*, 12 Nov. 2002, §§ 180–202; IT-01-47-AR72, *Decision on Interlocutory Appeal Challenging Jurisdiction in relation to Command Responsibility*, 16 July 2003, §§ 37–57.

13. ICTY, *Mrkšić et al. (Vukovar Hospital)*, IT-95-13/1-A, *Judgement*, 5 May 2009, §§ 45–103. ICTY, *Popović et al. (Srebrenica)*, IT-05-88-T, *Judgement*, 10 June 2010, §§ 1981–1991; IT-05-88-A, *Judgement*, 30 Jan. 2015, §§ 1725–1765.

14. ICTY, *Mrkšić et al. (Vukovar Hospital)*, IT-95-13/1-A, *Judgement*, 5 May 2009, A. Vaz, Partly Dissenting Opinion, especially §§ 10–11 and fn 28.

15. ICTY, *Perišić*, IT-04-81-T, *Judgement*, 6 Sept. 2011, §§ 1753–1769.

16. ICTY, *Perišić*, IT-04-81-A, *Judgement*, 28 Feb. 2013, §§ 77–79 and 86–118.

17. ICTY, *Tadić (Prijedor)*, IT-94-1-A, *Judgement*, 15 July 1999, §§ 187–193 and 220.

18. ICTY, *Stakić (Prijedor)*, IT-97-24-A, *Judgement*, 22 Mar. 2006, § 38. ICTY, *Krstić (Srebrenica-Drina Corps)*, IT-98-33-T, *Judgement*, 2 Aug. 2001, §§ 617–618. ICTY, *Brđanin (Krajina)*, IT-99-36-A, *Decision on Interlocutory Appeal*, 19 Mar.

2004, §§ 5–10. ICTY, *Đorđević* (Kosovo), IT-05-87/1-A, *Judgement*, 27 Jan. 2014, §§ 73–84.

19. ICTY, *Kvočka et al. (Omarska, Keraterm, Trnopolje)*, IT-98-30/1-T, *Judgement*, 2 Nov. 2001, § 307. ICTY, *Brđanin (Krajina)*, IT-99-36-A, *Judgement*, 3 Apr. 2007, § 422.

20. ICTY, *Stakić (Prijedor)*, IT-97-24-T, *Judgement*, 31 July 2003, § 435. ICTY, *Krnojelac (Foča)*, IT-97-25-T, *Judgement*, 15 Mar. 2002, § 82. ICTY, *Vasiljević (Višegrad)*, IT-98-32-T, *Judgement*, 29 Nov. 2002, § 67; IT-98-32-A, *Judgement*, 25 Feb. 2004, § 111. ICTY, *Milan Milutinović et al. (Kosovo)*, IT-99-37-AR72, *Decision on Dragoljub Ojdanić's Motion Challenging Jurisdiction—Joint Criminal Enterprise*, 21 May 2003, § 20.

21. ICTY, *Martić (RSK)*, IT-95-11-A, *Judgement*, 8 Oct. 2008, *Separate Opinion of Judge Schomburg*, §§ 2 and 5.

22. ICTY, *Mrkšić et al. (Vukovar Hospital)*, IT-95-13/1-A, *Judgement*, 5 May 2009.

23. ICTY, *Simić et al. (Bosanski Šamac)*, IT-95-9-A, *Appeal Judgement*, 28 Nov. 2006, §§ 75 and 301. ICTY, *Dragomir Milošević (Sarajevo)*, IT-98-29/1-A, *Judgement*, 12 Nov. 2009, §§ 279–282. ICTY, *Krstić (Srebrenica-Drina Corps)*, IT-98-33-A, *Judgement*, 19 Apr. 2004, §§ 138–139 and 143–144.

24. ICTY, *Slobodan Milošević (Kosovo, Croatia and Bosnia)*, IT-02-54-AR73.5, *Decision on Interlocutory Appeal on the Admissibility of Evidence in the Form of Written Statements*, 30 Sept. 2003. ICTY, *Tolimir (Srebrenica)*, IT-05-88/2-A, *Judgement*, 8 Apr. 2015, §§ 16–40.

25. ICTY, *Tadić (Prijedor)*, IT-94-1-T, *Opinion and Judgement*, 7 May 1997, §§ 256 and 535–539.

26. ICTY, *Karadžić (Bosnia and Herzegovina)*, IT-95-5/18-T, *Decision on Appointment of Counsel and Order on Further Trial Proceedings*, 5 Nov. 2009, §§ 14–16 and 19–27. ICTY, *Slobodan Milošević (Kosovo, Croatia and Bosnia)*, IT-99-37 / IT-02-54-AR73.7, *Decision on Interlocutory Appeal of the Trial Chamber's Decision on the Assignment of Defence Counsel*, 1 Nov. 2004, §§ 11–14. ICTY, *Šešelj Case*, IT-03-67-PT, *Decision on Prosecution's Motion for Order Appointing Counsel to Assist Vojislav Šešelj with his Defence*, 9 May 2003, §§ 20–21; IT-03-67-AR73.3, *Decision on Appeal against the Trial Chamber's Decision on Assignment of Counsel*, 20 Oct. 2006, § 8; IT-03-67-AR73.4, *Decision on Appeal against the Trial Chamber's Decision (No 2) on Assignment of Counsel*, 8 Dec. 2006, § 19.

27. ICTY, *Blaškić (Lašva Valley)*, IT-95-14-PT, *Decision on the Defence Motion Filed pursuant to Rule 64*, 6 Jan. 1997.

28. See, for an example of the latter type: ICTY, *Slobodan Milošević (Kosovo, Croatia and Bosnia)*, IT-99-37 / IT-02-54, *Transcripts*, 19–20 Apr. 2005, pp. 38592–38597, 38605–38606 and 38615–38617; IT-02-54-T, *Order on Contempt concerning Witness Kosta Bulatović*, 20 Apr. 2005; IT-02-54-R77.4, *Decision on Contempt of the Tribunal*, 13 May 2005; IT-02-54-AR77.4, *Decision on Interlocutory Appeal on Kosta Bulatović Contempt Proceedings*, 29 Aug. 2005.

29. ICTY, *Haradinaj et al. (Kosovo)*, IT-04-84-A, *Judgement*, 19 July 2010, §§ 34, 37 and 48–49.

30. ICTY, *Haradinaj et al. (Kosovo)*, IT-04-84-PT, *Order on Disclosure of Memorandum and on Interviews with a Prosecution Source and Witness*, 13 Dec. 2006, pp. 1 and 9; IT-04-84-T, *Decision on Motion for Video-Link*, 14 Sept. 2007, § 3; IT-04-84-A, *Judgement*, 19 July 2010, §§ 41 and 48, notes 130 and 158.

31. ICTY, *Haradinaj et al. (Kosovo)*, IT-04-84-R77.1, *Order on Contempt concerning Shefqet Kabashi*, 5 June 2007.

32. ICTY, *Final Report to the Prosecutor by the Committee Established to Review the NATO Bombing Campaign against the Federal Republic of Yugoslavia*, 13 June 2000, especially §§ 90–91.

33. Court of Appeal of The Hague, *Mustafić*, No 200.020.173/01, & *Nuhanović*, No 200.020.174/01, 5 July 2011.

34. HR Chamber BiH, *Selimović et al. v. Republika Srpska (Srebrenica)*, 7 Mar. 2003, §§ 202–203.

35. Tribunal of Grande Instance of Paris, *Kovac v. Karadžić and Plavšić*, 14 Mar. 2011.

36. New York District Court, *Doe v. Karadžić, Kadić v. Karadžić*, 1994. US Second Circuit, *Doe v. Karadžić, Kadić v. Karadžić*, 1995. US Supreme Court, *Doe v. Karadžić, Kadić v. Karadžić*, 1996.

REFERENCES

Alvarez, Jose E. (1999). 'Crimes of States, Crimes of Hate.' *Yale Journal of International Law* 365–483.

Arendt, Hannah. (1963). *Eichmann in Jerusalem*. New York: Viking Press.

Bachmann, Klaus, and Aleksandar Fatić (2015). *The UN International Criminal Tribunals*. London: Routledge.

Badar, Mohamed Elewa. (2006). 'Just Convict Everyone!' *International Criminal Law Review* 293–302.

Benvenuti, Paolo. (2001). 'The ICTY Prosecutor and the Review of the NATO Bombing Campaign against the Federal Republic of Yugoslavia.' *European Journal of International Law* 503–29.

Chouliarias, Athanasios. (2010). 'From Conspiracy to Joint Criminal Enterprise.' In *Future Perspectives on International Criminal Justice*, edited by Carsten Stahn and Larissa Van Den Herik, 545–82. The Hague: Asser.

Colangelo, Anthony J. (2003). 'Manipulating International Criminal Procedure: The Decision of the ICTY Office of the Independent Prosecutor Not to Investigate NATO Bombing in the Former Yugoslavia.' *Northwestern University Law Review* 1393–436.

Damaška, Mirjam. (2008). 'What Is the Point of International Criminal Justice?' *Chicago — Kent Law Review* 329–65.

D'Amato, Anthony. (1994). 'Peace *versus* Accountability in Bosnia.' *American Journal of International Law* 500–506.

Darcy, Shane. (2007). 'Imputed Criminal Liability and the Goals of International Justice.' *Leiden Journal of International Law* 377–404.

Dembour, Marie-Bénédicte, and Emily Haslam. (2004). 'Silencing Hearings?' *European Journal of International Law* 151–77.

Drumbl, Mark A. (2007). *Atrocity, Punishment, and International Law*. Cambridge: Cambridge University Press.

Fatić, Aleksandar (2000). *Reconciliation via the War Crimes Tribunal?* Aldershot: Ashgate.

Fichtelberg, Aaron (2008). 'Liberal Values in International Criminal Law.' *Journal of International Criminal Justice* 3–19.

Fletcher, George P. (1998). *Basic Concepts of Criminal Law*. Oxford: Oxford University Press.

Futamura, Madoka. (2008). *War Crimes Tribunals and Transitional Justice*. London: Routledge.

Gaynor, Fergal, and Mark B. Harmon. (2007). 'Ordinary Sentences for Extraordinary Crimes.' *Journal of International Criminal Justice* 683–712.

Hagan, John, and Sanja Kutnjak Ivković. (2011). *Reclaiming Justice*. Oxford: Oxford University Press.

Hart, Herbert L. A. (1958). 'Murder and the Principles of Punishment.' *Northwestern University Law Review* 433–61.

Hazan, Pierre. (2000). *La justice face à la guerre*. Paris: Stock.

Humanitarian Law Centre. (2000). *Spotlight on War Crimes Trials*. Belgrade: HLC.

ICTY. (1994). *First Annual Report*, 28 July 1994, UN Doc., A/49/342; S/1994/1007.

ICTY. (2002). *Ninth Annual Report*, 14 Aug. 2002, UN Doc., A/57/379; S/2002/985.

ICTY. (2006). *Independent Audit of the Detention Unit at the International Criminal Tribunal for the Former Yugoslavia*, 4 May 2006, http://www.icty.org/x/file/Press/PR_attachments/DU-audit.pdf.

International Law Commission. (2001). *Draft Articles on Responsibility of States for Internationally Wrongful Acts Adopted by the Drafting Committee on Second Reading*, UN Doc., A/CN.4/L.620/Rev.1.

Kerr, Rachel. (2000). 'International Judicial Intervention.' *International Relations* 2: 17–26.

McGonigle Leyh, Brianne. (2011). *Procedural Justice?* Cambridge: Intersentia.

Milgram, Stanley. (1974). *Obedience to Authority*. New York: Harper.

Pradel, Jean. (1995). *Droit pénal comparé*. Paris: Dalloz.

Reiter, Axelle. (2013). 'Kafka's Legacy.' In *Međunarodna Krivična Dela: Dvanaesti Tematski Međunarodni Naučni Skup*. Belgrade: ICLA.

Robinson, Darryl. (2008). 'The Identity Crisis of International Criminal Law.' *Leiden Journal of International Law* 925–63.

Robinson, Darryl. (2010). 'The Two Liberalisms of International Criminal Law.' In *Future Perspectives on International Criminal Justice*, edited by Carsten Stahn and Larissa Van Den Herik, 115–60. The Hague: Asser.

Schabas, William A. (2003). '*Mens Rea* and the International Criminal Tribunal for the Former Yugoslavia.' *New England Law Review* 1015–36.

Schabas, William A. (2006). 'International Justice for International Crimes.' *European Review* 421–39.

Scharf, Michael P. (1997). 'A Critique of the Yugoslavia War Crimes Tribunal.' *Denver Journal of International Law and Policy* 305–12.

Security Council, Resolution 827 (1993), 25 May 1993, UN Doc., S/25704.

Smeulers, Alette. (2008a). 'Perpetrators of International Crimes.' In *Supranational Criminology*, edited by Roelof Haveman and Alette Smeulers, 233–65. Antwerp: Intersentia.

Smeulers, Alette. (2008b). 'Punishing the Enemies of All Mankind.' *Leiden Journal of International Law* 971–93.

Smeulers, Alette, and Wouter Werner (2010). 'The Banality of Evil on Trial.' In *Future Perspectives on International Criminal Justice*, edited by Carsten Stahn and Larissa Van Den Herik, 24–43. The Hague: Asser.

Stover, Eric. (2005). *The Witnesses War Crimes and the Promise of Justice in The Hague*. Philadelphia: University of Pennsylvania Press.

Tolstoy, Leo. (1869, reprint 2008). *War and Peace*. New York: Penguin Random House.

Zimbardo, Philip George. (2007). *The Lucifer Effect*. New York: Random House.

Chapter 2

Transitional Justice, Democracy and the Justification of State Coercion

Thomas Hancocks

Transitional justice is concerned with how states should progress to a more just political order while coming to terms with legacies of wrongdoing. An essential element of transitional justice concerns the problem of political legitimacy — how societies can move from periods of conflict, illegitimate rule and human rights abuses to a legitimate state. Naturally, this process of political transition invites a number of questions about what political legitimacy is and why it should matter that a state is or is not legitimate. The aim of this chapter is to consider the problem of political legitimacy with respect to transitional justice contexts. More particularly, I will attend to a central aspect of political legitimacy — the moral justification of state coercion — and develop a novel account of justified coercion which is sensitive to some of the problems faced by transitional societies.

Most commentators on transitional justice hold that the process of transition from conflict or illegitimate rule should seek to achieve democracy. This view is common in policy documents on transitional justice — for instance, a UN document on transitional justice claims that a central aim of transition is to 'reinforce the possibilities for . . . democracy' (United Nations, 2008), and the International Centre for Transitional Justice writes that 'transitional justice should be designed to strengthen democracy' (International Centre for Transitional Justice, 2009). According to this widely shared view, the fields of transitional justice and democratisation are broadly synonymous — the transition to a state that is legitimate (where this means in part is morally justified in coercing) is taken to be a transition to a state that is democratic. In this chapter, I want to challenge this view by making two arguments about democracy as it relates to state coercion. First, I will argue that democratic participation is neither necessary, nor sufficient, to morally justify the use of coercion through law by the state. Second, I will argue instead that the protection of basic human rights morally justifies the content of laws and the way in which they are enforced coercively by the state.

These arguments are significant, I will argue, because they impact on the sort of state that transitional justice should seek to achieve, and the way in which this process of transition should be carried out. First, according to this view, the process of transition should seek in the first instance to achieve the protection of human rights through law, *prior to* establishing democracy. Second, it follows from this view that undemocratic states may be morally justified in coercing citizens if they succeed in protecting human rights. I will explore these two implications towards the end of the chapter.

My account relates to the Bachmann and Fatić (2015) volume *The UN International Criminal Tribunals: Transition without Justice?* in the following ways. Like Bachmann and Fatić, I am interested in the problem of legitimacy with respect to transitional justice contexts. Yet where the arguments from Bachmann and Fatić for the most part concern the legitimacy of international criminal trials, in this chapter I will be interested in state legitimacy — in particular, the justification of the state's use of coercive laws (as I outline in the following section). Second, I adopt a view of legitimacy that is importantly different from that adopted by Bachmann and Fatić (again, I explain this in the following section). Despite these differences, I share the view, outlined by Bachmann and Fatić (2015: 28–29), that 'outcome-legitimacy' is important — that the legitimacy of a political agent or process (in their case international trials, in my case state law-making) is in large part shaped by the justness of the outcomes.

The chapter will run as follows. In the following section, I consider the feature of political legitimacy that interests me in this chapter — the moral justification of coercion. In the third section I consider the democratic justification for state coercion — an account both implicitly and explicitly endorsed by both political philosophers and commentators on transitional justice. In the fourth section I develop an argument against the view that democracy is necessary or sufficient to morally justify state coercion. The argument takes the form of an *ad absurdum* challenge in the form of the tyranny of the majority which (I claim) is supported by two descriptive observations about the nature of transitional states. In the fifth section, I sketch the outline of an alternative, human rights-based justification of state coercion. In the sixth section, I introduce three hypothetical test cases to support the view of coercion I defend. In the seventh section I consider the implications of this view for the broader issue of the legitimacy of transitional states.

POLITICAL LEGITIMACY AND THE
JUSTIFICATION OF STATE COERCION

One of the main challenges of transitional justice is how to move from a period of state illegitimacy where governments are undemocratic, fail to respect the rule of law and routinely violate the rights of citizens to a period of state legitimacy.[1] This process of transition from illegitimate rule invites questions that have long preoccupied social scientists and political philosophers — what is political legitimacy? And why is it important that a state possesses it?

To begin, we may note a distinction between the *normative* and *descriptive* senses of legitimacy. The descriptive sense of legitimacy is adopted by Bachmann and Fatić (2015: 27–31). On this view, first developed by Weber (1964: 71–74), the problem of whether a political agent, or process, is legitimate is grounded in (empirical) considerations about whether citizens *believe* said agent or process to be legitimate, and whether they habitually *obey* said agent.[2] This descriptive sense is distinguishable from the normative sense, which I will adopt in this chapter.[3] The normative account of legitimacy appeals not to empirical questions about whether citizens believe an agent, or process, to be legitimate, but to moral questions of permissibility and justification. On this view, a political agent is legitimate if she meets the conditions required to rule with moral justification.

According to the normative view, political legitimacy concerns the way in which a state exercises its authority over citizens. In the broadest terms, to say a state is normatively legitimate (from hereon I will simply say 'legitimate') is to say that a state possesses a *right to rule*. Importantly, this sense of legitimacy as the right to rule comes in degrees. Thus where a just foreign power may be justified in coercing citizens in a state that is illegitimate (say, to prevent human rights violations), we would not want to say that this power possesses the right to rule. Indeed, one reason for this is that the foreign power has not come to power through democratic measures. This spectrum of legitimacy that ranges from the weaker sense of justified coercion to the stronger sense of the right to rule is important to my argument. I will be concerned with the former, weaker sense of legitimacy and I will provide an account of when a state is morally justified in coercing and does not rely on an appeal to the value of democratic procedures. Importantly, I do not wish to provide a full account of state legitimacy as the right to rule (the stricter standard),[4] and it is an open question as to whether democracy should feature in a broader view of a legitimate state. My claim is the more modest one that democracy is not required for a political agent to be morally justified in coercing.

Although I am interested in this weaker sense of legitimacy as morally justified coercion, it is important to note that an account of why the state is morally justified in coercing is essential to any account of legitimacy.[5] To say a state is legitimate is to say (at least in part) that it is justified in coercing and, conversely, to say that a state is illegitimate is to say that it does not coerce with moral justification — perhaps because it routinely violates human rights, or persecutes a minority group, or fails to respect the rule of law, for instance.

We want states to be morally justified in their use of coercion for a number of reasons. One is that laws are liberty-restricting. Laws direct the otherwise free conduct of individuals in certain ways, chiefly by imposing positive and negative legal duties on individuals, duties whose violation comes with the threat of punishment or sanction. The central tenets of criminal law, for instance, impose negative duties of noninterference on citizens (to not kill, steal and so on). Given that it is *prima facie* wrong to restrict the liberty of individuals, the authority of the state to introduce and enforce these laws requires moral justification.

Second, states not only coerce, but they claim to have authority over a particular jurisdiction or territory. As such, they impose laws and demand compliance not only from those who are born within the territory which the state has authority over, but also over foreign nationals who by entering this jurisdiction become subject to the state's coercive authority. Again, the fact that a state claims authority over all those within a particular geographical territory — including non-nationals — requires an explanation. We need a reason, or set of reasons, as to why the state is morally justified in exercising its authority in this given territory, over individuals who are not nationals of the state, country or region.

Third, states claim to possess a *monopoly* of force and authority over a given jurisdiction. States use coercion exclusively — in such a way that the laws of the state have supreme power and no other group has a moral claim to impose laws. Buchanan (2002) captures this notion that states attempt to monopolise when they make law, 'a state not only uses coercion to secure compliance with its rules, it also attempts to establish the supremacy of those rules and endeavours to suppress others who would enforce its rules or promulgate their own rules' (p. 690).

Given that legitimate states not only coerce citizens, but seek to have *exclusive* authority to coerce, this requires moral justification. We require a reason as to why the state, and the state alone, is morally permitted to create and enforce laws and to do so in such a way as to exclude other potential law-making bodies. It is for these three reasons that we want states to be morally justified in enforcing coercive laws.

In what follows, I will be interested in this question of the moral justification of coercion as a central (though not sufficient) explanandum of state legitimacy.

THE DEMOCRATIC JUSTIFICATION OF COERCION

In this section, I consider the view that democracy is required to morally justify the state's use of coercion. In the scholarship and policy around transitional justice this view is common. Many commentators argue (or indeed often simply assume) that democracy is required to legitimise the state — where this means to morally justify its use of coercion. Indeed, this view is so ubiquitous, that the processes of transitional justice and democratisation are deemed to be synonymous.[6]

De Greiff (2010), for instance, writes that, 'as justice measures . . . instruments of transitional justice should be understood as contributing to democratisation. Democracy is valuable both inherently (as an expression of individual autonomy) and as a means for citizens to give concrete content to their understanding of justice by means of law' (p. 29).

For de Greiff, part of the reason that democracy morally justifies coercive laws is that it makes laws more just, where this means that laws become more representative of the views and interests of citizens. For this reason transitional justice should seek to achieve democracy.

Winter also claims that establishing democracy is an essential aim of transitional justice, one that is required for the legitimacy of states. For Winter (2013), 'a state has legitimacy when it is permissible for it to issue and enforce laws and regulations' (p. 231). In this light, democracy is an essential requirement for the justification of coercive law, 'It is a necessary condition of a legitimate political order that it enables those governed to play equal and meaningful roles in the process of government' (Winter, 2013: 237).

Finally, Mihr (2013: 299) writes that democracy is essential for legitimate institutions — the more democratic the institution, the more legitimate they are. Transitional justice measures are seen over a period of time as catalysts to enhance democratic performance by increasing accountability, transparency or participation of, among, and with democratic institutions, and consequently strengthening and legitimising them.

The element of these passages that interests me is the claim that the legitimacy of the state (it's being justified in coercing through law) is conditional on democratic procedures of political participation that establish the nature and content of these laws. For all of these commentators, democracy is essential for the legitimacy of states. It follows, on this view, that the process of democratisation — of moving towards democratic governance — is an essential goal of transitional justice.

To be sure, there are a number of reasons for thinking that democracy should play some role in morally justifying the state's use of coercion.[7] From simple observation, we know that democratic states generally introduce laws that are relatively just, and, at least compared to authoritarian states, generally do a reasonable job in protecting basic human rights.[8] We may also appeal to the value of representative governments and legislatures — that in order for laws to be justified, they must be shaped by and reflective of the views and interests of those who are subject to them. Others have appealed to the value of public reason and the role that deliberative democracy plays in 'justify(ing) the exercise of collective political power . . . on the basis of a free public reasoning among equals' (Cohen, 1997: 412). Others still have sought to ground the justification of democracy on more substantive moral values. Buchanan (2002), for instance, grounds his justification of democracy on the value of equality. Buchanan claims that the exercise of coercion can only be justified if it is exercised in such a way as to respect the natural equality of individuals (what he terms the 'robust natural duty of justice'). Buchanan further argues that only democracy can confer legitimacy to states in such a way that respects this natural equality.[9]

Despite these different views of the value of democracy and its role in morally justifying state coercion, democratic accounts of state coercion share the same broad view — that a state derives its authority to coerce from political decision-making procedures that afford all individuals the opportunity to participate. In Cohen's (1997) terms, 'the fundamental idea of democratic legitimacy is that the authorization to exercise state power must arise from the collective decision of the members of a society who are governed by that power' (p. 407).

In the following section, I challenge this view that democratic participation is required to morally justify the state's use of coercion.

AGAINST THE DEMOCRATIC ACCOUNT OF COERCION

The democratic account of legitimacy appeals to the normative force of democratic procedures in providing the state with the moral authority to coerce. Here I will outline a simple and by no means original challenge to democratic authority — an *ad absurdum* challenge in the form of the 'tyranny of the majority.'[10] The argument points to the implausibility of the view that democratic participation can, by itself, justify coercion by showing that democratic authority, without further restrictions and conditions on majority rule, will license injustice. Democracy can, therefore, not be sufficient to justify coercion. To see this challenge consider the following example.

Suppose a territory is composed of three factional ethnic groups. Group A represents 15 percent of the populace, group B 25 percent and group C 60 percent. Suppose a democratic majoritarian procedure is introduced to determine which political group ought to have the monopoly of coercive authority, and that the representatives from each of the respective groups have vowed to implement persecutory laws against members of the other groups. The vote affords each individual within each respective group one vote and considers each vote equally. Law-making power and the authority to coerce is then granted to the majority.

Assuming that each voter votes for the representative of their respective groups, the tyranny of the majority challenge states that in such a case group C will have the authority to persecute the members of B and C. For the reason that it looks to license such injustice, democratic authority, taken as a sufficient condition for coercive authority, is morally impermissible.

Of course, one may think that the problem of tyranny of the majority as presented in such a hypothetical case is only theoretical, and does not realistically problematise democracy in practise. Yet two further observations suggest that the problem of the tyranny of the majority poses a serious challenge to an account of democratic authority in transitional contexts.

First, transitional contexts are commonly composed of rival factional religious, ethnic or racial groups. Think of the Tutsis or Hutus in Rwanda, or different ethnic and racial groups in South Africa or the Balkans, or Iraq.[11] The distribution of rival ethnic groups in a given territory increases the chance of injustice carried out by a majority government against a minority group. Brian Barry (1991) makes a similar observation about the problem of the tyranny of the majority in certain contexts:

> To be subject to a majority of a different language, religion or national identity is ... threatening. In an area where nationalities are intermingled, like the Balkans, every move to satisfy majority aspirations leaves the remaining minorities even more vulnerable. (p. 35)

The thought is that implementing a majoritarian democratic system to establish the content of laws in territories where there are pre-existing tensions between racial, ethnic or national groups will only intensify the problem of the tyranny of the majority.

The second observation is that transitional states do not generally have systems or institutional safeguards in place that protect minority rights by limiting the power of a majority elected government in ways that more developed democratic states do. These safeguards include,

1. A strong judiciary that is independent from and uninfluenced by the state/ majority elected government.
2. Judicial review — a process that gives judges the last word on aspects of law and limits the legislative decisions of a majority.
3. Developed police forces to ensure law and order.

4. Legal systems that are sufficiently developed such that they may enforce human rights law.
5. Institutions that protect free speech and the freedom of the press (affording an outlet for expression to minority groups).

In developed democracies, these institutional procedures play a role in protecting minority rights and limiting the power of a majority. The absence of such procedures in fragile transitional contexts serves only to compound the problem of the tyranny of the majority.

The *ad absurdum* challenge of the tyranny of the majority, twinned with the two descriptive features of transitional societies, together support the view that democracy should not, without further conditions limiting the power of the majority, be sufficient to justify the state's coercive authority. Of course, one may argue that democratic participation is *necessary* to justify coercion, twinned with other conditions. I want to resist this view, however, and I will appeal to three intuitive hypothetical cases that support the view that democracy should not feature in an account of what morally justifies state coercion.[12]

A HUMAN RIGHTS-BASED
JUSTIFICATION OF COERCION

One question that immediately presents itself with respect to the relation between human rights and justified coercion concerns the now much discussed issue of the moral status of human rights. In the burgeoning literature on the philosophy of human rights it is possible to identify two broad schools of thought concerning the justification and content of human rights. The *naturalist* or *moral* view holds human rights to derive from natural properties or values intrinsic to human beings — which we possess by virtue of our humanity or personhood.[13] The rival, *political* view of human rights holds that human rights serve a broadly political function in the sense that they function as claims against states, institutions and international bodies, and define the standards of legitimacy that these agents possess.[14]

I do not want to take a stance on this issue of the philosophical justification of human rights. This is not because such questions are not interesting or philosophically important, but rather because they can be separated from that which chiefly interests me here — the relationship between human rights and justified coercion. The debate between the moral and political schools is a debate about the moral grounding (or lack thereof) of human rights. The question that interests me here is that of *function* — the role that human rights play with respect to the question of whether the state is morally justified in coercing.[15] These two questions are distinguishable. For instance, it is perfectly intelligible to claim that by systematically torturing citizens states are no longer justified in coercing through law (a claim about function), without being committed to a view about what is wrong about torture and why a human right against it exists — that it violates human dignity, agency or personhood for instance (a claim about content). I thus proceed to consider the function of human rights in justifying state legitimacy, without taking a stance on the issue of content.[16]

THE FUNCTION OF HUMAN RIGHTS IN AN ACCOUNT OF JUSTIFIED COERCION

What we require from a human rights-based view of legitimacy is an account of why states are morally justified coercing in the interests of protecting basic human rights.[17] In this section, I make three points on this score. First, I argue that the protection of human rights provides the basis for a justification of the use of some level of coercive force by appealing to analogous cases in which coercion looks permissible to protect rights. Second, I argue that the protection of human rights provides the basis of a justification for the creation of a system of coercive laws. Third, I argue that human rights serve not only to vindicate the use of coercion by the state, but also to set limits on the sorts of coercive measures that are permissible.

The first principle states that the protection of human rights[18] serves to morally justify coercion. One may defend this principle by appealing to a broader principle about the protection of rights.

Protection of rights principle: It is sometimes permissible to use force to protect the basic rights of individuals.

The protection of rights principle is supported by other cases in which some level of coercive force — even violence — is permitted to protect rights. Think of cases of self-defence, where some level of force is permitted to prevent culpable attack against oneself or other innocents. Or think of a rescue case. Imagine a case in which some level of force is required to save a child from drowning. Suppose, for example, that the only way to save the child is by (nonfatally and causing minimal harm) pushing a nearby adult into the water so the child may climb onto the individual to save themselves. In both cases, it seems justified to use some level of coercive force to protect rights.[19] Both of these cases thus support the *protection of rights* principle.

By itself, the protection of rights principle is not sufficient to explain why the use of coercion by a state is permissible. This is because states do not use force to protect rights in only one-off cases, but systematically. What we want is a principle that justifies the coercive use of force not only in particular cases, but through the *systematic* coercion of law — laws that seek to disincentivise rights violations with the threat of sanction and punishment. Therefore, we must provide some positive support for such a system.

HUMAN RIGHTS AND THE JUSTIFICATION
OF A SYSTEM OF COERCIVE LAW

To defend the second aspect of a human rights-based account of legitimate authority consider a second principle.

System of rules principle: It is sometimes permissible to impose a system of coercive rules (backed up with threats of sanction or punishment) to direct the conduct of individuals in such a way so as to protect basic rights.

There are two arguments which support the system of rules principle. First, consider cases in which it looks permissible to impose a system of rules to direct the conduct of others in such a way as to prevent rights violations. Suppose there is a community comprised of a small group of attackers (A) and a larger group of innocents (I). Suppose further that one of the ways in which A may be disincentivised from attacking I is if a system of rules backed up with the threat of sanction is implemented. Even if the imposition of such a system is only *one* way of protecting group I (it need not even be the best way), it looks to be permissible to implement such a system, assuming further conditions are met such as that the rules do not impose sanctions that are extraordinarily draconian or brutal. Grounding this is the thought that morality requires the protection of the basic rights of individuals in group I, and thus justifies the implementation of such a system.

The second argument draws upon a principle that has been developed by Buchanan (2002: 703–9). This principle states that no one has a right against being coerced to do that which they have a natural obligation of justice to fulfil. If this is correct, then a system of laws does not violate an individual's moral rights if said individual possesses a moral duty to do the things that the law prescribes. More formally: 'a coercive law prescribing x does not violate the moral rights of an individual y if y has an independent moral obligation to do x.'

This argument requires some qualification, however. It may be the case that laws which coerce individuals to fulfil certain duties of justice — say, to give half of their income to those in poverty — are overly demanding, given that some level of discretion should be afforded to individuals over their decisions about how they wish to distribute their wealth. There are two ways around this challenge. This first denies that such duties — such as that of giving half of one's wealth to charity — are indeed duties of justice. One may argue that such duties are over-demanding, for instance. The second restricts the principle to negative duties of noninterference. On this view, an individual does not possess a right against coercive laws that coincide with their negative duties such as those against killing, stealing or restricting the liberty of others. This view is supported by the thought that it would be implausible to suggest that the negative duties imposed by the criminal law violate the rights of individuals, because individuals have a moral obligation to not violate the basic rights of others (through killing, theft, etc.). Similarly, it would be implausible to suppose that I have a right against the policeman who restrains me to prevent me from killing another innocent individual.

We should be careful about endorsing this second response. Restricting the principle to only apply to laws that coincide with our negative duties would only justify a very minimal set of libertarian laws that prohibit interference. Yet there are good reasons for thinking we want coercive laws to enforce some positive obligations as well, such as those which impose obligations to pay tax for the common good. Indeed, the human rights-based account can help to explain why some positive obligations should be enforceable under law. Article 22 of the Universal Declaration posits the following right to a dignified standard of life 'everyone . . . is entitled to realization . . . of the economic, social and cultural rights indispensable for his [or her] dignity.' This would serve as the basis of a justification of tax laws that impose positive obligations on individuals to contribute to a state system of welfare and healthcare, for instance.

The previous two lines of argument support the coercive rules principle. First, that it is at least sometimes permissible to introduce coercive laws if this serves as one means of protecting human rights. Second, individuals do not possess a right against coercive laws that impose obligations and coincide with their preexisting moral obligations. It follows that a system of coercive law is (at least sometimes) (1) justified and (2) not impermissible because it does not violate the rights of those it imposes obligations on.

HUMAN RIGHTS AND RESTRICTIONS ON THE LIMITS OF COERCIVE AUTHORITY

A third way in which human rights play a role in an account of coercion concerns the nature of the coercive laws in question. Human rights serve to prescribe limits on the nature and content of the coercive laws that may be permissibly implemented. This is a central function of modern day human rights law, which imposes obligations on states to respect the human rights of their citizens. In failing to do so, states lose their claim to legitimacy under international law and, sometimes, their right to sovereignty — their right against interference by other states or international bodies. Indeed, it is a central principle of international law that illegitimate states are those that violate the human rights of their citizens.

Human rights can inform an account of the sorts of limits that apply to the content of legislation and the way in which it is enforced. Laws that seriously and systematically violate the human rights of citizens are impermissible, according to both human rights law and the human right-based view of legitimacy I defend here. Thus a state that legally licensed the systematic torture of its citizens, or imposed cruel and unusual punishments,[20] would no longer be justified in coercing.

In this section I have sought to defend the following three principles, each of which explains how human rights serve to both justify the use of coercive authority, and also prescribe limits to the extent of that authority.

1. It is sometimes permissible to use coercive force to protect basic human rights.
2. It is sometimes permissible to impose a system of coercive laws to protect basic human rights.
3. In order to be justified a system of coercive laws must not violate basic human rights.

In the following section I will introduce three test cases to support the human rights-based view. These cases also support the claim that democracy is neither necessary nor sufficient to justify the use of coercion.

THREE TEST CASES

In this section I want to introduce three cases to support the human rights-based justification of coercion defended in this chapter. Importantly, according to the human rights-based account, in each case the state (or the government in charge of the state) is morally justified in coercing, even though they are undemocratic. Where the tyranny of the majority argument shows why democracy should not be sufficient to justify state coercion, these cases support the view that democracy should be necessary to justify state coercion. Consider the following examples,

1. *Coup d' état case*: Suppose that an illegitimate government responsible for serious rights violations against its people is overthrown by a rich elite group that forms a government, takes charge of the state's legislative institutions and implements laws that protect the human rights of citizens.
2. *Transitional government case*: Suppose, in the wake of a civil war between rival groups, a transitional government is put in place (undemocratically)

and succeeds in securing political stability and the protection of basic human rights through the imposition of law.
3. *Military intervention case*: Suppose an international military power intervenes in a state in the midst of conflict, succeeds in ceasing the conflict, and implements (and funds) a government that keeps the peace and protects the basic human rights of citizens.

According to the human rights account, in each case the respective state agents are morally justified in coercing through law. Furthermore, I take it that the intuitive plausibility of these cases supports the view that democracy is neither necessary nor sufficient to justify the use of coercion by the state. Would we really believe these state agents to be unjustified in coercing through law by virtue of the fact that they have not come into power through democratic election? It seems difficult to motivate such an argument, given that in all of these cases citizens are substantially better off insofar as their basic human rights are better protected. The main lesson I take from these cases is that the burden of proof is on those who do believe that democracy is required to justify coercion, to explain why in these cases the respective state agents are not justified in coercing.[21] Importantly, my claim here is not that these agents have the right to rule (the stronger sense of legitimacy) but is the weaker claim that these agents are justified in coercing. It may be that democracy is required for the right to rule — though I do not take a stance on this.

Democratic participation offers an account of the procedures in accordance with the question of who should rule the state are determined. According to the argument in this chapter, these procedures cannot be sufficient (or, if the agents are justified in the three hypothetical cases [as I have argued they are], even necessary) to justify state coercion. To many this conclusion may seem controversial. I take it that even the most ardent advocate of the democratic account of state coercion will see some sense in the human rights-based alternative. This is because effective (and safe) democracy *requires* the protection of human rights. That is, given that the protection of basic human rights is essential, if not a necessary condition, for the political association required for democratic procedures — one's rights must be protected if they are to even vote at a voting booth. The human rights-based view is sensitive to the thought that (effective and just) democratic procedures require certain preconditions to be in place. According to the human rights-based justification of legitimacy, it is precisely the need to establish these preconditions for democracy which justifies the coercive use of force.[22]

IMPLICATIONS FOR TRANSITIONAL JUSTICE

In this section I want to draw out some implications of the view I have defended on how we understand political legitimacy and justified coercion with respect to transitional societies. The main implication of the human rights-based account is that undemocratic states and governments may be morally justified in coercing if they succeed in protecting the human rights of citizens. To many, this implication may problematise the account. Yet three broader arguments support this conclusion. First, recent experience about the process of democratisation in Iraq and Afghanistan, among other locations, informs us that democracy is not necessarily either easily or nonviolently implementable, nor is it well-suited to all parts of the globe.[23] Second, the more expansive human rights-based defence of state coercion I have defended here leaves scope for nondemocratically elected political agents such as those in the hypothetical cases above (rich elite groups, transitional governments and agents in charge of military intervention). In each case these agents are not democratically elected yet they are morally justified in coercing (according to the human rights-based account) insofar as they better protect the human rights of citizens through the implementation of laws. I take this to be an intuitively plausible consequence of the account; we want these sorts of agents to be morally justified in implementing laws that serve to better protect human rights in fragile or violent political contexts. Third, we may point to the examples of 'benevolent dictatorships' as a case of states which are undemocratic yet still reasonably just insofar as they protect human rights.[24] According to the human rights-based view these regimes may be morally reprehensible in a number of ways but to the extent that they protect human rights, they retain their claim to being morally justified in enforcing coercive laws.

If we think about this in terms of how we understand the process of transitional justice, the main implication is as follows. One may apply this to the case of transitional justice by emphasising that the first step of transition from illegitimate rule is to bring about a state of affairs in which human rights are protected. That is, political agents (including undemocratic governments in the form of rich elites, imposed transitional governments or governments formed undemocratically after military intervention) may bring it about that rights are protected *prior* to bringing about democracy and other goals of transition (reconciliation, lustration of past political officials, amnesties and war crimes trials, among other measures). According to the human rights-based view defended in this chapter, if such agents succeed in protecting human rights, they are justified in coercing citizens.

We may represent this view of transitional justice in figure 2.1:

Illegitimate state ➡ Transitional political agent ➡ End-goal state

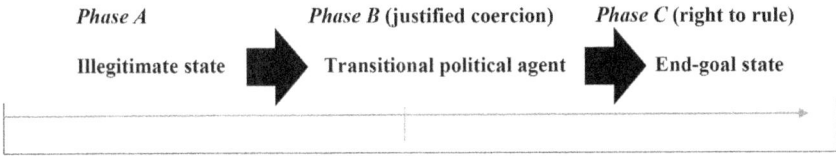

Figure 2.1.   Three stages of transition[25]

Phase A represents a period of illegitimacy where governments are authoritarian (or otherwise undemocratic), commit systematic rights violations and fail to respect the rule of law. Phase B is the stage of justified coercion, and, according to the human rights-based view defended in this chapter, requires the protection of human rights. Phase B, on this view, must be secured *prior to* phase C which represents the end-goal state, which is legitimate in the sense that the state has the right to rule and in which the broader goals of transition are achieved — establishing democracy, securing compensation for victims, war crimes trials and amnesties, forgiveness and reconciliation, among other transitional goals. The important point is that these features of the democratic, end-goal state *presuppose* the protection of human rights such that the latter must be secured prior to the former. It is precisely the protection of human rights (and not democracy) that serves to justify coercion, according to the view defended in this chapter.

In this chapter I have argued that democracy should not play a role in morally justifying state coercion and that the protection of human rights should instead be seen to be sufficient to justify this coercion. In developing this account I have sought to challenge the mainstream view that democracy is required to morally justify state coercion which is endorsed in much of the scholarship and policy around transitional justice. Fair, safe and effective democracy presupposes the protection of human rights. Establishing the conditions for democracy should be a priority — that which morally justifies the state's use of coercion.

NOTES

1. Transitional justice is concerned not only with the transition from illegitimate rule, but also transitions from conflict, civil war and foreign occupation, among other periods of belligerence. My argument applies to all of these cases of political transition.

2. In Bachmann and Fatić's (2015) terms: 'For Weber, on whom we draw in this book, those to whom a ruler or his agent address their decisions must have a choice whether to carry them out or not. And the ruler's decisions are legitimate if they chose to obey them, despite having another choice' (p. 27).

3. Without delving too much into detail, here are three reasons for favouring the normative view of legitimacy, over the descriptive account. First, the descriptive view counterintuitively holds that a radically unjust political agent or process is legitimate, if it is the case that some citizens believe in the legitimacy of said agent or process. Second, people hold mistaken or ill-informed beliefs or habits. Thus grounding our evaluation of legitimacy in beliefs or habits alone is arguably an indeterminate basis. Third, it seems probable that the justness or moral status of a process or agent would play a large role in citizen's evaluation of the legitimacy of an agent or process. Thus we may ask whether the descriptive view of legitimacy is a standalone view, independent of evaluative moral concerns.

4. My point here is that a full account of state legitimacy will be richer in the sense that it will include a more expansive criteria including, for example, an evaluation of a state's policies of distributive justice, retributive justice and of the procedures in accordance with which its officials have come to power, among other functions of the state. A state that systematically failed to allocate welfare to the poor, or which allowed radical divergences in the distribution of wealth, or which failed to give healthcare to the ill could be justifiably challenged on the grounds of its legitimacy, even if it was justified in using its coercive authority through law.

5. Wellman (1996) takes this view, claiming legitimacy concerns whether a state has a moral right to impose its coercive authority on citizens (pp. 211–12). Dworkin (1986) also endorses this view (p. 191).

6. The view that democratisation and transitional justice are synonymous is particularly common in legal scholarship and policy documents around transitional justice. To give one representative passage: 'Rwanda's best hope for achieving democracy — and thereby preventing future interethnic violence — lies in its transitional justice experiment' (Wierzynska 2004, 1939).

7. The role that democracy plays within a wider account of the state needs not be restricted to its function in justifying state coercion, of course. J. S. Mill (1946), for instance, argues that one of the ways in which democracy is valuable is that it cultivates the character of citizens (pp. 136–51).

8. Some political philosophers (Arneson, 1995) have provided instrumental arguments in favour of democracy on the grounds that democracy tends to lead to the protection of human and political rights (privacy, freedom of expression, religious expression). While it may be descriptively true that democracies tend to better protect political rights (i.e., as an observation about the state of the world), it is important to distinguish between democracy and human rights protection — it is possible to have one without the other.

9. He writes: 'If the wielding of political power is morally justifiable only if it is wielded in such a way as to recognise the fundamental equality of persons, and if democracy is necessary for satisfying this condition, then political legitimacy requires democracy' (Buchanan, 2002: 712).

10. De Tocqueville presents the earliest detailed engagement with the problems of the tyranny of the majority in his *Democracy in America* (1963: 254–70); It is important to note that my arguments against democracy only apply to majoritarian forms. There is a debate in the scholarship on democracy about the extent to which

democracy implies or requires majority rule. Yet majority rule is implemented by most, if not all, democracies worldwide. Majority rule is so essential to our understanding of the constitution and operation of democracy, that I take it that the concerns I raise about the tyranny of the majority are forceful.

11. For a scholarly engagement with the problem of the tyranny of the majority in Iraq, see Bapir (2010).

12. Of course, one may argue that even if democracy is neither a necessary nor sufficient condition for the justification of state coercion, it may provide a weighty *pro tanto* reason in favour of certain forms of coercion. This option is an open one. Indeed, according to the human rights-based view of coercion I defend in the next section, it may well be the case that if a state protects human rights *and* is democratic, then this provides extra-justificatory force (given the values of democracy highlighted earlier). The main point I want to make is that it is the protection of human rights that does the work in justifying coercion, and while democracy may be a *pro tanto* moral reason in support of certain forms of coercion, it is neither necessary nor sufficient to justify this coercion.

13. Some philosophers in the moral school appeal to values such as equality and human interests (Buchanan, 2005), others to aspects of human agency and personhood (Griffin, 2008) and others still to a plurality of values grounded in concerns with human dignity (Tasioulas, 2013).

14. Rawls (2003), for instance, claims that human rights establish the 'justifying reasons for war and its conduct, and they specify limits to a regime's internal autonomy' (p. 79). Similarly, Raz (2013) claims that human rights 'set limits to the sovereignty of states' (p. 328) by which he means that in committing human rights violations states lose their presumptive rights to sovereignty and freedom from intervention.

15. I don't want to suggest that questions of content have no impact whatsoever on questions of function; there will be some level of cross-over such that the issue of content will have some bearing on the issue of function. The point I wish to make is that the two questions are distinguishable such that we can pursue the question of function without having to first commit ourselves to an account of what morally grounds human rights.

16. It is also worth highlighting the point that there is a reasonably comprehensive list of human rights under international law. And while philosophers may argue about penumbral cases, many of the rights captured by these documents would feature in any plausible moral account of human rights (rights against torture, arbitrary arrest, to a minimally decent existence, to life, liberty, freedom, and so on).

Focussing on the function of human rights with respect to justified coercion may seem like an implicit endorsement of the political justification of human rights. This is incorrect. To repeat, I seek to remain neutral about questions of content. Moreover, both schools of human rights justification, in order to be normatively interesting, will have to explain the function of human rights in political contexts, and it is likely that these accounts of the function of human rights will be at least in part analogous (i.e., practises like torture would have to undermine the legitimacy of states on any plausible account of human rights content).

17. There is a sense in which this claim is uncontroversial, and does not need any defence. We generally take it for granted that states should protect human rights. Yet given the controversial view of this chapter that democracy is not required to justify coercion, I will spend some time developing and defending the different elements of the human rights-based alternative.

18. I should emphasise that I use the term 'human rights' — rather than 'moral' or 'natural' rights — to capture the more expansive list of liberties included in most human rights declarations. These include political rights to free expression, freedom of thought and religious freedom, alongside the more basic rights to life, liberty and possession which are generally accepted to be basic moral rights, as well as human rights.

19. I say 'some' rather than 'any' to capture a proportionality requirement. It would not be that any level of force is justified but only a level that is not proportionate to that which is required to protect/save/prevent harm.

20. Torture is prohibited in most international human rights treatises. Article 7 of the International Covenant on Civil and Political Rights includes a right against cruel and unusual punishment — 'No one shall be subjected to torture or to cruel, inhumane or degrading treatment or punishment.'

21. Again, this leaves open the view that democracy may be a weighty *pro tanto* reason in favour of a particular system or government. If we were to amend the cases such that the state agents *both* protected human rights *and* were democratically elected, this could mean these agents are *more justified* in coercing compared to a state agent that only protected human rights. The important point I want to emphasise is that state coercion is still morally justified without democracy. To reiterate, the burden is on the defender of democracy to explain why the state agents are unjustified in coercing in the three examples.

22. It is important to note that I have only denied that democracy should play a role in the use of coercion. On this account there is still scope for democracy in other features of the state — that is, deciding on who comes to rule, determining some issues of distributive and retributive justice and other state policies. My arguments in this chapter do not preclude these roles of democracy, only its role in justifying state coercion.

23. There has been extensive scholarly discussion about the problems of democratisation in Iraq. See, for instance, Anderson and Stansfield (2004: 225–36), Diamond (2004: 47–52) and Moon (2009).

24. Benevolent dictatorships are regimes which are undemocratic and authoritarian yet which are benevolent in the sense that they do a reasonable job of protecting human rights. Examples include regimes in the former Yugoslavia, Jordan and Oman.

25. Of course, it is unlikely that the process of transition will be as seamless as the process implied by this diagram. The process will unlikely be a swift transition from illegitimate rule to a context of protected rights and then on to democracy. Second, this tripartite process would most plausibly be *scalar* in the sense that it would require a state to achieve *more* or *greater legitimacy*.

REFERENCES

Anderson, Liam, and Stansfield, Gareth. (2004). *The Future of Iraq: Dictatorship, Democracy, or Division?* New York: Palgrave Macmillan.

Arneson, Richard. (1995). 'Democratic Rights at National and Workplace Levels.' In *The Idea of Democracy*, edited by D. Copp, J. Hampton and J. E. Roemer, 118–48. New York: Cambridge University Press.

Bachmann, Klaus, and Fatić, Aleksandar. (2015). *The UN International Criminal Tribunals: Transition without Justice?* Oxon: Routledge.

Bapir, Mohammed Ali. (2010). 'Iraq: A Deeply Divided Polity and Challenges to Democracy-Building.' *Information, Society and Justice* 3(2): 117–25.

Barry, Brian (1991). *Democracy and Power*. Oxford: Clarendon Press.

Buchanan, Allen. (2002). 'Political Legitimacy and Democracy.' *Ethics* 112(4): 689–719.

Buchanan, Allen. (2005). 'Equality and Human Rights.' *Politics, Philosophy and Economics* 4(1): 69–90.

Cohen, Joshua. (1997). 'Procedure and Substance in Deliberative Democracy.' In *Deliberative Democracy*, edited by J. Bohman and W. Rehg, 407–38. Cambridge, MA: MIT Press.

de Greiff, Pablo. (2010), 'A Normative Conception of Transitional Justice.' *Politorbis* 50(3): 17–29.

de Tocqueville, Alexis. (1963). *Democracy in America*. New York: Random House.

Diamond, Larry. (2004). 'Transition to Democracy in Iraq?' *The Brown Journal of World Affairs* 11(1): 45–53.

Dworkin, Ronald. (1986). *Law's Empire*. Oxford: Hart.

Griffin, James. (2008). *On Human Rights*. Oxford: Oxford University Press.

International Centre for Transitional Justice. (2009). *What Is Transitional Justice?* Retrieved from https://www.ictj.org/sites/default/files/ICTJ-Global-Transitional-Justice-2009-English.pdf.

Mihr, Anja. (2013). 'Transitional Justice and the Quality of Democracy.' *International Journal of Conflict and Violence* 7(2): 298–313.

Mill, John Stuart. (1946). *On Liberty and Considerations of Representative Government*. Oxford: Basil Blackwell.

Moon, Bruce E. (2009). 'Long Time Coming: Prospects for Democracy in Iraq.' *International Security* 33(4): 115–48.

Rawls, John. (2003). *The Law of Peoples*. Cambridge, MA: Harvard University Press.

Raz, Joseph. (2013). 'Human Rights without Foundations.' In *The Philosophy of International Law*, edited by S. Besson and J. Tasioulas, 321–38 Oxford: Oxford University Press.

Tasioulas, John. (2013). 'Human Dignity and the Foundations of Human Rights.' In *Understanding Human Dignity*, edited by C. McCrudden, 291–312. Oxford: Oxford University Press.

United Nations. (2008). *What Is Transitional Justice?* Retrieved from http://www.un.org/en/peacebuilding/pdf/doc_wgll/justice_times_transition/26_02_2008_background_note.pdf.

Weber, Max. (1964). *Basic Concepts in Sociology*. London: Peter Owen.

Wellman, Christopher. (1996). 'Liberalism, Samaritanism and Political Legitimacy.' *Philosophy and Public Affairs* 25(3): 211–37.

Wierzynska, Aneta. (2004). 'Consolodating Democracy through Transitional Justice: Rwanda's Gacaca Courts.' *New York University Law Review* 79: 1934–70.

Winter, Stephen. (2013). 'Towards a Unified Theory of Transitional Justice.' *International Journal of Transitional Justice* 7(2): 224–44.

Chapter 3

Organised Crime as a Challenge to Transitional Justice

Nataša Radovanović

THE BEGINNINGS AND INITIAL FUNDING OF ORGANISED CRIME IN TRANSITIONAL SOCIETIES

At a surface, the concept of transition is usually associated primarily with just one segment of what transition really is, namely with the changing economies of transitional countries, including the adoption of a liberal or at least liberalised market, the gradual achievement of a macroeconomic stability, the restructuring and privatisation of companies and the introduction of a culture of competition and rule of law throughout society. One often overlooked phenomenon that regularly attends transitional processes is the emergence of systemic or structural corruption and organised crime.

The beginnings of organised crime in the postconflict societies of Eastern Europe were the same as in Western societies, namely in the form of racketeering criminal organisations. The very name of the American RICO law (the Racketeer Influence and Corrupt Organizations Act) suggests that racketeering lies in the very genetic code of organised crime, just like corruption does. In Eastern Europe, after the breakdown of communism, institutions were in crisis and room was wide open for the services provided by criminal organisations instead of those normally due by state institutions. Criminal organisations thus started to collect debts or offer 'protection' to small enterprises from other criminal groups where the police could not do this. In some countries, including Serbia, criminal organisations started by providing physical protection of individuals, and later of corporate subjects. All of these activities allowed organised crime to quickly accumulate extremely large profits. Just like with the RICO law in the United States, such high profits of criminal groups caused the enactment of new legislation, which allowed a speedy confiscation of property from criminal groups and their members.

Such seizures of property became possible even before a full criminal conviction was secured, on the basis of a civil procedure (Hammil et al., 2014).

The distinguishing feature of civil procedure as opposed to criminal one is that in the former the standard of proof is less demanding than in the latter. In civil procedure decisions are made based on a balance of probability, while the criminal procedure requires a proof at the level of certainty, or 'beyond reasonable doubt.' The reason is that the civil cases confront one citizen against another, with relatively equal arms and resources, and with relatively less serious consequences in case of loss. However, in criminal proceedings it is the state that prosecutes a citizen, and the resources and legal arms available to the state are incommensurably greater than those available to any private citizen, while the consequences of conviction include a loss of liberty, even life or limb. Thus the standard of proof of culpability in criminal cases is considerably above that required in civil cases.

When the so-called criminal property is seized through a civil procedure, this casts serious consequences for the conceptualisation of guilt. Taking away someone's property based on a balance of probabilities that it is 'criminal property,' while the criminal proceedings are underway and the person is legally innocent (until proven guilty) threatens to prejudice the outcome of a criminal trial. It is even possible for the prosecution to use the fact that the defendant's property has been seized as 'criminal property' in a civil case as evidence of one's criminal guilt in the criminal case. In Serbia and in southeastern Europe as a whole the most infamous example has been that of the seizure and public sale of assets taken away from drug lord Darko Šarić, who at the time of writing of this chapter was being tried for the crimes that had allegedly led to his acquisition of all the seized property. In other words, the procedure to prove that he has committed the crimes allowing him to gain the property has not been concluded, and the property has long been seized and sold at public auction as 'criminal' (*Blic Daily*, 2014).

In the course of time, the activities of organised crime have expanded so as to include extortion, kidnappings, trade in stolen vehicles, the smuggling of narcotics and weapons, cigarettes and other restricted commodities. Criminal groups ventured into the trade in human organs and in the process became involved in collaboration with murderers and war criminals. All of these activities allowed organised crime to become deeply entrenched in the very structure of the 'grey' and 'black' (semi-illegal and illegal) economies in the transitional countries. Criminal groups have succeeded in establishing a sound market, with a large number of customers in the black market relying systematically on organised crime as a supplier of goods and services in structurally the same way as the citizens at-large tend to rely on legitimate companies and institutions. In transitional states the legitimate sector simply cannot offer effective services such as debt collection or the implementation of justice, thus opening the room for criminal groups to offer the same kind of services, however on criminal terms.

This particular aspect of organised crime sets it apart fundamentally from the so-called standard or classical crime. While standard crime is a sort of aberration or violation of the ordinary structure of relationships in a legitimate society, organised crime impacts the social structure and social system as a whole in a systematic, broad way. By being able to offer a wide range of goods and services illegally, criminal organisations destabilise the very foundations of a system of legality and legitimacy in society, not on a case-by-case basis, but in principle. Namely, in transitional societies institutions tend to be less effective and of a lower quality than in democratically advanced societies. This, for example, means that the court systems in transitional countries tend to be clogged with cases, dependent on political influence and command far less public credibility than court systems in advanced democracies. If such a situation persists for a relatively long time (several decades), this means that a relatively substantial proportion of the population will gradually likely start to rely on resolving their differences not in front of the courts, but with the aid of criminal groups. After all, nobody can wait several decades for the collection of a debt or an important decision on property; criminal groups have the ability to solve such issues within days in criminal ways. In light of institutional dysfunction, the increasing resorting to the services of organised crime starts to emerge not as an aberration of the system, but as an alternative, perhaps necessary, system of provision of services previously reserved for the state. This undermines the very foundations of legality and legitimacy in society and has profound consequences for the various aspects of political, ideological and institutional transition. This is the reason organised crime is an essential part of any transitional crisis and of any transitional process; it is a key challenge to societal management as a whole during the sociopolitical transitions. At the same time, anti-organised crime policy is a key aspect of transitional justice, although the theme of organised crime is rarely mentioned in the existing studies of transitional justice.

In southeastern Europe the few decades spanning the very end of the twentieth and beginning of the twenty-first centuries have seen an explosive expansion of organised crime, which was facilitated by the wars in the former Yugoslavia (the wars in Slovenia, Croatia, Bosnia-Herzegovina and Kosovo), as well as the 1999 NATO intervention against Serbia over Kosovo's secession attempt. The region became flooded with public controversies over the connections between political personalities and organised crime and the increasingly obvious influence specific criminal groups were able to exert on legal economic and political institutions. Criminal organisations had started to launder their criminal proceeds from narcotics, cigarette and human smuggling, mainly through investments in real estate, construction or the hospitality industry. This gave them the publicly recognised status of 'contro-versial businessmen,' some of whom proceeded to buy formerly state-owned enterprises through the privatisation process, and to fund political parties. All of this allowed them to take part in the making of political decisions and appointments in key parts of the public sector.

In the region affected by the civil wars in the 1990s, one of the main challenges of transition has become the fight against organised crime, espe-cially against the most effective and well-organised 'queen' of the narcotics market, the Kosovo Albanian mafia. Kosovo has been a particularly con-venient area to experiment with the various modalities of organised crime because it has long been affected by systematic lawlessness and has thus grown into a regional 'hub' for the storage and transfer of large quantities of narcotics towards Europe.

In southeastern Europe, like elsewhere, the main source of funding for organised crime has been the narcotics trade. Hence, the fight against large criminal groups almost always involves some kind of action against the organised drug trade. Serbia is a particularly interesting country in this con-text, as it has traditionally been among the top five countries where drugs have been the cheapest and most accessible, with the exemption of the countries where the specific types of drugs are actually grown or produced. However, up until the 1980s, the number of heroin users in Serbia was very low; they were mainly young people from wealthy families. During the 1980s the use of heroin became massive, because the drug, produced in Afghanistan, had started to be transported to Serbia via Istanbul and Sofia, and then across Macedonia and Kosovo. The heroin trade established itself as the most profitable criminal business, which allowed criminal groups to amass large amounts of liquid cash in a very brief amount of time. For example, at the time the 70 percent pure heroin cost 15,000 German Marks in Turkey, and was subsequently mixed with other substances to double the quantity. This final substance was then sold in the former Yugoslavia and Europe for 30,000 German Marks a kilo, meaning that the profit was quadrupled in relation to the initial price paid by the traffickers in Turkey. A similar modus of operation in the heroin distribution and pricing is used today (Golubović, 2005). A 2008 report by the International Committee for the Control of Narcotics, an inde-pendent UN body for the implementation of monitoring of the UN Program for the Control of Drugs specifies that the southern route of the so-called Balkan drug route (Istanbul-Sofia-Belgrade-Zagreb) was increasingly used for the trafficking of heroin into the Russian Federation (*Politika Daily*, 2017). Similarly, according to the reports by the US State Department on drug control strategy, Serbia, and especially Kosovo, is a key transit country on the Balkan corridor of the narcotics trade, including heroin, cocaine, mari-juana and the various synthetic drugs. The corridor starts in Afghanistan and

Turkey, even in South Africa, and stretches across Bulgaria and Macedonia to reach central and western Europe (*Politika Daily*, 2017). So far mainly American sources have claimed that the narcotics have only transited through Serbia, while only a small quantity remained there to supply a market of sixty to eighty thousand consumers, where the main points of trade were the regions of Sandžak (border region between Serbia and Montenegro) and Kosovo. According to the same sources, the majority of heroin is destined for western Europe (*Politika Daily*, 2017). According to the UN Office for Drugs and Crime (UNODC) 2009 report, the overall profit from the narcotics trade globally amounts to $320 billion annually (USD), which *exceeds the double budget of the European Union* (*Blic Daily*, 2017).

A prime example of a large criminal group detected in Serbia is the so-called Zemun Clan, a highly structured group which started with the trafficking in stolen upmarket vehicles. The group then joined up with another major group, the 'Surčin Clan'; having found the narcotics trade far more lucrative than the trafficking of stolen cars, they have since focused exclusively on drugs. The drug trafficking operations of these regionally significant criminal groups spanned two decades. Initially, they had started with a small group of selected members who distributed narcotics in the streets of Serbia's capital Belgrade; however this quickly transformed into a large dealer network which was registered in police databases already in the 1990s. At one stage, they gained the support of the most influential leaders of paramilitary formations in the postconflict transitional state after the wars of disintegration of the former Yugoslavia, and within just four years they grew into one of the most threatening criminal groups in southeastern Europe. During and immediately after the civil wars in the former Yugoslavia, the clan enjoyed the support of various state institutions, first of all the state security service of the time. The group was thus able to develop a high level of internal discipline and control the various precisely defined roles for its members, which made it a highly hierarchic criminal group. The transitional context was a condition of the group's survivability due to the transitional state's inability to stamp out criminal influences on the institutions. Systematically, particularly cruel individuals with large experience on the battlefield were recruited to perform the most brutal tasks for the group, including the executions of potential competitors. These individuals trained the other members of the clan in the skills they had gained on the front line of the civil war, which militarised the group and increased the overall level of the threat it posed to society. The next stage in the clan's development included abductions of high-profile business people. A series of such abductions, along with the drug trade, allowed them to generate enormous profits. They thus grew into a serious narcotics empire whose ambitions went beyond merely ruling the criminal underworld: the clan started its attempt to take over all the important levers of power in the government by influencing both the government and the opposition political parties. In 2003, they organised and executed the assassination of Serbian Prime Minister, Dr. Zoran Đinđić. The immediate motive for the assassination was that the members of the clan had sensed a threat from the new political coalition, led by Đinđić, which was preparing a repressive campaign against them. In an attempt to avoid the state's strike and the arrests of its members, they orchestrated the execution in order to demonstrate their power and superiority, which they though would make it easier for them to de facto take over political power in the country through the political figures whom they controlled. It should be noted that the way in which the assassination was carried out clearly reflected the close intertwining between the state institutions and the criminal underworld in a transitional society: the prime minister was shot by deputy commander of a special unit of the State Security Service, Colonel Zvezdan Jovanović.

The example of the Zemun Clan illustrates how organised criminal groups in transition can use the institutional weakness and disorganisation and, thanks to the enormous accumulation of financial wealth and social capital in an unstable, transitional society, cause not just serious aberrations of social justice and social control, but an implosion of the entire system of state institutions. The abrupt enrichment of criminal groups and their ability to corrupt and influence officials leads to rapid changes in the factual distribution of power in society. Transitional processes themselves often give rise to sharp differences in wealth between the citizens, who tend to become divided into just two groups: the wealthy and the poor, with the middle class disappearing. The mechanisms of social control stall, and values in society become brutally materialistic. All this leads to wealth automatically determining one's overall social status. This often happens in formerly highly egalitarian societies, where, for example, the level of one's education or the type of one's profession (e.g., artists) were far more important for determining one's social status than one's wealth. The sudden shift to barren materialism causes a confusion of public values and makes it difficult for ordinary people to understand their place in society and the norms through which they should judge their choices and those of others. As a result, the legitimacy of the democratic system becomes reduced, because through all of the described phenomena the public loses trust in the quality of the institutional order, the legality and propriety of behaviour of the state institutions. In such a situation, organised crime is particularly well placed to present itself as a viable alternative to the legitimate state. This idea, of swapping the legitimate institutions for criminal organisations, is built in all phases of the development of organised crime, from the initial 'racket'-based activities to more advanced ones where criminal groups openly challenge the state. It is this developmental logic of organised crime that explains why transition is an ideal social and political environment for an in-depth criminalisation of society.

This is the main reason organised crime is not only a challenge to internal security and social control, but also a broader social issue for transitions. Organised crime's quest to legitimise itself vis-à-vis the largely dysfunctional state institutions in transition renders an effective anti-organised crime policy not just a matter of enforcement, but also an issue of struggling to preserve a legitimate social culture where crime continues to be seen as illegitimate. This is a fundamental facet of the transitional anti-organised crime policy that has to do with values, rather than merely with control policies.

Policing organised crime in transitional societies is thus an exemplary *social process*, which makes democratic values credible and helps preserve the moral integrity of a society. In transitional circumstances, policing is a particular contribution to the legitimacy of the system, because it increases public confidence that the 'main' way of conducting social transactions is still the legal and legitimate way, despite the threat arising from the alternatives presented by organised crime. This is particularly important in light of the 'systemic' features of the various threats to the security of transitions, where, for example, 'systemic' corruption threatens to hijack the public agenda in the way of making the corrupt way of conducting social transactions — the main way. Organised crime as an equally systemic threat links up with corruption and seeks to impose an overall culture of illegitimacy as more efficient and indirectly, socially more acceptable way of solving problems than the legitimate and, in transitions, often inefficient ways of doing the same.

DOMINATION OF A NETWORKED MODEL OVER THE HIERARCHIC MODEL OF CRIMINAL ORGANISATION

In transitional societies, the social pressures to achieve financial success and prestige tend to be combined with unjust and discriminating social conditions and mechanisms of social promotion that facilitate the success of some, which debilitating others from achieving the same, either due to their class, race or some other aspect of identity. According to one of the most influential theories of criminal deviance, it is this tension between the pressure to succeed and the reality where access to success for many is systematically barred by social conditions, that gives rise to the propensity by many young people to resort to criminal careers. According to Robert Merton, the Western society imposes an ideal of social affirmation which is articulated in terms of wealth and power; the message behind this ideal is that one's social value is confirmed if one achieves wealth and power, and contrariwise, one's social value is denied if one is a 'failure.' In a system that, on the described terms, causes most people to be 'failures,' the drive to 'achieve' in terms of wealth and influence is easily deformed into choosing a criminal career (Merton, 1938). The logic thus becomes: achieving illegally bestows value on a person that is lower than the value of achieving legally, but considerably greater than failing to achieve wealth and power altogether. Consequently, to achieve a full social affirmation one might decide to strive to achieve more illegally than is considered sufficient for 'success' by legal means, thinking subconsciously that this will 'equalise' one's social value and recognition with those who are privileged and able to attain legitimate wealth and social prestige. Within a criminal subculture, organised crime is considered an 'elite' crime. The most 'successful' criminals are those who operate criminal organisations or play important roles in such organisations. For many members of organised criminal groups in transitional societies their logic of 'success' vacillates between their inability to attain legitimate success in the face of ineffective transitional institutions on the one hand, and the 'Mertonian' narrative of success at any cost, on the other. That is why the development of organised crime in transitional, postconflict societies conforms so well to the models well known from the history of development of organised crime in the more developed societies: the conditions, the social pressures and the mechanisms are the same.

In the context of a criminal career being a conscious choice, it becomes clearer why such careers are rarely broken by the individual's serving a prison sentence. While some offenders will be taken out of their ordinary orbit of associates and activities by being sent to prison, others will be able to continue organising or coordinating a criminal group, or a particular activity within such a group (e.g., the production of synthetic narcotics) from prison. This means that once they are released they find it easy to reconnect with criminal co-operators and continue their 'work' as though it was never interrupted. One aspect of this type of continuity of criminal careers is that such individuals are relatively easily detectable: the authorities know that they continually operate in the criminal arena, and are thus able to follow them continually. Such criminals thus shift in and out of prison most of their lives. Their profits grow, as do their groups, but they themselves, as persons, are constantly under police surveillance and tend to pay a high price in prison time for their business. Because they are able to sacrifice their liberty and pay such a hefty price for the criminal profits, they are respected by other criminals. The described profile of a criminal leader is particularly beneficial to hierarchically organised groups: such groups are characterised by a high degree of division of labour and considerable control of the participants. Hence, the physical absence of one or more of the ringleaders, if they are dedicated and continue their involvement from prison, does not necessarily diminish the stability of the organisation and its ability to control its members. Such stability is vital to the medium- and longer-term survivability of hierarchical groups. This type of leaders see themselves as professionals, and the cost of crime is seen as the cost of their profession. They often enjoy the support of their family and immediate community, which makes it additionally difficult to control and repress them because the local support reduces the stigma that trials and punishments are meant to bring to bear on the perpetrator.

The mechanism of family support also operates on lower levels of the criminal organisation, vis-a-vis ordinary criminals, who are often younger men and women who enjoy the support of their parents. Often such a criminal would be a person who has grown up in a broken family, alone with the mother, in difficult financial circumstances and in a social group heavily affected by unemployment and poverty. When such a person resorts to drug trafficking, the family starts to live 'decently.' The prior state of poverty is seen as a result of social injustice (which it usually really is), and the later stage, after the person's involvement in crime, is seen as a 'rectification' of social injustice by criminal means. Both the immediate and wider family offer support, and even actively participate in the illegal activities, because the new 'business' is seen as a redemption from poverty which had been inflicted on the family through discriminating and unequal social circumstances. This is a 'political' pathology of organised crime that needs to be considered, especially in changing, transitional societies where a massive redistribution of wealth and privilege is underway.

Criminal organisations tend to behave in much the same way as legal businesses on the market. They follow the market conditions and contribute to the creation of an entire parallel illegal market where the so-called grey (semi-legal) and black (illegal) goods and services are exchanged. This is why modern criminology describes criminal organisations as 'criminal enterprises'; the term reflects the logic behind the operation of such groups. Unlike legitimate enterprises, they are able to offer the participating individuals easy and fast profits. In transitional societies, dominated by high unemployment and widespread poverty organised crime is an extremely attractive choice of career for some.

The evolution of the criminal organisation has gradually led to a gradual overcoming of the hierarchically structured criminal groups. Hierarchic criminal organisations are ones characterised by a strict division of roles, more or less permanent membership and the existence of a hierarchical command network consisting of various 'leftenants' who control specific criminal activities and report to higher brass. Such leftenants have their own prerogatives for instilling discipline in their parts of the group, while their own destiny, often their lives, lie in the hands of those they report to. The lines of responsibility are very clear and the sanctions for any breaches of the rules are severe, often including the physical elimination of those responsible. The recruitment of group members is based on various criteria, including similar places of origin, prison experience, similar level of prestige in the group and so on. Unlike less well-structured groups, hierarchic criminal organisations are capable of exerting greater discipline within their ranks; they can mobilise very quickly and have far greater control over various parts of their operations. They also have a stronger collective identity and allow a greater mutual identification between their members, whose 'professional' and private lives tend to be highly intertwined with those of other members of the group. Members of networked organisations, which are not hierarchical, on the other hand, tend to lead private lives that are largely independent of those of their colleagues.

The more recent, networked groups, conversely, have much fewer permanent members, while most of the collaborators simply join the particular activities of the group and then continue their careers as independent criminals. People who participate in networked crime are often highly specialised for specific types of crimes (robberies, theft of artefacts, counterfeiting of documents, automobile theft, human trafficking, etc.). When several specialists for various types of crime join in a complex criminal enterprise, this leads to an ad hoc criminal group, which expands or contracts in time depending on the number of the participants, dynamics of criminal activity or simply the type of crime they commit at a particular time. As a result, at certain points in time the group may seem very weak; it may even seem that it has faded away, while in the next moment the group can become maximally engaged, 'swell' in numbers and even resemble a highly structured hierarchic group. This fluidity of the limits of group members makes the detection of networked groups more difficult.

When observed over longer periods, it is noticeable that networked groups tend to expand overall: they tend to increasingly engage individuals charged with specific activities who do not necessarily even know about most other activities of the group: people who organise the transport of narcotics, the guarding of the narcotic crops (with organic narcotics such as cocaine or marijuana) and the like. Some of these individuals are recruited as unemployed persons who are trustworthy because of their family or social connections. Such people are often, strictly speaking, not really criminals, and are otherwise in search of legitimate jobs.

Networks are occasionally broken due to conflicts between criminals, but they usually successfully heal because the social 'glue' of the group is interest or profit, which most members cannot have at the same level anywhere else. Thus the basic group of ringleaders who keep the network together tends to be stable. Clearly the mechanism of survival of the networked group described here is different from that of a hierarchic group, where conflicts are controlled through intragroup enforcement and any disintegrative tendencies are punished severely. Hierarchic groups rely on authority that rests on a person's capacity to enforce obedience, while in networked groups the logic of cohesion is mostly that of interest and rational calculation. Thus the need for brutality in networked groups is lower than that in hierarchic groups.

In southeastern European transitions, the new trend of networked groups is also increasingly present, especially in drug-related crime. Narcotics traffickers often hire various independent criminals who are there only for a limited time and are then changed for other similar individuals. They perform simple tasks, such as keeping watch over 'safe houses' used by fugitives from the law or over apartments used for the growing of marijuana and other crops in urban environments. Such individuals are given housing accommodation, food, money for expenses and a certain fixed amount of fee after all expenses, usually for a period of six months, depending on their residency and visa status in a particular country. This is the type of arrangement that often attracts individuals who are neither criminals, nor necessarily aware that they are participating in serious crime. They do not see themselves as members of a criminal group. The influence of this type of recruitment is particularly damaging for the broader social interpretation and stigmatisation of organised crime because the group appears as an almost legitimate employer. Such an 'employer' is then seen both by the 'employees' and their families, as well as their broader social circle, not as a major threat to society, but rather as a type of occurrence that ought to be tolerated because it generates benefits for 'ordinary people.' Such a way of recruiting gives organised crime a width and depth of social reach through its contacts with 'ordinary people,' and gains a degree of social acceptability. This makes the work of control agencies difficult, especially in transitional societies which, by definition, are socially unstable. Transitional societies often suffer from high unemployment, including structural unemployment. In other words, there are entire layers of the population whose members are systematically unable to find employment in a transforming and changing economy.

The latest stage in the evolution of a criminal organisation appears, however, to be a complex structure that goes beyond the now already well-established divide between hierarchic and networked groups: the contracting of individuals who belong to one group for crimes committed by another group, where various criminals hold various positions and roles in different criminal groups, all of which are so intertwined that the entire structure of organised crime in a particular country becomes *one single criminal network*. Fighting these groups requires the use of infiltrated insiders, a variety of criminal intelligence methods, and prosecutorial collaboration at a fast pace and high institutional level. Such methods are often less than fully effective because of information leakage and the use of different methods in different countries. Some perpetrators who participate in such complex structures have a strong social influence, and their mere presence within the criminal network may deter the development of an efficient police and prosecutorial collaboration, especially when warrants for arrests or requests for detection assistance come from another country and target a high-profile person in the country where action is required. Highly influential businesspeople in small and underdeveloped economies are not exactly the preferred target for the police forces and prosecutors of those countries, especially when the crimes have occurred outside their own country. The relative social and economic significance of such persons is often sufficient for the police and prosecution to 'look the other way.'

In some countries the implementation of intrusive surveillance, for example, is easier and more liberally regulated than in other countries. In still other countries resources are sparse. In practise, effective police and prosecutorial collaboration requires also the ability to arouse interest by the police officials and prosecutors abroad. This does not always happen easily, because each country has its own priorities, depending on the perceived threat posed by particular types of crime. For example, the institutions of a foreign country may not be willing to react to synthetic drugs or crop-growing of marijuana, because they focus their priorities on cocaine as the major drug problem. This is the case in Spain and the Netherlands, whose institutions have been known to fail to react to information received from abroad about marijuana crops, because they judged it too expensive to engage their resources given the expected amount of marijuana to be seized. Such a logic pushes the threat to society from the growing and sale of narcotics to second place compared to the cost-effectiveness of the control effort. In some countries all specific police actions, ranging from secret surveillance to the use of extra personnel, make up a calculation of operational costs to be justified to the superiors, given the expected results. Organisationally, this logic might be inevitable, but it does not always contribute to fighting organised crime overall. On the other hand, in the transitional states of the former Yugoslavia, resources are often lacking or there is such corruption that effective cross-border collaboration is hindered. Such situations necessitate the use of traditional policing, including various types of field work. This calls for skills, training and adaptability of police officers. That is why the Balkan countries usually combine traditional policing with the use of advanced technology. In more advanced countries, the technology tends to play a dominant role.

A NEW FOCUS ON SYNTHETIC DRUGS

As most criminal organisations depend for their funding on the narcotics trade, the recent trend is a reliance on synthetic drugs rather than the traditional natural drugs such as heroin or cocaine. Synthetic drugs are harder to detect and always available independently of complicated supply chains and transport routes from areas where the opiate cultures naturally grow. The production of synthetic drugs requires a chemical expertise, and it also allows experts to change the molecules and the various ingredients of the drug so as to create a substance that influences the brain of a consumer in the same way as forbidden substances, while the new substance is not even on a list of banned chemicals. The profits from synthetic drugs are approximately the same as in the sale of heroin or cocaine, but the conditions of their availability are far more favourable to the criminals.

The distribution of heroin occurs from the East towards the West, as the opium poppy is grown in Afghanistan and Pakistan, while the distribution of cocaine unfolds from the West towards the East, as coca plants grow in Latin America. These general directions of distribution dictate the way in which the drug market must adapt itself in various parts of the world. With synthetic drugs, however, production is possible anywhere in the world, and this makes the market larger and more accessible: synthetic drug cartels are able to position themselves in a favourable market and simply manufacture the drugs there, without depending on the geographical constraints of global cocaine or heroin trafficking. The 'geopolitics' of cocaine and heroin distribution are reflected in their prices in various parts of the world. In America, heroin is a greater challenge for control agencies: it is imported across the ocean, while cocaine comes from the neighbourhood, from Latin America. Thus the trafficking of heroin often includes large, transnational criminal networks with an extensive cross-border corruption potential and brutal methods of enforcement of discipline and debt collection. In the Balkans, on the other hand, heroin is a traditional, almost 'domestic' drug from the near abroad, so the move by organised drug traffickers from heroin to cocaine smuggling was a major change on the drug market and is now one of the main challenges to the region's police forces. New challenges include new types of narcotics, especially the synthetic drugs, some of which have been produced en masse in the Balkans.

The most common are the amphetamine drugs, including amphetamine itself, methamphetamine and MDMA (Extasy). They are particularly attractive for the criminal organisations because the initial investment in their production is lower than that required for the purchase of organic drugs. However, the production of synthetic drugs requires some expertise. Recently the synthetic drugs market has become dominated by synthetic Cannabinoids, because they are not on the lists of forbidden substances due to the wide variations in their molecular structure. The trend of producing new synthetic drugs is that two hundred to three hundred new psychoactive substances are detected annually that produce the desired effect, yet they are not on lists of forbidden substances. These psychoactive substances are commonly called 'designer drugs.' China is the greatest producer of synthetic drugs and their precursors, while the production in Europe is topped by the Netherlands and Belgium.

Criminal groups that produce and distribute synthetic drugs must have a person with a basic knowledge of chemistry and the skills and experience in the production process in illegal laboratories. Adequate premises are also necessary, as is the laboratory equipment and the precursors (substances used to produce the drug). Precursors are also regulated by lists of precursors, and their sale is controlled; they are not freely available on the legal market.

The need for expertise in those who coordinate the production of synthetic drugs is at the same time the chief weakness of the groups who are involved in this type of the narcotics business. Namely, the detection of such groups is primarily based on uncovering the presence of the known experts with criminal careers in synthetic drugs. The locating of such persons often leads to detecting new groups who supply the market with new types of synthetic narcotics, given that the circle of experts for production is limited and the same persons tend to be used by various groups.

As an illustration of the profits generated by trade in synthetic drugs, one kilogramme of amphetamine combined with four kilogrammes of cellulose, or some other 'filler' mass, is sufficient for the production of five kilogrammes of tablets, where one kilogramme is four thousand to five thousand tablets. One tablet is sold in the street for 3–5 Euro, which means that with about 1,000 Euro investment the return is about 75,000 Euro. The drugs are always available as long as the conditions for production are there, and the criminal group does not depend on any suppliers. In addition, the synthetic drug groups can always exchange their drugs for other types of drugs, including organic ones, because the supply-demand ratio in the drug market is always well balanced, namely the supply is always proportional to the demand. All of these facets of synthetics drugs make them exceptionally challenging for policing. In transitional societies that is even more so, because concealment and corruption are more feasible than in wealthier and better structured societies.

Organised crime based on the trafficking in synthetic drugs requires special attention by the control agencies and a continuous following of global trends that tend to be replicated in various locations around the world. The main control measures include monitoring the sale of precursors, equipment and other chemicals typically required for the production of synthetic drugs. It should always be kept in mind that the technological prerequisites for the production of synthetic drugs are at the same time the most reliable means of detecting the criminal organisations involved in this type of drug crime.

Among European countries, the Netherlands and Belgium are the greatest producers of amphetamine and MDMA, while Czech Republic is the leader in the production of methamphetamine. In Serbia, twenty or so illegal laboratories for the production of synthetic drugs have been found since the beginning of the 1990s. These labs ranged in capacity from professional ones to those improvised in homes. However, Serbia is particularly threatened by synthetic drugs because it is home to the production of all kinds of various synthetic drugs, including amphetamine, methamphetamine, methaqualone, MDMA, as well as the precursor benzil metil keton (BMK).

In wealthy countries the detection of these types of laboratories is based on high-level technology and considerable other resources, while in transitional countries the success in fighting synthetic drugs depends on the skilful use of traditional policing methods, primarily the use of informants. The maintenance of networks of police informants requires special skills, including the ability to acquire other's trust, keeping communication alive in difficult circumstances, as well as judgement in making decisions about the launching of repressive actions so as to preserve the network of associates, avoid compromising individual associates and informants, and generate a sense of trust in the informants. Police associates from the criminal world are compensated, either by money or by privileges. These may include a reduced level of prosecution, better prison conditions, protection of their families while they are serving prison sentences and so on.

Due to donations from France, a special training centre for the safe entry into illegal laboratories has been established in Serbia. This centre has since been listed within EUROPOL-S training centres. Other similar centres exist only in Poland, Belgium and Turkey. The centre is used for the training of police officers in the detection of and entry into illegal laboratories. It contains equipment that has been seized from criminal groups in order to facilitate simulations and exercises.

One often mentioned aspect of drug trafficking careers is that of exceptionally high recidivism. This might seem to suggest that any repressive action against high-level drug trafficking is automatically without an appropriate long-term effect. Given the strong connections between drug crime and other types of systemic criminal threats to society, such as corruption and co-option of public officials, the social damage inflicted by such crime, even if slightly reduced by successful control activity, justifies the expenditure of resources and effort in controlling drug trafficking rings dealing in synthetic drugs. In this context the traditional goals of repressive controls, namely general and special prevention, are relegated to the background, while the main aim of repressive action is a reduction of damage, given the destructive effects of drug-based organised crime. Recidivism is simply a structural and dynamic feature of organised crime anywhere in the world today and it needs to be accepted as the way organised crime operates, with or without a successful repressive action.

INFLUENCE ON INSTITUTIONS

A culture of informality and corruption that organised crime helps engender in society generates such disintegrative effects on public institutions that members of criminal organisations are even able to appoint public officials in particularly sensitive parts of the state administration. Such persons, once brought to positions of public influence and power by organised crime, enter into a deeply entrenched relationship of clientelism with the criminal organisation. The main feature of clientelistic relationships is their binary character and the extreme difficulty of exiting such a relationship at any point in time. The relationship is binary because each participant is both a client and a sponsor: the criminal group is a sponsor for the public official whom it helps appoint to a high-level office, however the person later becomes the sponsor of the criminal group, because she is able to provide protection to the group from any institutional action. The relationship involves deeply set interests which make the severing of the relationship very difficult and very risky. Namely, in clientelistic relationships (and any clientelistic relationship in the public service is a form of corruption) usually one side starts to desire to distance themselves from the other side (typically the corrupt public official, once the risks and burdens become unbearable), however any such exit would place such serious risks on the criminal group that it would not allow the person to go away from the relationship. Any attempt to exit thus leads to conflict, often causing the killing of the person wishing to go away. Clientelistic relationships are thus long term and are considered a structural feature of organised crime and systemic corruption.

In light of this, the very survival of public institutions in transition depends on the existence of a critical number of legitimate public officials who are not corrupt. Whether there is such a critical mass or not determines whether the state is systemically corrupt or not. Systemic corruption sets in once the main way of functioning of the institutions becomes corruption, so that fighting corruption, strategically speaking, makes no sense. Preventing systemic corruption is perhaps the main challenge for transitional states. Fighting organised crime, in a sense, 'buys time' for the institutions in transitional countries to pick up pace and start protecting the interests of the public in optimally satisfactory ways so that the actual demand for corruption on the society-wide market might decrease. This is a slow process whose results, in some societies, appear distant for a long time.

The main problem in the corruption of institutions lies in a particular overlapping of the legal and illegal aspects in their work, namely of the discretionary decisions which public officials are legally required to make (and which, obviously, lead to some people being satisfied, and some not, wherever there is a conflict to address), and the criminal influences on the way these discretionary prerogatives are exercised within the institutions. It is important to keep in mind that criminal influences will not always, or even not typically, lead to decisions being made in an openly illegal way: public officials who are corrupt may act *within* the legal bounds of what they are entitled to do, however their motivation will be to further the interests of particular groups or individuals. This is how 'good governance' is lost due to criminal influences, however any legal action in such situations is difficult because it is hard to establish that any particular law has been broken. In fact the law is not being broken; it is being used in ways which *pervert its purpose*. Policing, especially criminal intelligence, is crucial here, because only by successful advanced policing is it possible to determine the intent to abuse the law by corrupt public officials and single out their specific actions which might incriminate them. This is why in political transition policing remains a key aspect not only of fighting organised crime directly, but also of fighting informality as a generalised problem of public administration and the public sector more generally.

POLICE RESOURCES, INTERCEPTION OF COMMUNICATIONS AND CRIMINAL PROFILING

Within the general bounds of intelligence-led policing, quality analytic work is crucial. Crude criminal intelligence material, which is often spectacularly presented as a 'result' of intelligence is rarely operationally useful or legally acceptable. Often, it can be deceitful and lead either to misled repressive action, or to missing important clues if it is not adequately and creatively interpreted. Once the intelligence material is gathered, it requires a careful analysis and systematisation. An important aspect of analytics is the elimination of operationally irrelevant information and the classification of the rest so that it can be used adequately within the relevant context, not necessarily that in which it has been gathered. For example, information received from intercepted communications by specific persons may be useful in addressing some type of criminal activity by completely different persons, but at first sight it may seem irrelevant if the entire intelligence material is interpreted only in light of the specific perpetrators who are investigated. This is why analytics should be separated from intelligence gathering, not only in terms of the individuals involved in the two specific phases of intelligence work, but also in terms of methodology, space and time: analytics should be able to take some time to sift through the information and consider whether and where it 'fits' and can be used. This is often contrary to the demands placed on the police to act quickly and produce visible and actionable results, which can be presented to the public as achievements of the government.

An excess of intelligence material, if it is not critically appraised through analysis, can be dangerous as well. In addition to compromising citizen privacy and rights, it can generate the so-called crying wolf syndrome, where many signals that something is about to happen mobilise institutional resources and, when nothing happens a sufficient number of times, the next time the signals come the institutions might respond sluggishly or not at all. It is thus important to reduce the number of false alerts and to maintain a reserved view on intelligence data unless it is matched with other information or fits with patterns which suggest the need for action. The judgement of a threat within any particular body of intelligence material is the primary responsibility of an intelligence analyst, and the importance of the analyst's knowledge, creativity and experience can hardly be overestimated. It is the analyst's work that allows the intelligence material to be filtered and processed in a way which turns it successfully into a quality intelligence product. Only the final intelligence product is actionable intelligence. It is a part of educating the police in transitional institutional settings that the gathering of criminal intelligence material is only the first phase of criminal intelligence and that it is insufficient on its own for any type of operation.

Transitional countries in southeastern Europe use the so-called special investigative methods (criminal intelligence techniques) for the detection of specific types of crimes. In Serbia, for example, the law specifies the special investigative methods of secret surveillance of communications ('wiretapping'), physical surveillance and recording, simulated transactions, computer intelligence, controlled delivery of goods and the use of informants or 'secret interrogators' (police officers disguised as criminals who extract confessions or information on specific crimes or criminal careers) (*Official Gazette of Serbia*, 2014).

Wiretapping, or the surveillance of electronic and phone communications, has been in use for quite some years in most countries of the region, and this has led to the development of a high level of security culture within the criminal circles. Individuals with criminal convictions in the past, especially the recidivists, are familiar with the ways in which their communications are intercepted, given that trials are public, transcripts of intercepted communications are used in such trials, and that even the media often publish such transcripts when they are 'leaked' to journalists. Hence, the use of wiretapping is largely an outdated method of criminal intelligence. Even when the conversations between underage perpetrators are wiretapped, they rarely provide information which might incriminate them, because they understand that their conversations are monitored. More serious criminals have long abandoned communication by telephone and tend to use various applications which they consider more difficult to tap: Viber, WhatsApp or Skype. In the past, criminals had resorted to using only public phones for sensitive conversations. They are acutely aware of the threat that wiretapping poses to them and they act in ways to reduce the value of this method for detection.

While tapping telephones may be of limited value directly, when the information received in this way is adequately interpreted and combined with standard policing methods, its value is increased. Persons whose conversations are tapped reveal their personalities, abilities, inclinations, weaknesses and habits through their communications. Such conclusions are valuable for planning the approach to such persons or for making predictions of their behaviour. In addition, although most telephone conversations will not contain directly actionable information, they may reveal the person's contacts, movements and habits, all of which may be useful for standard police work. Finally, this type of information is useful for criminal profiling, namely for the exploration of the personalities of the perpetrators or potential perpetrators of organised crime and the development of their psychological profiles.

In the process of criminal profiling, the profiler typically goes through several phases. The first phase is the detection of phonetic characteristics of the subject, namely the analysis of the way the person speaks, their voice, their use of colourful words, accent, and rough age based on speech assessment. If there is some type of speech pathology or consistent pattern of grammatical mistakes that the person makes, these can be strong phonetic 'markers' for the future recognition of the person based on their speech.

The next task for the profiler is to decide about the sociological profile of the person: their relationship to their primary family, especially to individual family members to whom they are particularly attached, to their friends, extended family and acquaintances. The profiler then looks at whether the person is skilled at establishing new social contacts, whether they are xenophobic, whether they are extroverted or introverted, promiscuous, what kind of sexual orientation they have, and what kind of a social circle they generally spend their time in. This speaks about the person's emotional, social and general intelligence level, whether they are self-confident or feel inferior to others, whether they see themselves as a professional in their work, whether they are a perfectionist, what their temperament is and so on.

Third, the profiler may be able to determine, based on the information received from the tapping, the financial status of the subject, whether they have some previously invisible source of income, their hobbies, interests, whether they suffer from physical or mental illnesses, addictions, if they are married or in a relationship, and learn about other persons for whom the subject shows strong affection, either positive or negative. The phone tapping information can also reveal the person's daily routine.

The value of criminal profiling is manifold. First, it can assist operational action by helping plan the placement of a police agent in the criminal environment. Such placement is a very complex task that requires a detailed and precise prior analysis of the persons with whom the agent will be in contact. Second, profiling can assist the placement of information and disinformation by police. For example, in order to gain insight into the perpetrators and manner of perpetration of various offences, the police often place true, half-true and entirely false information to various members of the criminal environment with a view of provoking specific types of reactions, so that the target persons may do or say things that they would otherwise not, and which reveal operationally relevant information. All highly developed police structures possess special organisational structures that are dedicated to this type of propaganda. Third, criminal profiling gathers information about the psychological makeup of the person that can be used in interrogation. Finally, profiling does not only serve the detection of crime, but increasingly the mapping of trends and the acquisition of information and knowledge useful for prediction and long-term planning, thus also for long-term crime prevention. In the confusing environment of a transitional society, understanding trends is even more important for prevention because it allows an efficient allocation of the limited resources and timely action against the emergence of new structures and transformations of organised crime. Criminal intelligence, and especially profiling, also contribute to the achievement of institutional transparency, including the transparency of the police force itself, and that in itself is a way of fighting systemic corruption.

Profiling requires a high level of skill and creativity, talent and intuition in the profiler. While police work contains many tasks which can be performed by almost anyone, in any police force there are only a few highly specialised profiling experts whose work is highly valued. The transitional states in southeastern Europe are on their way of developing this type of structures in their police forces. Profiling represents the most advanced and most sophisticated tool of criminal intelligence. When the use of advanced technologies for intelligence gathering is combined with quality analytics and profiling, the value of the intelligence product is maximised. Conversely, even with the use of the most advanced technical equipment, it is sometimes impossible to resolve particularly complex crimes without an expert profile. Thus profiling, although it benefits from technology, is a skill in itself which is independent of technology.

CONSEQUENCES OF CRIMINAL INTELLIGENCE
FOR OVERALL POLICING IN TRANSITIONS

Criminal intelligence is the most important part of overall policing today; this is the case to such an extent that, overall, policing is considered to be 'intelligence-led policing.' Without such intelligence, addressing the main criminal threats today, namely organised crime and systemic corruption, would not be even possible. However, the increasing use of criminal intelligence leads to certain general consequences for the understanding of policing in general, and these consequences are even more pronounced in transitional countries, which are more unstable and more prone to criminalisation than those with better entrenched institutions and norms of legitimacy.

The first consequence is that criminal intelligence does not necessarily serve only the detection and repression of crime. It is equally useful for prevention, without necessarily being used as evidence in the court. This leads to a general understanding of the mission of policing: since the introduction of intelligence, policing is no longer seen as limited to resolving crimes; it is perceived as a broader social function of identifying and neutralising threats before they develop, much like standard (military) intelligence does.

Second, criminal intelligence does not rest on the assumption that some kind of general or special prevention will be attained in the traditional sense; the kind of prevention it seeks is a generalised social prevention of most severe consequences of serious crime, not the prevention of continuation of individual criminal careers. Such a change of perspective is important because the effects of organised crime on society go far beyond the immediate effects of individual criminal careers of organised criminals.

Third, the priority of criminal intelligence within overall policing has led to a change of the traditional reactive model of police activation. The traditional model of activation, where the commission of a crime 'triggers' police action in detecting the crime, is outdated today. The very essence of criminal intelligence is in the proactive anticipation of trends and long-term planning with a view of achieving transparency and maximising effectiveness in removing the most significant threats, or in repressing crime quickly after it is committed. Given these structural characteristics of criminal intelligence with regard to policing not just the society at large, but specifically the transitional institutional development of postconflict societies, the use of intelligence methodology in the transitional countries is extended and the level of its development is relatively high. In fact, it is higher than the level of development of most other institutions and tends to be above the level of the overall economic and political affairs in such countries, because it is the very foundation of the transitional countries' security policy.

REFERENCES

Blic Daily. (2014). 'Šta je sve zaplenjeno Darku Šariću: Stanovi, kuće, firme, hoteli' ('Property seized from narcotics boss Darko Šarić: apartments, houses, hotels'). http://www.blic.rs/vesti/tema-dana/sta-je-sve-zaplenjeno-darku-saricu-stanovi-kuce-firme-hoteli/yz7nkev, 25 November.

Blic Daily. (2017). 'Trgovci drogom godišnje zarade dva budžeta EU' ('Drug traffickers make two EU budgets annually'). www.blic.rs/vesti/svet/trgovci-drogom-godišnje-zarade-dva-budžeta-eu/rrvvzgd.

Golubović, Slobodan R. (2005). *Droga — istine i zablude* (*Drugs: the truth, and the misconceptions*). Belgrade: Zograf.

Hammil, John, et al. (2014). *Practice Series: RICO. A Guide to Civil RICO Litigation in Federal Court.* Chicago: Jenner and Block LLP.

Merton, Robert. (1938). 'Social Structure and Anomie.' *American Sociological Review* 3(5): 672–82.

Official Gazette of Serbia. (2014): *Law on Criminal Procedure*, no. 72/2011, 101/2011, 121/2012, 32/2013, 45/2013 i 55/2014.

Politika Daily. (2017). 'Heroin iz Srbije ide za Rusiju' ('Heroin from Serbia destined for Russia'). www.politika.rs/sr/clanak/35402/heroin-iz-Srbije-ide-za-Rusiju.

Chapter 4

Economic Justice and Economic Efficiency in Postconflict Societies in Transition

Mrdjan Mladjan

TRANSITION AS A CONTEXT FOR ECONOMIC JUSTICE

Transition could refer to any period of change in the state of a society, its political or economic order. Recently, it has been associated with the process of change from a centrally planned economy to a market economy, as well as with changes in the political system from the rule of a single party or individual to a representative democracy (Kaličanin, 2010). Initiated in the last decade of the twentieth century, the process interacted with the concurrent wave of globalisation and led to changes in the distribution of wealth, income and political power, both across and within countries. Although apologetics of the changes emphasised the achievement of economic and political freedoms and economic efficiency as their goals, the justness of many phenomena that characterised them was often questioned (e.g., Kluegel, Mason and Wegener, 1995; Fatić, 2004), while many changes actually led to economic decline.

The question of economic justice in transition was additionally emphasised by the frequently sharp contrast between the expectations that had preceded the changes and reality. Not all countries and individuals realised their hopes of economic prosperity. Recessions associated to structural changes were so long, with an average duration of 3.6 years, and so deep, with an average decline in GDP of 33.6 percent (Fischer, Sahay and Vegh, 1996) that they were more severe than those in industrial economies during the Great Depression (in which the worst performer, the United States, experienced a GDP decline of 30 percent; Wicker, 1996: 4). The changes were also associated with a rise in corruption (Rakita and Marković, 2013), a partial collapse of money economy through reverting to barter and money-alternatives (Woodruff, 2000) and increasing inequality (Milanović, 1998), causing severe hardship to many in societies previously accustomed to high

123

levels of income equality.[1] The question of equity featured even more prominently in those multiethnic and multireligious societies in transition that had experienced armed conflict, frequently not for the first time in the twentieth century. Wars have led to extreme transfers of wealth, disruptions of the production process, and life itself, creating new economic and other injustices.

The direction of economic changes was determined by a great faith in the power of market forces to lead to dynamic economic growth. It was believed that as soon as the 'chains' of central planning were broken, and the government was banished from the economy, economic prosperity would result. To faster unleash the forces of market economy, simultaneously making it less likely that the process of transition could later be politically reversed, changes were frequently sudden and deep rather than gradual (Popov, 2007). What added to the reformers' zeal was the concurrent wave of globalisation: one of its distinct marks was the implementation by many countries around the world of the set of policies contained in the so-called Washington Consensus (Williamson, 1990). These recommendations went beyond what could arguably already be a reversion of the economic legacy of the communist revolutions that had shaken the east of Europe in the twentieth century. For instance, they not only demanded the respect of private property rights, upon which the communist governments had infringed in the previous decades, but also the privatisation of those government-owned enterprises that may have never been private, and that were still public even in many Western European economies.

The simultaneous privatisation of a multitude of enterprises accounting for much of domestic product, coupled with trade liberalisation that exposed to competition from abroad previously protected industries, unsurprisingly led to large disruptions of economic activity. The resulting changes made few rich, while many were impoverished, made unemployed or even found themselves unemployable (due to inadequate skills) in the new structure of the economy (Kupets, 2015). Death rates soared (as evidenced in figure 4.1), not in the least for psychological reasons, and especially among the adult men who lost their jobs and were unable to find another one, but were culturally still expected to provide for their families.[2] Because the changes in economic and human condition related to transition were already well documented in the preceding literature,[3] they are not the focus of this chapter. Instead, I argue that a concern for economic efficiency need not exclude that for economic justice. Moreover, historical evidence suggests the contrary: that the pursuit of economic justice can lead to more efficient economic systems and social economic equilibria. I believe that my argument need not remain a mere historical narrative but can also be used to advise on modifications to already completed transitional processes and on a design of the remaining ones.

The rest of the chapter is structured as follows. I continue by discussing the role of the Marshall Plan in supporting the 'losers of transition' during the reform of West European economies following the Second World War, and in contributing to the formation of a cooperative social contract that led to outstanding economic performance in the following decades. The section after that compares the Eastern postcommunist transition to the Western European post–World War II transition, while the one that follows provides an illustrative overview of market failures characteristic of postcommunist economies. The final section analyses the features of postconflict societies that make the achievement of both economic justice and economic efficiency in transition even more difficult.

THE SOCIAL DIMENSIONS OF SUCCESS OF THE POST–WORLD WAR II MARSHALL PLAN

By the type and importance of change, as well as the size and population of the affected region, Eastern Europe after the fall of the Berlin Wall has a natural counterpart in Western Europe after World War II. In both periods, large parts of the European population experienced economic transition from command to a market economy. The contrast between the two historical episodes in the importance given to caring for the most vulnerable social groups, 'the losers of transition,' is telling about both economic justice and economic efficiency during the postcommunist transition. In contrast to Western Europe after World War II, where the care for the vulnerable was the key to unlocking the process of economic change and assuring its success in the decades to come, it played a much smaller role in postcommunist Eastern Europe. While the weaker care for the vulnerable in the postcommunist transition could in part reflect a strong faith that limiting government's involvement in the economy would quickly lead to economic prosperity, it also ought to reflect the weakness of a political opposition to postcommunist transition and a contemporary lack of intrinsic concern for economic justice.

West European governments at the end of World War II, similarly to Eastern European governments in the late 1980s, were heavily involved in their economies. Regulation of prices, direct allocation of goods and government ownership of companies, especially in heavy industries, were widespread. This resulted from a discrediting of the market economy by the events in the preceding two decades, starting with the Great Depression, and the need for government intervention in the economy during the war itself. That future would bring a change towards more market, within a mixed economy that contained both command and market elements, was not at all clear: communist parties were strong also in the West of the continent, and there was fascination with Soviet Union's command economy, not in the least because of its military successes.

Most of the economics profession would, however, agree that, were it not for reforms for a 'purer' market economy, Western European economies would have been much less successful in the decades after World War II. De Long and Eichengreen (1991) argue exactly that when they compare post–World War II Western Europe to contemporary Argentina. In Argentina 'the government allocated goods, especially imports, among alternative uses; the controlled market redistributed income . . . in Western Europe market forces allocated resources . . . the government redistributed income, and the outcome was much more favourable' (p. 42). Starting as rich as a large Western European country at the onset of the Great Depression, Argentina had less than two-thirds of the GDP per capita of West Germany or France in 1960.

What then, in spite of the strength of contemporary support for government intervention, enabled economic reform and the impressive development of West European economies in the decades after World War II?[4] Were reforms and economic growth that followed indeed related, as the comparison with Argentina suggests? For Western Europe's economic wonder, both the popular opinion and more recent research ascribe an important role to the European Recovery Program of the United States, administered in the period 1948–1952 and better known as the Marshall Plan.[5] However, while the Marshall Plan is commonly believed to have led to strong recovery by providing funds for investment in rebuilding a destroyed Europe,[6] the prevalent view by more critical economists is that its role was primarily in helping to create a consensus for economic reform that then led to economic prosperity.

The timing of the events after 1945 and the information on the content of the aid package, as persuasively argued by De Long and Eichengreen (1991) and Eichengreen and Uzan (1992), simply do not support the folk wisdom on the Marshall Plan. First, although the magnitude of the Marshall Plan was significant, it was much humbler than believed. It accounted to $13.3 billion dollars (Marshall Foundation, 2018), less than 3 percent of the recipients' combined GDP over the period of the programme. Second, by the time Marshall Plan came into force, the reconstruction of the damaged infrastructure was mostly over. Third, even investment in production, rather than infrastructure, was not a major component of the Marshall Plan; not more than one-sixth of the total funds were spent on machinery and vehicles (that could be used in production). One could, however, argue that the Marshall Plan relaxed the budget constraints of the recipient countries. A part of the money that would otherwise be spent on consumer goods and production inputs could be redirected towards private investment. However, Eichengreen and Uzan (1992) estimate that this channel could not have added more than 2 percent to the recipients' national products in 1951. In a similar vein, De

Long and Eichengreen (1991) estimate that the plan's contribution to making the scarce production inputs available, by direct provision or by rebuilding the intra-European trade, was also limited. While these contributions are not negligible, they are simply insufficient to explain the large economic growth in the years of the plan and later.

Did the Marshall Plan help set the post–World War II West European economies on a dynamic growth path? According to De Long and Eichengreen (1991) and Eichengreen and Uzan (1992), it did so by resolving several aspects of uncertainty that surrounded both the immediate and longer-term future. Although the Marshall Plan was not much larger in size than the United Nations Relief and Rehabilitation Administration (UNRRA) aid and similar programmes that had preceded it in the period until 1948, it was a three-year commitment, while the UNRRA aid could be abolished at any quarter. Committed to providing aid for several years to societies that were deeply divided about the preferred role of government in the economy, the Marshall Plan removed much uncertainty about the direction of future economic changes in the recipient societies. The recipients namely had to match each dollar of aid with one dollar of their own funds, and had to accept that all these funds are spent in agreement with the US government. The US government used their power over all these funds to direct the European economies away from command elements: trade barriers, price controls and allocation mechanisms (for food, coal and industrial inputs such as fuel) were gradually abolished or reduced. The changes allowed the comparative advantages of each economy to be reaffirmed through mutual trade. They also ended the shortages by giving an incentive to producers to bring their goods to the market, allowing them to charge a market price (higher than the previous, regulated one) for their goods. Resolving the uncertainty about the future economic policy increased the overall participation in the economy. This means that, instead of hoarding wealth, investors and creditors were willing to invest and lend because the uncertainty about inflation and tax rates was reduced. In a similar vein, instead of being unwilling to learn and invest effort at work, workers were willing to acquire new skills and work hard because the job prospects and the expected compensation became more certain (Eichengreen and Uzan, 1992).

For the proponents of a market economy to achieve such a political victory, a political compromise was needed. The Marshall Plan provided the means to pay for the initial compromise; it increased the overall size of the pie to be divided by the social groups competing for scarce resources. Importantly, the budgets expanded by the Marshall Plan facilitated the provision of help for the poorest, who were affected the most by liberalisation of markets for food and coal. Immediate care for the most vulnerable, and positive effects of the

reforms on economic growth in the years of the plan,[7] weakened the critique
of the economic left and enabled the transition.

Despite these challenges, a mere transition to a market economy is not
enough to explain the stellar economic performance of Western Europe
following World War II. De Long and Eichengreen (1991) argue that the
Marshall Plan helped establish a new cooperative social contract, enabling
crucial social compromises that made the high Western European growth
rates politically and socially sustainable over two and a half decades. The
new social agreement encouraged the workers to supply more labour when
demanded, instead of responding by asking for higher wages. Similarly, it
encouraged the management to reinvest the profits in pursuit of a further
output and productivity growth, instead of spending them on personal luxury
goods, accepting that some of the resulting profits would go to the workers.
To the extent that the care for the less well-off in the initial phases of transition helped establish a mutually accommodating approach of the different
social groups to the economy, it helped raise economic efficiency: sacrificing
immediate partisan gains enabled faster growth and larger medium and long-
term gains for one's own group, as well as for everyone else.

From these suggestions it appears that the post–World War II transition
was tied to a serious concern by policy elites about securing economic
justice within the transitional societies. The future prosperity was not built
by risking the lives of less fortunate countrymates. An effort was put into
avoiding a situation where most of those who had survived the terrors of
war might paradoxically die of cold and hunger in peacetime. Those for
whose better future the war itself had been fought did get a chance to have
one, and those cared for just after the war responded by carrying their part
of the burden of economic compromise for a better future of all. In this way,
the concern for economic justice itself also resulted in an economic system
and a social agreement that improved economic efficiency in the decades to
come. It is however unclear how much the care for the 'losers of transition'
resulted from a genuine concern for economic justice, and to what extent it
was an emotionally cold political compromise. Namely, even if there was no
concern for economic justice, workers, managers and the state could realise
that forging an agreement would help avoid an internal conflict such as that
which characterised the European societies between the world wars, as well
as escape economic decline and help create growth. Such a compromise
would also save the reforms that could cause some harm in the short run, but
are beneficial in the long run, from being politically challenged and reversed.

While it may be hard to differentiate a genuine concern for economic
justice from a dry compromise in the post–World War II transition, we can at
least try to reason about how a difference could be recognised. The fact that
a transition was not made possible before the Marshall Plan may suggest that

solidarity was not strong enough to enable the transition in the absence of external aid. It could, however, also simply mean that there was no internal agreement on the direction of economic changes before the US involvement. The fact that, once the changes started, the participants in the transition process were able to realise that a cooperative social contract could make everyone better off, suggests that at least some positive predisposition by the various social groups towards one another — a precondition for solidarity — was present. Another piece of evidence to infer about the genuineness of the post–World War II concern for economic justice could be the durability of the cooperative equilibrium that was reached at the time. If it resulted from interest, then it would last only until each of the groups is strong enough vis-à-vis the others. A change in the balance of power would break the agreement and some groups would pursue their own interest against the well-being of the others. Interestingly, once the political competition of Western social market economies and Soviet Union disappeared, following the latter's demise, these economies became less 'social' and more 'market,' with a pronounced rise in inequality within high-income countries (Milanović, 2016). While this may suggest that the initial cooperation was motivated purely by interest, it could also mean that solidarity was gradually lost. If solidarity were indeed lost, one could try to comprehend it by keeping in mind that the living standards rose well above subsistence as Western European GDP increased around four times during the 1945–1990 period (Maddison, 2003), and that one is more prone to feel compassion for someone in severe need.

I do not necessarily claim that a weakening of inter-group cooperation in Western European societies had resulted in rising inequality, a feebler economic growth and a major economic crisis, although the events are suggestive of such a conclusion. I would rather limit myself here to expressing a belief that a cooperative economic equilibrium, one that also allows the less well-off to reach their full professional and overall human potential, ought to be able to lead to greater well-being for everyone.

MARKET FAILURES OF THE EASTERN EUROPEAN POSTCOMMUNIST TRANSITION IN THE MIRROR OF THE POST–WORLD WAR II TRANSITION

Given that its similarity with post–World War II Western Europe was obvious even at the beginning of the postcommunist transition, historical lessons could have been drawn to make the recent transition successful. Judging from the comparison between Western Europe and Argentina following World War II, one such lesson would have suggested pursuing a transition towards a market economy, just as it was done. Another lesson would have supported making any aid or loans to Eastern Europe conditional on reforms towards a market economy, a principle which was in fact widely practised.[8] However, perhaps the most important recommendation would have been to provide substantial aid, through a mechanism similar to the Marshall Plan, in order to protect the losers of the initial recession phase of the transition. Such aid would have been an expression of solidarity and concern for economic justice in at least two ways. First, it would have made sure that no member of the nation is left behind in a moment when national identity is revived and rebuilt, following the decades of communism, during which time national identity had frequently been suppressed. Second, it would have been the least that transitional political elites could have done for the workers who were likely to lose their jobs in transition, but whose support was crucial in initiating the transition and bringing the same transitional elites to power (e.g., a decisive driver for the postcommunist transition in Poland was an independent labour union called 'Solidarity'). A major plan to support the vulnerable would have both bought time for the effects of reform to bear fruit, ensuring that reforms are not later reversed by their discontents, and helped forge a social contract similar to that which had enabled dynamic growth in post–World War II Western Europe.

In spite of the well-acknowledged importance of the Marshall Plan, there was no single major programme dedicated to aid provision during the postcommunist transition, either externally or internally financed, that could parallel it. Admittedly, there were many smaller initiatives that provided aid to support the postcommunist transition process. The aid arrived from multi-lateral institutions (such as the EU, World Bank, International Monetary Fund, European Investment Bank and the European Bank for Reconstruction and Development), but also from nation-states and private donors. Slim (2001) estimates that the aid received by Central and East European countries (CEECs) in 1990–1995 amounted to 86.24 billion euros — around 4 percent of GDP of these countries — a greater percentage compared to that of the Marshall Plan. However, it mostly consisted of loans rather than grants: while about 90 percent of the Marshall Plan aid were grants, they amounted to only about a third of the overall international aid to CEECs.

It is of course possible that care for the vulnerable was taken through the usual social care programmes of the states, potentially helped by this external aid. While this could in principle be so, the data on death rates and birth rates during transition, presented in figure 4.1, suggest that any such care was far from sufficient. Figure 4.1 shows the average (population-weighted) birth rate and death rate in the European countries in transition. While the birth rate started to decline sharply even before the end of communism, poten-tially suggesting some deep dissatisfaction by the population, the death rates exploded with the start of the transition and remained high. The two crossed as early as 1992, with more people dying than being born. How is it possible that the postcommunist transitional elites, brought up on ideas of social justice and presumably inspired by ideals of national revival, had allowed such suffering of so many members of their nations? Was a broader social contract of the type enabled by the Marshall Plan missing in Eastern Europe during the recent transition? If so, what could explain this? To answer these questions, one should attempt to better understand the ideas and the atmosphere that dominated Eastern European elites, and their relations to the rest of the society, at the time.

While the atmosphere varied from country to country, it is fair to say that the political and intellectual elites were divided, and that their substantial parts were not in favour of a change towards a market economy, especially in the former Soviet Union. But the historical dynamics of 1990 were very different from those of 1945. Market economy was discredited during the pre-1945 period, and the Marshall Plan was needed to change the historical dynamics

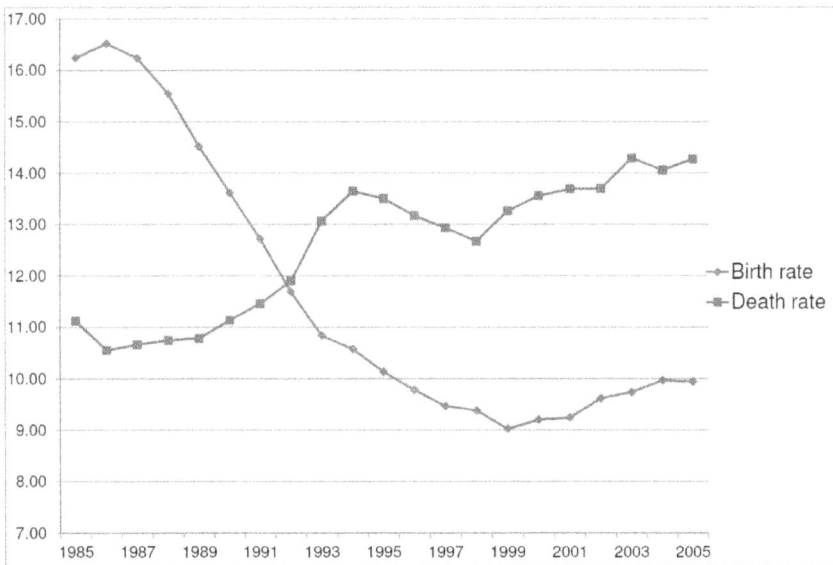

Figure 4.1: Birth Rate and Death Rate during the Postcommunist Transition
Note: The graph shows average crude birth rate and death rate (equal to number of live births and of deaths per 1,000 people) as the average of the Russian Federation, Ukraine, Belarus, Moldova, Poland, Czech Republic, Slovakia, Hungary, Romania, former Yugoslav republics, Bulgaria and Albania. The average is weighted by the 1990 population.
Source: World Development Indicators (World Bank, 2018), Maddison (2003) and author's calculations.

of the moment. The opposite is true of the early 1990s, when the command economies were discredited, having failed to satisfy the expectations of their citizens. Those who did not want changes, especially those members of the elites with vested interests in the current system, were on the defensive. Those who wanted changes had more élan and a strong argument in the form of the economic successes of the post–World War II West European market economies. The contemporary international environment further raised the popularity of transition: the role of government in the economy had recently been reduced in the Western economies which served as role models (such as through privatisations carried out in the United Kingdom in the 1980s during Margaret Thatcher's premiership and the contemporaneous policies in the United States during Ronald Reagan's presidency). In such an atmosphere, no Marshall Plan equivalent was needed for a transition towards a market economy; there was no need for persuasion or containment of a defeated ideological enemy. When support from abroad did arrive, it typically added both speed and depth to the transition process, which, however, on average, made the initial recession deeper (Popov, 2007).

The feeling of riding the victorious wave of history must have added to the reformers zeal. Carrying a passionate belief that market economy would solve all economic problems, dampening the impact of transition on their more vulnerable countrymates was not their first priority. Instead of a concern for economic justice, the object of fascination of Eastern European reformers was the achievement of economic efficiency. In part, this was the case because the reforms were expected to quickly compensate for any temporary losses. However, not all motives and attitudes by the transitional elites could be characterised as benevolent or naïve. The idea of being special, unique, chosen by history to do something great,[9] may have inhibited reformers from checking their beliefs against reality more frequently. The widespread human hardship, presented as a necessary short-run sacrifice, may have attracted less attention by the reformers because the suffering was seen as in part 'deserved,' limited to the 'insufficiently educated,' those not 'enlightened' or those not 'appropriately skilful,' or 'adaptable.' Many members of the elites actually believed that the suffering of those who were deemed not suitable for a new age of market economy was somehow excusable. A part of the elite may have been driven by a desire to be seen by foreign elites as modern and culturally advanced, a fashionable manner of the time being to look down on one's own nation. In addition, for some members of the national elites, concern for economic justice would have taken time away from maximising their own illicit gains through the privatisation process.

Ironically, the great zeal of Eastern European reformers compared to their Western European predecessors was in contrast to their limited knowledge of the workings of a successful market economy and the preconditions required to establish one. This resulted from a lack of experience: decades of heavy governments' involvement in the economy and only very limited private property in the communist societies. While privatisation was seen as the magical solution to most economic problems, it was overlooked that even in a market economy there are instances when government intervention may be both justifiable and desirable, so as to prevent market failures and the associated loss of economic efficiency. The pursuit of economic efficiency without concern for economic justice thus prevented the achievement of economic efficiency itself. It did not only deprive many Eastern European societies of a type of cooperative social arrangement which made possible the high output growth rates in Western Europe for several decades after World War II. In addition, it resulted in many instances of market failure that further degraded economic efficiency and social well-being.

MARKET FAILURES CHARACTERISTIC OF POSTCOMMUNIST TRANSITIONAL ECONOMIES

What the Eastern European reformers may have overlooked is that a market economy leads to efficient outcomes only when markets are competitive. When the requirements for competition do not hold, this gives rise to market failures[10] associated with economic inefficiency. Any inefficiency is necessarily suboptimal for an economy because it means that, by reallocating final goods or inputs to production, it would be possible to increase the utility (a measure of well-being) of at least someone without decreasing the utility of anyone else. Given that solutions to market failures do exist, typically involving some form of government intervention, the challenge is to identify the failures.

Several market failures, caused by fast privatisation and a deregulation that was intended to increase economic efficiency, have endangered both efficiency and justice in the postcommunist transitions (Mladjan and Marković, 2016). One such failure was that of corporate markets. A rushed privatisation overlooked that time was needed for competitive corporate markets to form. A simultaneous offering of many valuable companies for privatisation was problematic in countries of great income equality, where few people could legally have the necessary funds to acquire such companies. Both economic efficiency and justice suffered whenever incompetent individuals with suspicious funds got hold of valuable firms at low prices. They often resold them, rather than using them productively. During this process, markets were lost and technology made more obsolete, leading to a reduced capacity of the economy. Having increased their power through privatisation, such individuals spread corrupt practises into other spheres of the society, making life even harder for the rest of their countrymates. This happened in spite of the fact that the same companies were frequently built during communism through the tax contributions by those same countrymates and their parents.

Another group of frequent market failures were those of market power (in the form of monopolies or cartels). Complete or near complete privatisation of previously government-owned sectors with few companies allowed the producers to agree on higher prices than would have been the case in a competitive market. While this could have in principle been avoided through regulation, transition countries did not have sufficient experience to do so, or may have had too easily corruptible institutions in order to prevent the formation of monopolies and cartels. The well-being of consumers was thus reduced, because they were able to consume fewer goods at higher prices.

Several other market failures related to culture: for instance, the positive externality of the birth of children and the negative externality of 'reality programmes' (Mladjan and Marković, 2016). In countries that experience demographic decline, parents benefit the whole society by bringing up the labour force that would pay for the pensions of the retired generation, without the political tension that immigrants of a different culture may bring. For this, they should be compensated in some way, which would likely lead them to having more children (as evidenced in Russia after the introduction of maternity capital in 2007, a form of material support for families with two or more children; Slonimczyk and Yurkoc, 2014). On the other hand, reality media programmes that have become popular in many transition countries present violence, promiscuity, criminality and other forms of deviant behaviour in a positive and socially desirable way. They should thus be hugely taxed, which would make them less prevalent in media programming. The other market failures related to cultural change in transition economies could include the uncritical adoption of problematic aspects of foreign business culture (such as aggressive marketing strategies that breach the norms of decent behaviour) and language (such as bad translations from English that preserve a foreign syntax and massively resort to Anglicisms; Mladjan and Fatić, 2018). By spreading outside of the corporate world, these changes endanger not merely the business culture, but culture in general.

While the previous list of market failures is far from exhaustive, it indicates a pattern. A hurry to achieve economic efficiency through privatisation, moving to an economic system with which the societies still had to gain experience, led the Eastern European transitional economies to many market failures that endangered not merely their economic justice, but also their economic efficiency. Whenever they permanently reduced the productive capacity of the economy, or misallocated the factors of production, market failures led to losses which made it impossible to achieve that level of aggregate social welfare which could have been achieved in the absence of market failures.

ECONOMIC EFFICIENCY AND ECONOMIC JUSTICE IN EASTERN EUROPEAN POSTCONFLICT SOCIETIES

I also argue here that any transitional society is a postconflict society. This is because any transition should lead to a change in the extent to which different social groups are privileged. Any change should be associated with a resistance offered by the previously privileged groups, and the push for transition by those whose standing would improve in the new system. For the system to change, the upcoming groups must become powerful enough to overcome both the power of the incumbent groups by themselves, and the additional power that the entrenched system of privilege gives to the incumbents. Once the changes to the system, the transition itself, start to occur, it appears that the decisive phase of the conflict has already been ended with a defeat of the incumbents. Having been overpowered even while they had the system on their side, the incumbents are weakened. This does not exclude the possibility of further struggles before the new distribution of power stabilises. Of course, such conflicts need not be violent, and need not be associated with war.

Despite this, I argue that all East European postcommunist transitions were also postwar transitions. This is so at least because communist parties came to power after civil wars and conflicts contemporaneous with World War I in Imperial Russia and World War II in the rest of Eastern Europe. The wars in former Yugoslavia and in different parts of the Soviet Union in the 1990s only added another layer of armed conflict to societies that had already experienced at least one violent political transition in the twentieth century. The armed conflicts in the two periods were, however, different, as were the ideas for which they were fought. While those during the transition to communism were fought for the communist ideology, although frequently concurring with interethnic or interreligious conflicts, those during the postcommunist transition were interethnic and interreligious. It is true that the confronted ethnic and religious groups during the 1990s may have differed in their level of preference for market economy, not in the least because the upcoming economic transition was bound to a political one that could potentially change their relative power in society. However, an individual's allegiance was primarily determined by one's ethnic or religious group. The key question here is whether transitions from a system that was originally installed by war, and transitions that occur simultaneously with war, yield different outcomes with regard to economic justice and economic efficiency from those of peaceful transitions.

I argue that outcomes related to both efficiency and justice should be different in postwar societies, but whether they would be associated to better or worse outcomes should depend on the context. Two sets of factors appear decisive, one related to wars during the transition to communism, the other related to wars concurrent with the postcommunist transition. In regard to the effect of wars that happened during the transition to communism, the external involvement and the intensity of the conflict are most likely to affect both efficiency and equity. In particular, where communism was imposed by an external force (such as the Red Army in Poland, unlike a strong communist partisan movement in large parts of Yugoslavia) and where there were fewer killings of the ideological opponents to communism, there was subsequently more willingness and skill for a successful transition to an economically more efficient system: a market economy with few market failures. In such cases there was also more willingness by the state to restore to its former owners the property confiscated by the communists, and more living descendants of the original owners to receive the property. When communism is perceived by large parts of a nation as imposed from abroad, then the push to replace it is driven by an additional reservoir of energies to attain a national liberation. On the other hand, those countries where killings, expulsions and emigration of opponents to communism were common, with a civil war unfolding alongside the communist 'revolution,' were left deprived of many politically and economically productive people. The more intense was the conflict, the less human capital and knowledge how to successfully implement a transition to a market economy remained in the country. To illustrate the importance of the characteristics of the wars during the transition to communism, let us consider the examples of Russia, Poland and Serbia.

The Russian postcommunist transition was characterised by a very deep transitional recession, associated with many market failures in the form of corruption and cartelisation. The system change was in many aspects incomplete, and the economy's eventual recovery could in part be attributed to income from natural resources. One feasible explanation for Russia's incomplete system change was that she did not have enough people with a strong desire and skill to conduct a successful transition. During the Russian Revolution, the annihilation of the anticommunist forces was very thorough and complete. The communist revolution took place concurrently with World War I, thus a generation earlier than the transitions to communism in other parts of Eastern Europe, leaving in Russian families less memory of anything other than communism. Thus there was both a lack of skilled people and of knowledge of capitalism in Russia, and this accounted for difficulties in pursuing the postcommunist transition.

The situation in Poland was very different. Poland had a massive anticommunist resistance movement during World War II, and communism was imposed on the country by the advancing Red Army. Communist rule in Poland lasted for a generation less than in Russia. There was more desire and skill in the Polish population to facilitate a transition to a market economy, making the change faster and more successful. The attainment of a market economy was, however, seen as a national goal for which even economic justice, at least in the short run, was worth sacrificing. This was evidenced by the fact that the workers from labour intensive industries, participating in crucial protests in the initial phases of the political transition, were those whose jobs were among the most endangered in the initial phases of the transition.

The Serbian case is complex and controversial. The Serbs had two very large anti-German occupation resistance movements during World War II, one monarchist and one communist. Their mutual fighting was intense, with many victims, and so were the killings of the anticommunists after World War II. But they were perhaps not as intense as in Russia, where communism also lasted for a generation longer. Serbian communists, although stronger than in Poland, needed the help of the Red Army to assume power. Nevertheless, the major postcommunist transitional changes in Serbia started a decade later than in most other East European countries. One reason was that Serbs associated communism with Russia, and they had a strong cultural affinity to Russia. Another important factor that delayed the Serbian transition involved the civil wars in the former Yugoslavia during the 1990s. The communist political elite adopted a nationalist rhetoric in the 1990s and thus prolonged its hold on power.

With regard to the wars concurrent with the postcommunist transition, I argue that the historical context in which they were fought made their effects on economic efficiency and economic justice predominantly negative. With the exception of Romania, where the communist regime was removed following a brief but violent civil unrest with hundreds of casualties, and the somewhat less bloody 1993 Russian constitutional crisis, all other conflicts during the postcommunist transition, with a comparable or larger number of deaths, contained a strong ethnic or religious component. They occurred in the ethnically and religiously mixed areas of former Yugoslavia (in all of its republics) and the Soviet Union (in parts of Moldavia, Russia, and recently Ukraine in Eastern Europe; Georgia, Armenia and Azerbaijan in the Caucasus; and Tajikistan and recently Kyrgyzstan in Central Asia). The warring groups had a history of conflict: from the period of World War II, the time communism was imposed, or even earlier. Common to all affected regions was that the communist-era governments had previously maintained mostly peaceful coexistence and some balance of power between those groups. But discussion about the past and current problems in intergroup relations, just like any other public discourse in these countries, was constrained to the communist ideological framework. For this reason, it was harder for the wounds to heal. The suppressed frustration, fears and group ambitions of at least a part of the population contributed to an escalation of these conflicts once the communist era ended.

The pursuit of national independence or unification, deep-rooted and emotionally laden by each group's perception of history, was a set of goals that strongly dominated the pursuit of an economic transition; it was more important than economic efficiency or justice.[11] This may not be surprising, since a struggle for national independence typically involves a loss of lives, while systemic transitions need not. In environments where populations are intrinsically motivated for achieving national independence, the elites have less reason to seek to create a cooperative social contract similar to that facilitated by the Marshall Plan. In such societies reforms could be delayed or conducted corruptly as long as this could be justified as 'national interest' related to war. The elites and power centres formed during the war, thus not arising from a primary concern for economic efficiency and justice, tend to remain influential long after the wars are over.

Without underestimating the successes of the postcommunist transitions in winning political and economic freedoms, which in some countries have been achieved to a greater extent than in others, many of their aspects have been damaging both to economic efficiency and to economic justice. If the political elites in the transitional states had adopted the psychology of action behind the Marshall Plan, which had been to help win support for the transition by cushioning the losers of its initial phases, rather than providing funds for massive investment, such a strategy might have contributed to the formation of a cooperative social contract. In turn, an effective collaborative social contract might have led to several decades of faster economic growth than was experienced by the postcommunist countries in transition, especially by those that experienced conflict.

Several important questions remain open here. Can the attainment of cooperative equilibria, like the one in Western Europe after World War II, ever be the result of concern for economic justice or just a cold self-interested strategy adopted by each of the relevant social groups? Can a collaborative equilibrium, achieved through a type of thinking behind the Marshall Plan, survive beyond mid-term? Based on the considerations presented in this chapter, it seems reasonable to suggest that both the achievement and sustainability of favourable equilibria primarily depend on the elites, the values that inspire them and the values with which they inspire the rest of the society.

NOTES

1. Milanović (1998: 41–42) analyses the change in inequality, as measured by the Gini coefficient based on income per capita, in a sample of eighteen transition economies. Inequality slightly decreased only in Slovakia (Gini coefficient moving down from twenty in 1987–1988 to nineteen in 1993–1995), while it increased in all other countries, in many very significantly (for instance, moving from twenty-four to forty-eight in Russia and from twenty-three to forty-seven in Ukraine).

2. Mortality rate for adult males in transition countries (defined as the probability of a fifteen-year-old male dying before reaching age sixty, if subject to age-specific mortality rates of the specified year between those ages) rose from 26 percent in 1986 to a maximum of 37 percent in 1994, a 42 percent increase. The mortality rate for adult females also rose, but less from 11 percent in 1986 to 14 percent in 1994, a 27 percent increase. Unfortunately, during the years that followed the mortality rates only marginally decreased. These numbers are the averages for the Russian Federation, Ukraine, Belarus, Moldova, Poland, Czech Republic, Slovakia, Hungary, Romania, former Yugoslav republics, Bulgaria, and Albania, weighted by their population in 1990 (which results in obtaining the average rates for the whole region as a single country). They are based on World Development Indicators dataset of the World Bank (2018) and my calculations.

3. Both economic (e.g., Blanchard, 1997) and human (e.g., Izyumov, 2009) aspects of transition are a very well-studied topic. Moreover, a number of specialized scientific journals are dedicated to it, for instance, *The Economics of Transition*, *International Journal of Emerging and Transition Economies*, *Transition Studies Review*, *Economic Policy in Transitional Economies*, while the European Bank for Reconstruction and Development, in collaboration with the World Bank, periodically conducts a *Life in Transition Survey* (EBRD, 2018).

4. The uniqueness of the West European growth rates in the quarter of century following World War II is obvious both when compared to the preceding and the following period. In 1938, twenty years after the end of World War I, the GDP per capita of Britain, France and Germany was around 30 percent higher than at the end of World War I. In 1965, twenty years after the end of World War II, their GDP was around 90 percent higher than at the end of World War II (De Long and Eichengreen, 1991: 22). Similarly, the average growth rate of the West European economies aggregate real GDP per capita — using data for Austria, Belgium, Denmark, Finland, France, West Germany, Italy, Netherlands, Norway, Sweden, Switzerland and the United Kingdom — was 3.8 percent in the 1950–1973 period, while it declined to 1.7 percent in the 1973–1993 period (Crafts, 1995: 429).

5. Named so after General George C. Marshall, US Secretary of State at the time that the plan came into force.

6. The recipients of the plan's aid, which took the form of a mixture of grants and loans, were the following European countries: Austria, Belgium, Denmark, France, Greece, Iceland, Ireland, Italy, Luxemburg, the Netherlands, Norway, Portugal, Sweden, Switzerland, Turkey, the United Kingdom and West Germany (Marshall Foundation, 2018). Notice that none of these were allies of the Soviet Union, which

rejected the plan for ideological reasons. The predictability of its rejection must have also made the offer cheaper to make.

7. Although the structural changes of an economy can be bound to transitional recessions, just as those that marked the postcommunist transitions, the GDP growth rates during the reforms of the Marshall Plan even slightly rose (from 6 percent in the 1946–1948 period to 7.5 percent in the 1948–1951 period for the sum of GDPs of Germany, France, and the United Kingdom, based on my calculations using data from Maddison [2003]).

8. For instance, in deciding whether to finance a project, the European Bank for Reconstruction and Development (EBRD) evaluated its potential transition impact vis-à-vis a list of its predefined goals: to increase private ownership, to increase competition, to transfer skills, to set a standard of corporate governance, and the like (EBRD, 2017).

9. In 2002, the author of this chapter attended a talk given at Harvard University by several ministers of the Serbian transitional government of the late Prime Minister Zoran Djindjić. The talk took place on the same day, but prior to the presentation by the prime minister himself at the JFK School of Government (*Harvard Gazette*, 2002). The ministers were energetic and excited, and one could feel that they believed they could do something good for their nation. The Minister of Privatisation and Economic Reconstruction, Aleksandar Vlahović, went a step further. He stated that his people were accusing him for the hardship caused by the economic changes, but that they would later erect him a monument for the good that his work would bring. This was a potent illustration of the almost messianic vision that many reformist leaders tend to harbour.

10. These market failures traditionally take the following forms: market power of buyers or sellers (e.g., markets with a monopolist supplier), externalities, public goods and incomplete information (Pindyck and Rubinfeld, 2001: 591–92).

11. In some cases, the push for the economic transition itself could in part be interpreted as one of nation-building goals, a way to reaffirm national identity.

REFERENCES

Blanchard, Olivier. (1997). *The Economics of Post-Communist Transition*. Oxford: Clarendon Press.

Crafts, Nicholas F. R. (1995). 'The Golden Age of Economic Growth in Western Europe, 1950–1973.' *Economic History Review* 48(3): 429–47.

De Long, Bradford, and Eichengreen, Barry. (1991). 'The Marshall Plan: History's Most Successful Structural Adjustment Program.' *NBER*, Working paper no. 3899.

EBRD. (2017). *Transition Impact*. Retrieved from http://www.ebrd.com/what-we-do/economic-research-and-data/transition-impact.html.

EBRD. (2018). *Life in Transition Survey (LITS)*. Retrieved from http://www.ebrd.com/cs/Satellite?c=Content&cid=1395236498263&d=Mobile&pagename=EBRD%2FContent%2FContentLayout.

Eichengreen, Barry, and Uzan, Marc. (1992). 'The Marshall Plan: Economic Effects and Implications for Eastern Europe and the Former USSR.' *Economic Policy* 7(14): 13–75.

Fatić, Aleksandar. (2004). 'Anti-Corruption and Anti-Organized Crime Policy in Serbia: Regional Implications.' *Southeast European and Black Sea Studies* 4(2): 315–24.

Fischer, Stanley, Sahay, Ratna, and Vegh, Carlos A. (1996). 'Stabilization and Growth in Transition Economies: The Early Experience.' *Journal of Economic Perspectives* 10(2): 45–66.

Harvard Gazette. (2002). *Serbian Prime Minister Speaks*. Retrieved from https://news.harvard.edu/gazette/story/2002/09/serbian-prime-minister-speaks/.

Izyumov, Alexei. (2009). 'Human Costs of Post-Communist Transition: Public Policies and Private Response.' *Review of Social Economy* 68(1): 93–125.

Kaličanin, Đorđe. (2010). *Ekonomski rečnik*. Beograd: CID Ekonomski fakultet.

Kluegel, James R., Mason, David S., and Wegener, Bernd. (1995). *Social Justice and Political Change: Public Opinion in Capitalist and Post-Communist States*. Berlin: de Gruyter.

Kupets, Olga. (2015). 'Skill Mismatch and Overeducation in Transition Economies.' *IZA World of Labour* 224. www.voi.iza.org

Maddison, Angus. (2003). *The World Economy: A Millennial Perspective*. Paris: OECD Development Center.

Marshall Foundation. (2018). *Marshall Plan Payments in Millions to European Economic Cooperation Countries*. Retrieved from https://marshallfoundation. org/library/documents/marshall-plan-payments-millions-european-economic-cooperation-countries/.

Milanović, Branko. (1998). *Income, Inequality, and Poverty during the Transition from Planned to Market Economy*. Washington, DC: International Bank for Reconstruction and Development/ World Bank.

Milanović, Branko. (2016). *Globalna nejednakost: Novi pristup za doba globalizacije*. Beograd: Akademska knjiga.

Mladjan, Mrdjan, and Fatić, Aleksandar. (2018). 'Economics and Morality: How to Reconcile Economic Thinking with Broader Social Thinking.' In *Sustainable Growth and Development in Small Open Economies*, edited by Isidora Ljumović and Andrea Éltető, 199–217. Budapest: Institute of World Economics of the Hungarian Academy of Sciences.

Mladjan, Mrdjan, and Marković, Dušan. (2016). Problem neuspeha tržišta u Srbiji prilikom tranzicije na tržišnu privredu. In *Pravci strukturnih promena u procesu pristupanja Evropskoj Uniji*, edited by Jelena Minović, Duško Bodroža, Ivan Stošić and Božo Drašković, 130–47. Beograd: Institut ekonomskih nauka.

Pindyck, Robert S., and Rubinfeld, Daniel L. (2001). *Microeconomics* (5th ed.). Upper Saddle River, NJ: Prentice Hall.

Popov, Vladimir. (2007). 'Shock Therapy versus Gradualism Reconsidered: Lessons from Transition Economies after 15 Years of Reforms.' *Comparative Economic Studies* 49(1): 1–31.

Rakita, Branko, and Marković, Dušan. (2013). Praksa antikoruptivnog i društveno odgovornog ponašanja međunarodno preuzetih kompanija. In *Konkurentnost preduzeća u Srbiji*, edited by Nebojša Janićijević and Stipe Lovreta, 243–59. Beograd: Ekonomski fakultet.

Slim, Assen. (2001). 'Ten Years of Western Aid for the CEECs: A Mixed Outcome.' *Revue d'économie financière* (English edition). *Hors-série: Ten Years of Transition in Eastern European Countries*, 251–62.

Slonimczyk, Fabián, and Yurkoc, Anna. (2014). 'Assessing the Impact of the Maternity Capital Policy in Russia.' *Labour Economics* 30: 265–81.

Wicker, Elmus. (1996). *The Banking Panics of the Great Depression.* New York: Cambridge University Press.

Williamson, John. (1990). 'What Washington Means by Policy Reform.' In *Latin American Adjustment: How Much Has Happened?*, edited by J. Williamson, 7–20. Washington, DC: Peterson Institute for International Economics.

Woodruff, David M. (2000). *Money Unmade: Barter and the Fate of Russian Capitalism.* Ithaca, NY: Cornell University Press.

World Bank. (2018). *World Development Indicators*. Retrieved from http://databank.worldbank.org.

Chapter 5

Fighting Impunity or Containing Occupiers

How the Ukrainian Self-Referrals Reshape the ICC's Role in International Relations

Klaus Bachmann

In December 2013 the protest movement of students, who occupied the Independence Square in Kyiv after president Viktor Yanukovych had refused to sign an Association Agreement with the EU, became increasingly militarised, mainly as a result of police violence. Both sides — the protesters, led by the leaders of three opposition parties and representatives of the government — negotiated a possible solution, involving a change of the constitution, the resignation of Yanukovych from office and the participation by the opposition in an interim government. These negotiations came to a standstill after a sudden assault by some protesters on the Parliament, whose speaker had cancelled a debate on constitutional reform. During this assault, which took place on 19 February 2014, the protesters, and in some minor cases also policemen who tried to contain the protesters, were shot at by snipers, who had been deployed at various places around the Independence Square. The precise number of the casualties remains disputed, but there is a consensus that about one hundred people were shot. This so-called Maidan massacre is highly controversial for several reasons. The version put forward by the opposition and — after Yanukovych's escape from office the following day — also by the new interim government, claims that the massacre had been perpetrated by snipers from special police units ('the Berkut') and the secret service ('the Security Service of Ukraine,' the SBU) on behalf of Yanukovych and his government. This version was endorsed by anti-Yanukovych, pro-Maidan and pro-Western media in Ukraine. It is, however, rejected by the majority of Russian media, members of the Russian political establishment, as well as by politicians and media workers siding with pro-Russian movements. Evidence is scarce, scattered, often inconclusive and contradictory, mainly because of the chaotic events which have prevented a thorough forensic investigation. Besides, the events on 19 and

20 February 2014 constitute a turning point in the development of Ukraine, since they triggered the arrival of a 'troika' of foreign ministers from the EU (and President Putin's Human Rights ombudsman) to Kyiv, the signing of a transitional agreement, the escape of Yanukovych first from Kyiv, later also from the country, and his formal destitution by the majority in the Verkhovna Rada. The sniper massacre on Independence Square also contributed to an emotional reception of the conflict by the Ukrainian and, to some extent, international public. Later on, the casualties started to be honoured as 'the Heavenly Hundred' and are now widely regarded as national heroes in the central and western parts of the country.

Several days after Yanukovych's disappearance, on 25 February 2014, the Verkhovna Rada adopted a resolution urging the International Criminal Court (ICC) to extend its jurisdiction to Ukraine and investigate the crimes against humanity allegedly committed between 30 November 2013 and 22 February 2014 by the president of Ukraine, Viktor Fedorovich Yanukovych and other official persons, which the ICC prosecutor might identify (Statement by the Verkhovna Rada of Ukraine, 2014). The resolution goes even so far as to suggest to the ICC who should be punished after the conclusion of an investigation. In the final paragraph of the resolution, the former Prosecutor General, Viktor Pshonka, and the former Minister of the Interior, Vitaliy Zakharchenko, are mentioned as alleged perpetrators along with other officials. Later on, a group of four Verkhovna Rada members submitted an amendment, which added to the list of suspects for alleged crimes against humanity the former Minister of Defense, Pavlo Lebedyev, Justice Minister Olena Lukash, Andriy Portnov, the first deputy head of the presidential administration, the head of the Ukrainian Secret Service (SBU) Oleksandr Yakymenko and Stanislav Shulyak, Chief of Staff of the Ministry of the Interior's military units, together with Andriy Klyuyev, Head of the Presidential Administration under Yanukovych. On 9 April 2014, the Ukrainian Embassy in the Netherlands lodged an application at the ICC, in which the Ukrainian government 'recognizes the jurisdiction of the ICC for the purpose of identifying, prosecuting and judging the authors and accomplices of acts committed on Ukrainian territory between 21 November 2013 and 22 February 2014.' The letter also pledges Ukraine's 'cooperation without delay or exception, in conformity with Chapter IX of the Rome Statute' (Embassy of Ukraine, 2014).

After the Verkhovna Rada had declared Viktor Yanukovych unfit to fulfil his role as president and instituted an interim government, separatist movements organised demonstrations against the regime change in Kyiv in several towns in Ukraine's eastern territories. Mirroring the earlier takeovers of public buildings by anti-Yanukovych protesters in central and western Ukraine, some of these movements started to take over and occupy public buildings in the Eastern part of the country. On Crimea, the local parliament was occupied by armed men and subsequently passed a motion for a referendum about the future of the peninsula. A new prime minister of the peninsula was elected and he asked the Russian government for help to establish control over Crimea. After the Council of the Russian Federation had allowed the government to use military force in Ukraine, soldiers in unmarked uniforms, driving in vehicles without licence plates, spread across Crimea, occupying strategic crossroads and taking over military infrastructure from the Ukrainian military. In March, the Crimean parliament first adopted a declaration of independence, then organised a referendum, whose alleged (but internationally contested) outcome supported the peninsula joining Russia. Subsequently, Russia formally annexed Crimea.

In a timely overlap with the events on Crimea, pro-Russian movements in several Eastern Ukrainian towns tried to take over public buildings by force, mirroring the occupation of public buildings in central and western Ukraine by anti-Yanukovych protesters during the Maidan demonstrations. These attempts failed in two bigger towns, Kharkiv and Odessa, where the riots were countered by supporters of the new Ukrainian government and a number of people died in violent clashes. In the districts of Luhansk and Donetsk, units of local separatists, supported by well-armed unmarked fighters, managed to get hold of the government administration. Several attempts by the Ukrainian army to reconquer the inner cities of Luhansk and Donetsk failed and led to intense war-like conflicts, including the use of military aircraft and tanks. The gravest atrocity against unarmed civilians occurred on 17 July 2014, when an unidentified unit fired a rocket at Malaysian aircraft MH17 on its way from Amsterdam to Kuala Lumpur, killing all staff members and passengers immediately. According to the available evidence, collected by institutions independent of Ukraine and Russia, the rocket had been propelled from a BUK antiaircraft system from Russian territory, most probably because the shooters had confused MH17 with an Ukrainian military aircraft. The conflict in Donbass escalated into a war-like situation, in which regular Russian units with tanks and heavy artillery took part, defeating the Ukrainian army during the fights around Debaltseve in February 2015, and around the Donetsk airport in September 2015. In June 2015, Ukrainian forces managed to retake Mariupol from separatists, who had seized public buildings and the centre of town. After consolidating their military power, the separatist movements in Luhansk and Donetsk also created their own governments and conducted elections, asking Russia to annex these territories. However, Russia supported both entities diplomatically, with humanitarian aid and military assistance, but never responded to the wishes for annexation. On 8 September 2015, Ukraine lodged another self-referral at the ICC, this time accepting the court's jurisdiction 'over crimes against humanity and war crimes committed by senior officials of the Russian Federation and leaders of terrorist organisations

"DNR" and "LNR," which led to extremely grave consequences and mass murder of Ukrainian nationals' (Embassy of Ukraine, 2015).[1] Different from the first self-referral, the second one was completely unrestricted; it included an approval of ICC jurisdiction for international crimes committed after 20 February 2014 on the entire Ukrainian territory with no time limit.

THE POLITICAL AND LEGAL BACKGROUND
OF THE UKRAINIAN SELF-REFERRALS

The Ukrainian referrals came at a moment when the ICC was under fierce attack from African states and the African Union for its alleged 'anti-African' or even neocolonial bias. These attacks have their main origin in three cases — the arrest warrants against Sudanese President Omar Hassan Ahmad Al Bashir and several members of his entourage for crimes committed in Darfur, the proceedings against Saif Al-Islam Gaddafi in Libya and the cases concerning Kenya. Whereas in Libya and Sudan the ICC acted pursuant to a UN Security Council referral, the Kenya case was initiated *proprio motu* by the prosecutor subsequent to the failure by the Kenyan authorities to deal with the 2007 postelection violence. All three countries — Kenya, Sudan and Libya — have developed mechanisms and institutions to deal with the crimes investigated by the ICC.[2] They did so in order to prove the cases inadmissible before the ICC and demonstrate their eagerness and ability to prosecute international crimes before their national judiciaries. Whereas the ICC found one of the Libyan cases inadmissible and has become involved in a complex legal battle with Kenya about the country's measures to hold perpetrators of the 2007 crimes accountable, the Sudanese reaction to the ICC was widely regarded as a mockery, because none of the national judicial mechanisms, established to deal with the atrocities in Darfur, had issued any indictment against any high-ranking suspects. Nevertheless, most African governments refused to act upon the ICC arrest warrant against Al Bashir, and at its summit in Addis Abbeba in January 2014, the African Union urged its members *not to* honour ICC arrest warrants against sitting heads of states (Hale, 2014). In many African media, the ICC has also been accused of bias because arrest warrants had only been issued and trials initiated against politicians and militaries from the African continent, despite the evidence of massive human rights abuses in other parts of the world, all of which are still being investigated (Al Jazeera, 2014). Against this backdrop, the Ukrainian referral was likely to be welcomed by the ICC prosecutor, since it empowered the ICC not only to investigate a crime committed in a European country, which until then had shunned ICC jurisdiction. It also enabled the ICC to investigate events that could potentially involve a permanent UN Security Council member and one of the great powers, which had stayed away from the Rome Statute from the very beginning — Russia. The Ukrainian letter provided the ICC with a unique opportunity to demonstrate its zeal not only towards poor, postcolonial and often fragile states, but also with regard to one of the most powerful ones. This, however, was a political and diplomatic challenge, rather than a legal one, and it bore a lot of political risks, linked to the foreseeable need to collect evidence under very unfavourable circumstances. Some authors argued that these political considerations would not play a big role for the ICC since Europe had already been on the ICC agenda in the past, when Georgia had referred crimes committed in Abkhazia and South Ossetia to the ICC and the ICC prosecutor decided to launch a preliminary investigation (Heller, 2014). However, there is an important difference: When Georgia referred the case to the ICC, it had already been a state party since 2003, and the ICC had full jurisdiction over Georgia. Ukraine, though, has signed, but never ratified the Rome Statute, among others because in 2001 its Constitutional Court found the Rome Statute to be in contravention of the then Constitution (Constitutional Court of Ukraine, 2001). Ukraine has also ratified the Agreement on the Privileges and Immunities of the ICC on 29 January 2007, but that does not make it a state party.

A first attempt in that direction had been made in January 2000, when the Verkhovna Rada with a majority favourable to then prime minister Viktor Yushchenko voted in a bill ratifying the Rome statute and then president Leonid Kuchma challenged the bill before the Constitutional Court (Constitutional Court of Ukraine, 2001). The latter found the Rome statute incompatible with the constitutional provisions of Article 124, which restricted 'the administration of justice' to the 'exclusive competence of the courts' and forbade 'the delegation of judicial functions to other bodies or officials.' According to the judges, the complementarity issue did not remedy this contradiction, since supplementary jurisdiction had not been taken into account when the constitution had been drafted. The court found the immunity provisions of Article 27 and Article 89 (surrender of own nationals to the ICC) of the ICC statute compatible with the constitution and did not reject the provisions, which foresaw that its own citizens be imprisoned in a third country (Constitutional Court, 2001). Some authors have recently discussed whether this verdict still applied in the current situation (Heller, 2014). Actually, the self-referral was lodged under a different constitution from the one that had applied to the attempt to ratify the Rome Treaty in 2001,[3] but Article 124 of the constitution had remained unchanged. The hope of the current Ukrainian political establishment to ratify the Rome Treaty is not so much rooted in a different legal context, but in the fact that the composition of the Constitutional Court has changed and that it is now easier to amend the constitution, since the Party of the Regions and the Communist Party have vanished from the Rada after the parliamentary elections. The Rada is now dominated by a clearly pro-Western majority. The revision of the 2004 constitution is underway. It needs to be amended not only in order to fulfil the interim government's and the newly elected president's commitment to decentralisation, but also in order to facilitate the adaptation of EU law as required by the EU Association Agreement, which has already been ratified by the Rada. Its political part, which comes into force without delay, requires Ukraine to become an ICC state party.[4] On 14 April 2014, two weeks after the annexation of Crimea by the Russian Federation, the interim government decided to start the ratification process for joining the Rome Treaty. The decision was taken unanimously and the cabinet urged the Constitutional Court to issue an opinion on the matter as soon as possible (Press Service of the Ministry of Justice of Ukraine, 2014). Accession to the Rome Treaty was also supported by two prominent Rada members, who had belonged to the Yanukovych majority in 2013. One of them argued that an earlier ratification would have prevented the bloodshed in Ukraine.[5] However, the issue of joining the ICC seems not to be a consensual matter among the currently ruling political establishment. According to victims' organisations and lawyers acting for the relatives of the Maidan sniper victims, the Ukrainian investigation into the massacre is slow and recalcitrant and the new Prosecutor General, Valerij Jarema, has tried to block cooperation with the ICC.[6] There is also a lot of confusion about how strong the case against Yanukovych and his entourage actually is, because in January 2015, Interpol rejected several Ukrainian requests for putting members of the former ruling elite on 'red-alert' search lists (Tucker, 2015).

THE MAIDAN SNIPING — A CRIME AGAINST HUMANITY?

There are two main reasons why relations between the ICC and Ukraine will likely be controversial and problematic. One is domestic in nature and related to the current jurisprudence concerning crimes against humanity. The second is connected to the repercussions for the development of international law and international criminal law, and even international politics, which an ICC involvement might entail, if Ukraine accepts a complete ICC jurisdiction over its territory and citizens by ratifying the Rome Statute and referring the crimes committed after the Maidan sniping to the ICC on the basis of Article 12.3 of the Rome Statute.

   With regard to the domestic controversies, the content of the self-referral is of utmost importance.

   There are two big question marks that apply to the first of the Ukrainian self-referrals. The first is whether the crime in question meets the Rome

Statute's gravity threshold. The second is whether it meets the criteria for a crime against humanity and what is likely to follow if it does not. Paradoxically, the latter would not at all prevent the ICC from investigating and prosecuting it; instead, it could constitute a major stumbling block for the government in Kyiv — not only because it would discredit the self-referral, but because it could trigger an even more painful investigation than that in the case of a crime against humanity.

The gravity threshold of Article 17.1.d. of the Rome Statute is a tricky one for three reasons. First, jurisprudence on what gravity is for the ICC is very limited and the decisions of previous ad hoc tribunals may not apply as precedents, as they were based on the priority principle, rather than the complementarity principle, which guides the ICC. Second, the Rome Statute leaves it open, whether a case in itself has to be grave in order to be taken over by the ICC or whether the whole situation needs to be grave (Kontorovich, 2014: 379–99). Third, it is unclear whether the gravity requirement applies only to the crimes, or also to the status of the perpetrator. In the case of Ukraine, assessing gravity amounts to shooting at a moving target: until the start of the hostilities in the Donbass region, the Maidan massacre had indisputably been the gravest single crime committed during the crisis. In the meantime, with several thousand casualties on both sides[7] and hundreds of thousands of internally displaced persons and refugees abroad, with war crimes committed by both sides, the Maidan sniping appears to be a rather minor crime (UNHCR, 2014a; 2014b).

The issue of whether the Maidan sniping fulfils the requirements for a crime against humanity is even trickier than the gravity problem. In its resolution, the Ukrainian parliament described the Maidan massacre as such a crime, but the highly emotionally drafted document lacked any further explanation about how exactly the crimes committed in February in Kyiv related to the statutory definition of a crime against humanity. The ICC statute defines crimes against humanity as: 'any of the following acts when committed as part of a widespread or systematic attack directed against any civilian population, with knowledge of the attack,' then enumerating, among others, 'murder, extermination, imprisonment or other severe deprivation of physical liberty in violation of fundamental rules of international law and other inhumane acts of a similar character intentionally causing great suffering, or serious injury to body or to mental or physical health.' It is difficult to deny that such acts took place during the timeframe set by the referral. As long as the Maidan uprising lasted, people were being abducted and tortured by the police, as well as by anonymous perpetrators colloquially labelled 'titushki' (violent football hooligans, acting on behalf of the authorities). People had been shot at by snipers and sentenced to prison terms by obedient judges, many of whom were later vetted and fired under the interim government. There are two important reservations that cast doubt on the referral's claim about a crime against humanity. The first is linked to the definition of crimes against humanity, which, in the ICC statute, does not require the context of an armed conflict taking place (Schabas, 2006: 186–89). The crucial point, instead, is the requirement that murder and other inhumane acts have to be part of a *widespread* or *systematic* attack *directed* against any *civilian population*. It is difficult to regard the incidental (though often brutal) police violence during the first weeks of the Maidan protests as a widespread or even systematic attack, since it was directed against small groups, or against individuals who did not belong to any clearly identifiable group. The absolute majority of the Ukrainian civilian population was not affected by that violence. In light of the Rome Statute, the only events that possibly fulfil the definition of a crime against humanity are the events in February 2014 — the sniper massacre. Regardless of who was actually responsible for the majority of the sniper attacks, it is difficult to dispute their systematic character. As the overall balance of casualties shows, almost all sniper attacks were directed at protesters (with a very few exceptions, when policemen were shot.[8] The sniping took place during a brief time span and was spatially concentrated in one street. The attack was not widespread since the massacre took place only in the centre of the Ukrainian capital. The number of casualties is less relevant for assessing whether a crime against humanity has taken place. In the case of *Katanga* at the ICC, an attack on a small civilian settlement, Bogoro in Ituri (the eastern part of the Democratic Republic of the Congo), leading to thirty civilian casualties, was regarded as a crime against humanity (Kamiński, 2014: 289–301). But there the whole village had been under attack, which enabled the prosecutor to argue that the entirety of its civilian population had been targeted. The pre-trial chamber confirmed the charges, indicating the attackers had attempted to destroy the population of the village as a whole (on ethnic grounds). With regard to the requirements for a crime against humanity, the trial chamber emphasised in its judgement that any attack on civilians was in itself a constitutive element of either a crime against humanity or a war crime, no matter whether the attack had resulted in casualties or not. In light of this paragraph, all former discussions about how many victims have to be killed in an attack in order to make the killing an element of a crime against humanity were overruled by the ICC. After the ruling, victims are no longer necessary for proving a crime against humanity. This has several important consequences for assessing the situation in Kyiv in February 2014. On the one hand, the Maidan sniping could be regarded as a crime against humanity regardless of how many casualties the snipers had killed. On the other hand, the situation also considerably differed from the situation in Bogoro, Itury, which the ICC chamber had examined, since in Kyiv only individual protesters had been targeted, not the entire population of the town (nor of any other distinguishable group). In *Katanga*, the judges had been able to disentangle civilian victims from fighters who had been killed in the battle. This will also be much more difficult with regard to Kyiv in 2014. One may even argue that after the radicalisation and militarisation of the Maidan movement, the protest camp already had a unified command structure, its members were armed and bore clear insignia, which made them distinguishable from the enemy group. Thus, they could no longer be regarded as members of a civilian population. The ICC would then have to deal with crimes committed during an internal armed conflict rather than with a crime against humanity. Deliberately directing fire at unarmed protesters could still be seen as a violation of Additional Protocol II to the Geneva Conventions and would fall under the ICC's jurisdiction, but it would also require the ICC prosecution to investigate crimes committed by the opposition, for example, attacks on the police. Finally, the assumption about the existence of a crime against humanity also rests on the answer to the question whether the sniper attacks were *directed* against civilians, understood as an attempt by members of the police and the SBU to kill the Maidan activists. Together with the criterion for an attack to be 'systematic,' this assumes the existence of an understanding or central order on the side of the snipers (a *mens rea* to committing a crime against humanity) to kill protesters. These requirements are not satisfied if one assumes the casualties to have arisen from uncoordinated actions by perpetrators with different agendas — for example, if some snipers had acted upon orders from the police and SBU, and others on orders from a third party, either from within the protester camp or from abroad. Some might even have taken action without any order and on their own. There is some confusion about whether a crime against humanity needs to be the result of a state policy or not (Schabas, 2006: 192–94). However, it is not necessary to decide this issue in order to punish individual perpetrators, since they are not required to contribute willingly to a 'widespread and systematic attack'; they only need to know about the attack in order to be found guilty. Neither need their own actions be widespread or systematic; it is enough if they are a part of such an attack. Under such circumstances, even individual snipers, acting on their own or contrary to a central government's plan or state policy, could be held accountable for 'murder as a count of genocide,' or, alternatively, a war crime. In such a case, the Ukrainian referral could easily backfire at the current government, if it leads to an investigation of killings committed by members of the protest camp. This might be an explanation for the reluctance of the current Ukrainian Prosecutor General to cooperate with the ICC. Once a self-referral is lodged with the ICC, it can neither be withdrawn by the relevant state authorities, nor can the state oppose or prevent the ICC prosecutor from changing the legal categorisation of the crimes referred. In other words — the ICC prosecutor is free to change the qualification of the Maidan sniping from a crime against humanity to a violation of Additional Protocol II and then investigate the actions of both conflict parties on the Maidan, including the chain of command potentially leading from the snipers on the ground to their commanders. So far, the ICC prosecutor did not find the Maidan massacre to be widespread or systematic enough to fulfil the respective requirements of the Rome Statute, but she declared to continue the examination and clearly labelled the atrocities committed in Kyiv 'an attack directed against a civilian population' (OTP ICC, 2016). It is probably not as much the legal definition of a crime against humanity as the lack of evidence regarding the 'widespread' and 'systematic' character of the events that prevents the prosecution from treating the Maidan massacre as a crime against humanity. At any time in the future, an investigation based on the Ukrainian self-referral of the Maidan massacre (the first self-referral) may expose the Ukrainian government and its armed forces to an investigation about their own crimes.

The same is true with regard to issues linked to the second self-referral. In light of the reports by nongovernmental organisations, there is hardly any doubt that war crimes have been committed in the Donbass conflict. With the second self-referral, the ICC prosecutor has obtained an instrument to investigate and prosecute not only suspects acting for or on behalf of the pro-Russian separatists and the Russian government, but also suspects fighting for the Ukrainian government, including the units outside the chain of command of the Ukrainian army. Should this happen, the Ukrainian government would not be able to renounce its own self-referral, because the Rome Statute does not provide for such a legal exit option. Once a situation is referred to the ICC and the latter's jurisdiction accepted, the ICC's proceedings can go either way — according to the wishes of the self-referring government, or against them.

Under Article 19.2 of the Rome Statute, a self-referring government can still claim inadmissibility, either based on a lack of gravity of the crime or on its (recovered) ability or willingness to bring the perpetrators to justice. However, it would be much more difficult to claim inadmissibility under a self-referral than under a *propriu motu* investigation by the ICC prosecutor in a signatory country, or even under a UN Security Council referral. In other words, any Ukrainian government would have considerable difficulty convincing an ICC pre-trial chamber of its ability or willingness to bring the Maidan snipers (and their commanders) to justice after it had claimed that these perpetrators were beyond the reach of the Ukrainian authorities at the time of the first self-referral (the Maidan events). In case of the ICC prosecutor's investigation, the Ukrainian government runs only a low risk of exposure for crimes committed by its agents. This is very different with regard to the subject of the second self-referral (against Russian officials), which bears a great risk of having the Ukrainian army and Ukrainian paramilitary units exposed to an ICC investigation. There, an inadmissibility challenge would be even more difficult.

With regard to the Maidan massacre, an inadmissibility challenge could be grounded in the fact that the Ukrainian authorities have conducted investigations on their own from the very beginning. Several weeks after the self-referral was lodged at the ICC, the interim government, which had taken power in February 2014, started to investigate the Maidan atrocities. The first decision was to disband the Berkut units, which had fought against the protesters on Maidan, beaten up the Euromaidan youth in December and beleaguered the protesters until February. The Berkut were also regarded as responsible for at least some of the sniping. The Berkut was extremely hated by the protesters and a large part of public opinion in the western regions of Ukraine, where some units, surrounded by protesters, had even surrendered and publicly apologised. On 26 February the new interim Minister of the Interior issued an order disbanding the Berkut units, directing its approximately four thousand members to the staff reserves of the Ministry and requesting the heads of the Ministry's regional branches to decide their fate. The Ministry gave them only fifteen days to solve the problem. During that time, the internal investigation of the behaviour of individual officers during the Maidan protests had to be concluded (Press Service of the Ministry of Interior of Ukraine, 2014). The consequences of this popular decision became evident very quickly. Many members of the Berkut lost their jobs or quit the Ukrainian security service and went to Crimea, where they were praised as heroes. Next, the Russian government, which regarded the interim government as a band of putschists and Yanukovych as the legitimate ruler of Ukraine, invited the Berkut officers to accept Russian citizenship and join the Russian security forces (Press Service of the Ministry of Interior of Ukraine, 2014). In early April, officers of the Prosecutor General, the SBU and the Ministry of the Interior arrested three Berkut members under accusations of murder of Maidan protesters. According to press reports, there were nine other suspects being investigated in connection with the massive sniper attacks during 20 February. The next day, the number of arrested Berkut officers rose to twelve.

Victims' initiatives often criticise the efforts by the Ukrainian judiciary to elucidate the events surrounding the events in February 2014 in Kyiv because of their lack of efficiency and delays. However, these proceedings provide a better basis for an admissibility challenge than attempts by the Prosecutor General to investigate crimes in Donbass, where the Ukrainian judiciary did not have and still lack access to the territory, key witnesses and written evidence, all of which is in the hands of DNR and LNR authorities. Thus

Ukrainian authorities have problems even to investigate crimes committed
by Ukrainian forces.

REPERCUSSIONS FOR THE ICC'S FUTURE ROLE

In the specific Ukrainian case, it would have made a lot more sense to ratify
the Rome Statute as early as possible than to lodge separate self-referrals
to the ICC.[9] So far, Ukraine is only a consumer of the public good of international criminal justice, which the ICC provides, but the country does not
shape this public good. It bears all the potentially problematic risks and
burdens that signatory countries share, but it does not have any influence
on the way international criminal justice evolves since Ukraine neither
delegates judges to the ICC, nor does she take part in the ICC Assembly of
State Parties. She therefore has no say either about the assembly's debates on
the crime of aggression, which — in light of Russia's annexation of Crimea
and its role in Donbass — has become a concept of greatest interest for the
Ukrainian government.

Ratifying the Rome Statute would also have brought the whole territory
of Ukraine under CC's territorial jurisdiction, regardless of whether any
suspects were Ukrainian citizens at the time of commission of the crimes.
Due to Russia's annexation of Crimea, the peninsula is currently beyond
Ukrainian de facto jurisdiction and the Ukrainian judiciary is unable (though
perhaps not unwilling) to investigate, prosecute and judge international
crimes that have taken or will be taking place there. Russia is not a state
party to the Rome Statute, but since Crimea is *de jure* still a part of Ukraine,
this would not make such cases inadmissible to the ICC. Recent reports from
international human rights organisations have provided indications about
actions that may fulfil the requirement of 'deportation or forcible transfer of
population,' particularly of Crimean Tatars and Ukrainians, although these
cases may not meet the gravity threshold for crimes against humanity. At least
the ICC OTP seems to regard them as grave enough to be further examined.
The most recent Report on Preliminary Examination Activities (OTP ICC,
2016) mentions the harassment of Crimean Tatars, of which some nineteen
thousand have become internally displaced persons (IDPs) on the Ukrainian
mainland due to restrictions imposed on them by the Russian authorities on
Crimea. Killings and abductions were also reported, as well as compelled military service. This mentioned report does not leave any doubt about the ICC
prosecutor's determination to treat the conflict in Eastern Ukraine (including
Crimea) as an international armed conflict. As the report emphasises, the
mere fact that Crimea (including Sevastopol) was conquered and annexed by
Russia without noticeable resistance by Ukrainian forces does not preclude

such a finding, because 'an armed conflict may be international in nature if one or more states partially or totally occupies the territory of another state whether or not the occupation meets with armed resistance' (OTP ICC, 2016).

Gravity considerations play a minor role with respect to the hostilities in Donbass which, depending on the evidence, may either be regarded as an internal armed conflict (between separatist rebels on one side, and government troops and volunteer units on the other) or as an international armed conflict, involving unmarked (but distinctly military) fighters from the Russian Federation on the rebel side. War crimes have undisputedly taken place in Donbass, since all three sides (the Russian government, the rebel leaders, and the Ukrainian government) have deplored them and blamed the others sides of committing them. Crimes were also reported by international human rights organisations (Amnesty International, 2014; Human Rights Watch, 2014). Whereas the Russian 'Investigative Committee,' linked to the Prosecutor General of the Russian Federation, has only investigated war crimes allegedly committed by Ukrainian units in Donbass, the Ukrainian Prosecutor General has done so with regard to rebel crimes and crimes committed by pro-government volunteers (*Kyivpost*, 2014a). This provides a relatively stable basis for the Ukrainian government to control the outcome of ICC proceedings; if necessary, it can always claim inadmissibility by pointing to its own investigations.

In terms of public goods, Ukraine can but need not pay the price for involving the ICC. She can secure the advantage anyway. The country is currently unable to prosecute any crimes in the rebel-held parts of Donbass, whereas the ICC prosecution can count on the Russian authorities, at least as long as it seeks evidence for crimes which can be attributed to Ukrainian forces. ICC involvement also provides a platform for internationalising the conflict, which is more in the interest of Ukraine than in the interest of Russia. Both aims can be achieved with the self-referrals, but a full accession to the Rome Statute would give Ukraine the opportunity to influence the development of international criminal justice. Such a move would also provide the ICC with a new opportunity.

The ICC may be able to investigate crimes that no other institution would be able to examine for lack of access to the crime scene and to all sides of the conflict, but this does not yet mean that it will be able to prosecute the perpetrators. The low probability that the ICC will ever be able to apprehend the perpetrators it may identify as a result of the investigations in Ukraine does not preclude an investigation. Such considerations are natural, but they neither form part of the Rome Statute, nor of the practise of ICC prosecutions so far. Uncertain perspectives to apprehend and try suspects neither prevented the ICC from issuing arrest warrants against Al Bashir and Muammar Al Gaddafi, nor from (finally unsuccessfully) prosecuting

Kenyatta. The uncertainty about getting a verdict does not show up among the criteria set out by the ICC Office of the Prosecutor in its policy paper about the interest of justice, one of the most cloudy notions of the Rome Statute (ICC OTP, 2007). Neither should it be considered an argument against an investigation or prosecution in Ukraine because the chance to try a suspect may not be obvious when an investigation starts. The interest of justice as a statutory hindrance for prosecution has mostly been discussed in the context of nonretributive (or at least not entirely retributive) judicial measures, such as truth commissions or amnesties (Robinson, 2003). The ICC OTP sees several factors with a potential for preventing investigations and prosecutions due to 'interest of justice': lack of gravity, the interest of victims (their assumed 'right to justice' being counterweighed by their right to security and protection) and the situation of the accused. As the policy paper sets it out, '[f]or example, international justice may not be served by the prosecution of a terminally ill defendant or a suspect who has been the subject of abuse amounting to serious human rights violations.' Whereas the latter aspect and the gravity threshold are hardly relevant in the current context of the Ukrainian crisis (at least they are not predictable at the moment), the interest of victims plays a crucial role. The OTP's policy paper, in line with Article 53 of the Rome Statute, assumes the interest of victims to be one of the few arguments for not pursuing an investigation or prosecution, since the very wording of Article 53 makes it clear that its drafters saw 'interest of justice' as a 'potential countervailing consideration' to a launch of the proceedings. The policy paper clearly sees the security interests of victims as being closely linked to their role in court, or, in other words, such security concerns arise when victims become witnesses. However, not every victim is called in court and victims are not only victimised when compelled to testify or to confront their abusers. Witness protection — or, in extreme cases, withdrawal of the case, is not the only means by which the ICC can contribute to victims' security. This interest will also be served if an ICC investigation is likely to prevent or mitigate violence, either by deterring potential perpetrators from committing crimes, or (more likely) by raising the cost for the perpetrators. This describes the situation in Ukraine's eastern territories, including Crimea, very precisely: the sheer perspective of getting into the ICC's (and the world media) focus is likely to raise the cost for those who may contemplate the commission of crimes under the Rome Statute. Acknowledging this argument shifts the core of the ICC's *raison d'être* to prevention and containment, rather than punishment. It could constrain the actions of pro-Russian separatists in Eastern Ukraine and of the Russian authorities on Crimea. It would also tie the hands of Ukrainian forces fighting in Donbass, but the disadvantage for the government's freedom of action would easily be compensated by another factor, which is likely to cause trouble for both the

ICC and Russia, for different reasons. The mere start of an ICC investigation concerning Crimea would be a strong argument for Ukraine's case against Russia before the International Court of Justice (*Kyivpost*, 2014b). However, the Ukrainian government has been very reluctant to submit the Rome Statute for ratification, despite being obliged to do so under the EU Association Agreement. This was mostly due to misunderstandings about the functioning of international criminal justice among the political establishment of the post-Maidan Ukraine (Lyubashenko, 2017: 113–21).

Launching investigations and prosecutions concerning Donbass and Crimea would turn the ICC from an instrument of retribution to an instrument of prevention and deterrence, whose purpose is no longer only ending impunity for atrocities, but also the prevention and mitigation of violence in ongoing conflicts. This function has so far been sidelined by the trials conducted at the ICC and the controversies about ongoing prosecutions, arrest warrants and trials against suspects from Africa. But the Ukrainian case is not the only one with a potential to push the ICC into prevention and conflict mitigation. The situation in Georgia, which has been investigated by the ICC, also involves a disputed territory, over which the country to which it belongs *de jure* is unable (though not unwilling) to exercise jurisdiction. The same intention to instrumentalise ICC jurisdiction as a mitigating factor in an ongoing conflict and submit a disputed territory to international judicial surveillance lies behind the Palestinian authorities' motion to become a state party to the Rome Statute. Recently, the ICC prosecutor has even sought leave to launch an investigation into Afghanistan. The Office of the Prosecutor's previous examination reports included crimes committed by the Taliban, the Afghan government and US troops. An investigation in Afghanistan would therefore also bring another non-ICC member state and permanent member of the UN Security Council under the ICC's personal and subject matter jurisdiction, despite the refusal by the US government to ratify the Rome Statute.

In all these cases the ICC's chances to have arrest warrants served upon the suspects are much slimmer than in those cases and situations where a government urges the ICC to go after its armed opposition, whose leaders are usually not protected by immunity. But Georgia, Ukraine, the Palestinian Autonomy and Afghanistan also provide a much better occasion for the ICC to bolster its public image and strengthen the (otherwise questionable) preventative potential of international criminal law.

NOTES

1. The abbreviations of 'DNR' and 'LNR' relate to the self-proclaimed Donetsk People's Republic and the Luhansk People's Republic.

2. The ICC is a court of last resort. It can only investigate and take over cases if the ICC prosecutor can prove — before a pre-trial chamber — that the respective country is unable or unwilling to investigate and prosecute an international crime under the ICC's jurisdiction. Whenever that happens, the respective government is usually eager to prove its ability and willingness to prosecute the respective crimes in order to convince the pre-trial chamber of the inadmissibility of the case at the ICC.

3. The Ukrainian Constitutional Court had examined the compatibility of the Rome Treaty with the 1996 Constitution. This constitution was subsequently replaced by the so-called 2004 constitution, which entered in force by 2006. On the basis of the latter constitution, the Verkhovna Rada ratified the Agreement on the Privileges and Immunities of the International Criminal Court on 29 January 2007. This decision had never be challenged before the Constitutional Court until 2010, although the new constitution contained the same restriction for courts as the 1996 constitution. However, when the Verkhovna Rada voted on the motion to refer the Maidan massacre to the ICC in February, it did so under a different constitution than in 2007. In 2010, the Constitutional Court, under tense pressure from then president Viktor Yanukovych, overruled the constitutional amendments of 2004 and revived the 1996 Constitution, strengthening the role of the president. On 21 February 2014 the Verkhovna Rada reinstated the 2004 Constitution, although without the qualified majority required for constitutional amendments. The amendment, which was passed in a very controversial, hasty procedure, was never signed by President Yanukovych, who had left his office and disappeared and was subsequently dismissed by a Rada majority, stating that he had abandoned his office. Until the presidential elections in May 2014, the chairman of the Rada, Oleksandr Turchynov, served as acting president. In other words, when the Rada passed the ICC referral, it did so under the 2004 constitution, which had been reintroduced a few days before.

4. The economic part has been postponed in order to accommodate Russian grievances about economic disadvantages in Russian-Ukrainian trade, allegedly caused by the Association Agreement.

5. The two are Viktor Pylypyshyn, a Rada member, who had supported the so-called dictatorship laws in January 2014, which threatened any public protest with extremely harsh punishment in order to curtail the ongoing demonstrations on the Maidan, and Sergiy Kivalov, who had been member of Yanukovych's 'Party of the Regions.' Both were guests of Parlamentarians for Global Action, a lobby group supporting the ICC.

6. In December 2014, the Kyiv daily *Den* reported, relying on information from Vitalij Kupryj, Member of Parliament, about the refusal by Procurator General Vitalij Jarema to cooperate with the ICC, arguing that the Ukrainian judiciary was effectively prosecuting the case. However, as Kupryj, the Vice-Chairman of the Parliamentary Committee on Internal Security, revealed, out of twelve high-ranking suspects only four were subject to Interpol arrest warrants and no single suspect of the Maidan massacre had been brought to trial.

7. One might also speak about three or more sides (including Russia), since there are strong indications about the presence of Russian regular soldiers in the conflict.

8. During the Maidan uprising in February, there were incidents, when armed protesters shot at policemen from hunting weapons or self-made firearms.

9. Since the ratification of the Rome Statute does not retroactively extend the timely jurisdiction of the ICC (only crimes which were committed after the ratification can be investigated), Ukraine could have ratified the Rome Statute in February 2014 and additionally lodged a self-referral only for the Maidan sniping.

REFERENCES

Al Jazeera. (2014). 'African Union Urges United Stand against ICC,' 1 February 2014, http://www.aljazeera.com/news/africa/2014/02/african-union-urges-united-stand-against-icc-20142111727645567.html (accessed 21 November 2014).

Amnesty International. (2014). 'Eastern Ukraine: Both Sides Responsible for Indiscriminate Attacks,' 6 November 2014, http://www.amnesty.ca/news/news-releases/eastern-ukraine-both-sides-responsible-for-indiscriminate-attacks (accessed 15 December 2016).

Constitutional Court of Ukraine. (2001). Opinion N-1-35/2001, doc. 3-v/2001 'Conformity of the Constitution of Ukraine to the Rome Statute of the International Criminal Court (the Rome Statute case),' http://www.ccu.gov.ua/en/doccatalog/list?currDir=24370 (accessed 14 December 2014).

Embassy of Ukraine. (2014). No. 1219/35-673-384, *The Hague*, 9 April 2014, http://www.icc-cpi.int/en_menus/icc/press%20and%20media/press%20releases/Documents/997/declarationRecognitionJuristiction09-04-2014.pdf (accessed 5 January 2015).

Embassy of Ukraine. (2015). *The Hague*. 8 September 2015, https://www.icc-cpi.int/iccdocs/other/Ukraine_Art_12-3_declaration_08092015.pdf.

Hale, Kip. (2014). 'ICC on Trial.' *Foreign Affairs*, 11 December 2014, http://www.foreignaffairs.com/articles/142514/kip-hale/icc-on-trial?cid=nlc-foreign_affairs_this_week-121114-icc_on_trial_6-121114&sp_mid=47611240&sp_rid=ay5iYWNobWFubkBmZXBzLnBsS0 (accessed 30 December 2014).

Heller, Kevin Jon. (2014). *Thoughts on the Ukraine Ad Hoc Self-Referral*. Opinio Juris 18 April 2014, http://opiniojuris.org/2014/04/18/thoughts-ukraine-ad-hoc-self-referral/ (accessed 12 December 2014).

Human Rights Watch. (2014). 'Ukraine: Letter to President Poroshenko on Military Operations in Luhansk and Donetsk,' 18 July 2014, http://www.hrw.org/news/2014/07/18/ukraine-letter-president-poroshenko-military-operations-lugansk-and-donetsk.

ICC OTP. (2007). 'Policy Paper on the Interests of Justice,' September 2007, https://www.icc-cpi.int/NR/rdonlyres/772C95C9-F54D-4321-BF09-73422BB23528/143640/ICCOTPInterestsOfJustice.pdf (accessed 21 December 2014).

Kaminski, Ireneusz. (2014). *International law Aspects of the Situation in Ukraine*. In *The Maidan Uprising, Separatism and Foreign Intervention*, edited by K. Bachmann and I. Lyubashenko, 389–401. Frankfurt/M.: Peter Lang International.

Kontorovich, Eugene. (2014). 'When Gravity Fails: Israeli Settlements and Admissibility at the ICC.' *Israel Law Review 47*(3), 379–99.

Kyivpost (2014a). 'Ukrainian Prosecutors Investigate Volunteer Battalions' Crimes against Donbas Civilians,' 10 September 2014, http://www.kyivpost.com/content/ ukraine/ukrainian-prosecutors-investigate-volunteer-battalions-crimes-against-donbas-civilians-364085.html?flavour=mobile (accessed 16 December 2014).

Kyivpost. (2014b). 'Ukraine Mulling Appeals to UN International Court of Justice due to Annexation of Crimea by Russia,' 20 May 2014, http://www.kyivpost.com/ content/ukraine/ukraine-mulling-appeals-to-un-international-court-of-justice-due-to-annexation-of-crimea-by-russia-348541.html.

Lyubashenko, Igor. (2017). *Transitional Justice in Post-Euromaidan Ukraine. Swimming Upstream.* Frankfurt/M.: Peter Lang.

OTP ICC. (2016). Report on Preliminary Examination Activities 2016, https://www. icc-cpi.int/iccdocs/otp/161114-otp-rep-PE_ENG.pdf.

Press Service of the Ministry of Interior of Ukraine. (2014). 'Arsen Avakov pidpisav nakaz pro likvidatsiju spetspidrozdilu 'berkut.'' 26 December 2014, http://www. kmu.gov.ua/control/uk/publish/article?art_id=247057542&cat_id=244276429.

Press Service of the Ministry of Justice of Ukraine. (2014). 'Urjad pidtrymav rishennja pro nevidkladu ratyfikatsiju Ryms'kogo statutu,' 14 April 2014, http:// www.kmu.gov.ua/control/uk/publish/article?art_id=247219232 (accessed 16 December 2014).

Robinson, Darryl. (2003). 'Serving the Interests of Justice: Amnesties, Truth Commissions and the International Criminal Court.' *European Journal of International Law* 14, no. 3: 481–505.

Schabas, William. (2006). *The UN International Criminal Tribunals. The Former Yugoslavia, Rwanda and Sierra Leone.* New York, Cambridge University Press.

Tucker, Michael. (2015). Interpol Rejects Ukrainian Murder Charges against Ex-officials. Kyivpost, 12 January 2015, http://www.kyivpost.com/content/kyiv-post-plus/interpol-rejects-ukrainian-murder-charges-against-ex-officials-377233. html.

UNHCR. (2014a). 'The Approach of Winter Threatens Thousands of Displaced Ukrainians,' UNHCR News Stories, 4 December 2014, http://www.unhcr. org/548085426.html (accessed 12 December 2014).

UNHCR. (2014b). 'Ukraine Conflict Uproots Hundreds of Thousands,' UNHCR New Stories, 5 December 2014, http://www.unhcr.org/548190aa9.html (accessed 20 December 2014).

Chapter 6

The Political Economy of Transitional Justice in Ukraine[1]

Igor Lyubashenko

ESTABLISHING LINKS BETWEEN TRANSITIONAL JUSTICE AND POLITICAL ECONOMY

Under the term transitional justice I understand *extraordinary* measures undertaken in order to address the perception of injustice that exists in a given society, the sources of which can be found in more or less distant past. Two main features constitute necessary conditions enabling us to regard a given policy as one that fits into the category of transitional justice. The first one is *large-scale violence*. We might speak about situations when violence is personal and direct (when it is clear who commits violent acts, and against whom they are targeted), as well as about situations when violence is indirect or structural (when it is built into the social structure and shows up as unequal power) (Galtung, 1969: 170–71). In both cases the scale of violence is crucial. It is hardly possible to set a clear quantitative threshold that would distinguish large-scale from small-scale violence. An indicator that might be helpful for defining situations when extraordinary measures are applicable is whether we deal with the case when 'crime becomes the rule [and] no justice system can adequately cope with the fallout — least of all one in a state of transition and fragility' (Freeman, 2009: 18). The second feature is the inevitability of *involvement of politics* in order to deal with the described sort of problems. Transitional justice policies are thus situated on a continuum between purely political and purely legal motivations to apply them. They are influenced by several types of interests: wrongdoers wish to avoid prosecution, victims wish to obtain compensation (not necessarily a material one), and political parties wish to utilise the transitional justice policies in order to increase their share of votes in the electorate (Elster, 2004: 84–89).

The presented set of features can usually be found in two types of situations: (1) transition between political regimes and (2) postconflict settlement, or transition from war to peace (in some cases, however, the dividing line between the two is blurred). This explains why the discussed extraordinary measures are referred to as *transitional* — in both types of situations shifts in the existing political order occur, either as results of regime change or as outcomes of power-sharing — an important element of many peace agreements, which may have a transformative effect on political systems (McAuliffe, 2017: 138–57). What is important, however, is that in any type of situation transitional justice policies usually have some normative inclinations: an incoming political order aims at securing and enforcing the system of norms and values upon which it is based. In other words, values proclaimed by the political regime which implements the transitional justice policies constitute a kind of 'normative anchor' for those policies; a reference point allowing, among other things, the assessment of the policies.

The scope of transitional justice has recently widened considerably. In other words, it has undergone an 'emancipation from the bonds of paradigmatic transition' (Sharp, 2015). One of the main directions of this 'emancipation' has been transitional justice's increased attention to economic and social violence that accompanies conflicts. The research of this problem goes in two main directions. The first one can be called normative. Generally, it is focused on deliberations about whether and to what extent abuses of *economic* nature should be addressed by transitional justice mechanisms. The second is more interesting from the perspective of this chapter — it can be called the political economy of transitional justice. Here, the debate is concentrated around the complex interplay between the economic and political costs and benefits of different transitional justice mechanisms and strategies. Taking into account the well-known words by Carla del Ponte, former Prosecutor of the ICTY, that 'justice is not cheap' (cited after Beigbeder, 2011: 83), the general assumption in this field is that the available resources may play a decisive role in selecting the modality or set of transitional justice mechanisms to be applied. Conversely, there are attempts to analyse how the implementation of transitional justice in itself may influence the social and economic development of a state (de Greiff, 2009). Here, one of the central claims states that addressing the violations of economic and social rights by means of transitional justice should enhance the level of trust in a given society and thus support its economic development, which, in turn, is a necessary precondition for the state to secure its citizens' economic and social rights.

To a significant extent, these considerations are theoretical. The currently available empirical research based on quantitative comparative methods provides evidence that the implementation of transitional justice can be a function of economic performance of a state (e.g., Addison, 2009; Olsen et al., 2010). However, such studies usually show only correlations and do not explain the causal mechanisms which operate behind such links. Likewise, insightful case studies are not necessarily a good basis for generalisations. In other words, in the political economy of transitional justice there are many unfilled and not-yet-interpreted 'white spots.'

I will focus here on one of the newest — and thus probably least understood — cases of implementation of transitional justice policies: Ukraine. In what follows I present the main challenges to the Ukrainian transition from the perspective of political economy.

THE SPECIFICITY OF UKRAINE'S TRANSITIONAL JUSTICE PROJECT

Ukraine has become one of the newest 'club members' among the states designing and implementing transitional justice policies. The moment of onset of the Ukrainian transition in this case was marked by the mass protest that took place in late 2013 and beginning of 2014 and is widely referred to as 'Euromaidan,' or 'Revolution of Dignity.'[2] The violent mass protest, followed by the escape of President Viktor Yanukovych and his formal removal from office by the Parliament, was not a paradigmatic transition. The protest led to a change of government, but there was no significant alteration in the active political elites. The majority of 'postrevolutionary' officials had been active in public life and had held high positions of power before the 'revolution.' After Euromaidan, they continued to do so. Although the protest did not articulate the demand for a change of Ukraine's political regime, there was a clear demand to change the informal rules upon which the regime had been based. These were defined first of all by *systemic corruption* (the processes that had led to the outbreak of Euromaidan are discussed elsewhere: Bachmann and Lyubashenko, 2014).

The postrevolutionary authorities officially declared the goal of building a 'normal' European state as their priority.[3] This goal of 'normalisation' should be regarded as a mentioned 'normative anchor' for all kinds of transitional policies.[4] Based on the idea of democratisation, or democratic 'normalisation,' considerable new legislation within the realm of transitional justice has been introduced in Ukraine. The core of it included policies designed to address the prerevolutionary *ancien regime*.

It should be clearly stressed that the Ukrainian socioeconomic system, which was widely perceived by the society as unjust (the one that triggered Euromaidan) was not a direct result of Viktor Yanukovych's actions as president. Rather, the period of his presidency should be regarded as the culmination of a particular political system that had formed gradually since the beginning of the 1990s. The prominent and immanent feature of this system was corruption.

As an addition to policies addressing the injustices of pre-revolutionary authorities, steps have been taken to address the already distant communist past. This included symbolic measures which were supposed to mark a definite end of Ukraine's first transition from being a Soviet republic to becoming an independent state in 1991. The significance of these measures was increased by the fact that, almost immediately after Euromaidan, Ukraine faced Russia's de facto aggression, which resulted in the annexation of Crimea and an armed conflict in the east of the country. A number of steps have been taken addressing mass-scale crimes committed during the Donbass conflict: crimes against state security and, more importantly, crimes committed by persons directly involved in warfare, predominantly qualified by the Ukrainian authorities as terrorist attacks. These steps include investigations and trials of crimes associated with the conflict; debates about possible amnesties and attempts to involve international criminal justice (Lyubashenko, 2017). In fact, the Ukrainian is a combination of two transitions: that between political regimes (initiated by Euromaidan) and that between war and peace. The conflict is no longer an open war, but remains far from being resolved; in this case, transitional justice is implemented in the environment of a low-intensity conflict and can be regarded as an element of peace-building.

TRANSITIONAL JUSTICE AS AN EXTRAORDINARY ANTICORRUPTION POLICY

Policies addressing the legacy of Viktor Yanukovych's presidency constitute, without a doubt, the core of Ukraine's transitional justice project. They are designed to deal with the human rights abuses committed by the prerevolutionary regime: the mass violence that took place during the Euromaidan protests, but also the less obvious structural violence of predominantly economic nature, which had been the informal feature of the political system under Yanukovych.

These policies clearly contain elements of what was referred to earlier as the political economy of transitional justice. The policies prominently included the investigations of alleged crimes committed by public officials during the Yanukovych presidency. In December 2014, a special unit was created within the Prosecutor General's Office aimed at coordinating all efforts in this field. Investigations have addressed the embezzlement of public funds and property, tax evasion and smuggling, bribery, money laundering and the illegal use of fiscal and law-enforcement agencies to eliminate competition (Prosecutor General's Office of Ukraine, 2015). Essentially, it is a retrospective type of crime control, because it addresses only the abuses that had already been illegal as per the old regime's laws, but were not sanctioned with regard to selected suspects (because of their positions in the political establishment of the time). The investigations started with great enthusiasm, announcing that a return to the state budget was expected of large amounts of illegal profits which corrupt officials and their close allies had gained, hinting at a de facto confiscation. However, at the moment of writing, four years later, no investigation has been finalised in court. This makes the stated purpose of confiscations even more difficult to attain, and thus removes the hope of effective reparation of damage to the state budget even further. While criminal prosecutions are often announced as the decisive measures of transitional justice, because of their public appeal, they are rarely capable of serving as the primary tool for transitional justice, not only in Ukraine. The reason is that complex criminal trials take years to complete, and the various discretionary rights with which prosecutors tend to be equipped mean that investigations can take all kinds of directions, often meandering around the issues that trouble the transition most.

The fundamental transitional justice mechanism that addresses the issue of corruption is vetting. Corruption was characterised as a 'lustrable offence' in the law titled 'On the cleansing of government (lustration),' which was enacted on 16 September 2014.[5] The main edge of the law was against Yanukovych-era officials, but the regulation also introduced a ban from holding public office for individuals who cannot explain the origin of their assets (the so-called property lustration). This particular provision encompassed a period extending beyond that immediately preceding the Euromaidan. At the same time, the law did not introduce an automatic mechanism of screening the property of state officials, and it did not include any provision for the criminal investigation of alleged cases of illegal acquisition of property or illegal enrichment. In practise, the process appeared to depend on civil activism — the consistent efforts by investigative journalists and nongovernmental organisations to draw attention to undeclared property and force the initiation of formal screening, eventually leading to the official's dismissal. Without a court decision, however, one can easily argue that allegations of impropriety are just that — allegations.

The lustration based on the mentioned law was supplemented by a de facto vetting,[6] which was embedded in a number of institutional reforms. This applied first and foremost to the judiciary (prior to Euromaidan, courts were believed to be among the most corrupt institutions in Ukraine; they thus became 'natural candidates' for some form of 'cleansing'). In April 2014, a law 'On the restoration of trust in the judicial power in Ukraine' was enacted. The law was primarily intended to facilitate the screening of the judicial decisions taken against Euromaidan participants, but it also provided for the immediate dismissal of all current members of the self-governing and disciplinary bodies within the judiciary, as well as the High Qualification Commission for Judges (the state organ overseeing the overall structure of the judiciary, which was entrusted to ensure that all judges were properly qualified). The second wave of vetting of the judges came in September 2014, and in February 2015, a law 'On the right to a fair trial' was enacted, introducing an obligatory 'evaluation of qualifications' of all Ukrainian judges. The procedure was to be conducted by the previously 'cleansed' High Qualification Commission for Judges. Formally, the goal of the procedure was to ensure that all Ukrainian judges satisfied the appropriate standards of professionalism; it is clear, however, that the idea of getting rid of corrupt judges was one of the reasons behind the law — such a motivation was clearly mentioned in the explanatory note accompanying the bill proposed by President Poroshenko.

The fundamental problem with the procedure of dismissing judges on the basis of an evaluation of qualification was that it was inconsistent with the constitution, which contained a clear set of circumstances under which a judge could be removed from office. In June 2016, the Ukrainian Constitution was amended, providing, among other things, a groundwork for the assessment of the professional qualification of judges. Also, along with the mentioned constitutional amendment, a law 'On the judicial system and the status of judges' was adopted, introducing two more steps that fit into the logic of a de facto vetting. First, the Ukrainian Supreme Court was reformed, with no guarantee for its old judges to continue their service. Second, the law also obliged all Ukrainian judges to submit regular property declarations, as well as the so-called declaration of family connections, namely statements explaining whether and how specific judges are in family relations with state officials.

The logic of a de facto vetting was also visible in the reform of the prosecution. A new law on the prosecution, adopted in October 2014, has essentially 'relaunched' the lowest level of state prosecution in Ukraine. Namely, all existing district (Ukr. *районні*) public prosecutor's offices were reorganised into a smaller number of local (Ukr.: *місцеві*) public prosecutor's offices. All the prosecutors willing to continue their service had to go through newly established assessment procedures. Like with the courts, the desire to get rid of bad or corrupt prosecutors was a key motive for the reform.

Probably the most spectacular example of combining institutional reform with vetting was the reform of the police force, which was initiated in July 2015. The logic of the reform was simple: an entirely new police force was created, and it gradually replaced the old police (which was formally called militia, Ukr.: *міліція*) with no guaranteed continuity of service for any police officer.

Other anticorruption measures that have been taken in Ukraine do not necessarily fall within the category of transitional justice: they do not focus on past abuses, but are aimed at the prevention and control of corruption and increasing transparency of public bureaucracy in the present and future. In particular, in October 2014 the National Anti-Corruption Agency (aimed at preventing corruption among public servants), the National Anti-Corruption Bureau of Ukraine (specialized in the prevention, detection, investigation and disclosure of crimes of corruption) and the specialised anticorruption prosecution service within the General Prosecutor's Office were created. In 2016, Ukraine introduced a system of electronic declarations of property by all public officials; these are publicly available online. Overall, the anticorruption measures implemented by the post-Euromaidan authorities included *extraordinary* elements, such as the attempt to eliminate from public life the officials who had been associated with grand corruption, which had flourished in Ukraine since the beginning of the 1990s. On the other hand, these measures also included the *ordinary* anticorruption policies, aimed at eliminating risks of corruption from ongoing public affairs.

The results of these rather sophisticated transitional justice policies have not been spectacular. According to report published by the Ministry of Justice (which oversees the implementation of the major law on lustration) summing up first two years of implementation of lustration, only 110 persons lost their office as a result of property lustration. It is unknown, however, whether any additional steps — such as further investigation and confiscation — have been taken against these particular persons.

The whole process of 'cleansing' the state administration from dishonest and corrupt officials was often presented to the public as a step towards harsher punishment, including some form of confiscation. For this purpose, the Agency for Asset Recovery was created in November 2015 with the task to support investigations into the origin of the disputed property of public officials, store and manage the illegally gained assets. However, no formal mechanism was established that would automatically lead from any form of vetting to investigations and eventual confiscations. As a result, no significant progress was achieved in this field. According to an analysis by the Ukrainian NGO Anti Corruption Action Centre, less than 1 percent of the initially anticipated misappropriated assets have been returned to the state budget (Anti Corruption Action Centre, 2016).[7]

Igor Lyubashenko

THE ECONOMIC CONSTRAINS OF
POSTCONFLICT JUSTICE IN DONBASS

At the time of completion of this manuscript, the Donbass conflict has lasted for four years and there is no clear perspective of its effective resolution. In such conditions, the application of transitional justice in Ukraine is bound by particular constrains, primarily by the imperatives of conflict resolution itself.[8]

It is not my intention here to discuss the evolution and nature of the Donbass conflict in detail. What should be underlined, however, is its *hybridity*, by which I understand primarily the unclear status of the conflict. First, there is overwhelming consensus among analysts that an external actor — Russia — has played a crucial role in the emergence of the self-proclaimed 'republics' of Donetsk and Luhansk in the east of Ukraine. By extension, Russia has played a role in initiating the conflict itself which, in a sense, makes it a conflict between Ukraine and Russia. At the same time, the existence of some popular support for the 'republics' in the east of Ukraine cannot be denied either. It would thus be correct to say that the Donbass conflict is a hybrid internal and international conflict. However, the assessment of an actual balance between these two elements remains a matter of (often very emotional and not fact-based) debate. A proper evaluation of the various hybrid aspects of the conflict would require a comprehensive interpretation of different views of, and stakes in, the conflict. Such a process in itself could be regarded as a truth-seeking transitional justice mechanism.

An important aspect of the hybridity of this conflict is its legal side. Although the Ukrainian authorities widely refer to the conflict as a 'war' (sometimes even 'war for independence'), such a status of the conflict has not been legally confirmed. The actions by Ukrainian forces have been defined as a 'counterterrorist operation,' which was initiated in April 2014. This contradiction between the political and legal qualifications of the same events may have a significant impact on the final shape of postconflict justice, especially when it comes to the status of the participants and the assessment of particular acts of violence.

The hybridity of the conflict creates complex circumstances for the design and implementation of any transitional justice policies for Donbass. Any introduction of a perspective of punishment of actors in the conflict while the conflict goes on militates against a successful conclusion of the conflict, because the belligerents may be discouraged from seeking settlement to the conflict if they are personally at risk of being held accountable for it. Given that most belligerents are Ukrainian citizens, this makes things additionally complex. On the one hand, they are legally responsible according to

Ukrainian laws and thus have reason to protract the conflict. On the other, any prolongation of the conflict will likely lead to a 'freezing' of the conflict. This forces the Ukrainian authorities to seek a relatively fast resolution to the conflict. At the same time, the described situations requires 'smart' transitional justice policies, which may well require extensive amnesties, the granting of regional rights, and even concessions in the domain of Ukraine's geopolitical orientation and policies.

The injustices generated by the Donbass conflict have a significant economic aspect.[9] For the first time since achieving independence, Ukraine has faced the problem of internally displaced persons. The number is estimated at around 1.4 million persons (OHCHR, 2015). Most have suffered from a loss of property and income; generally, the conflict has had a direct negative impact on the quality of economic life of those affected. Available data suggest that, from the perspective of the majority of Ukrainians, negotiations would be the preferable option for ending the conflict. In other words, Ukrainians are predominantly ready to accept some concessions that would be given to the rebellious regions. At the same time, there are no clear indicators suggesting that there are widespread expectations of compensation for the experienced violence. This does not mean, however, that such expectations will not appear once the violence stops.

Some type of legal reparations for the displaced and disenfranchised in the Donbass conflict is additionally likely given that Ukraine has adopted several laws which guarantee the protection of rights of internally displaced persons (Yevseyev, 2017). Also, the so-called law on de-occupation, adopted by the Verkhovna Rada in January 2017 (the main goal of which is to define basic principles of Ukraine's policy towards the Donbass 'republics') includes a provision that protects property rights of Ukrainian citizens in the rebel-controlled Donbass. While Ukrainian laws protect these rights formally, no specific action can be taken until peace is achieved. In addition, catering to the economic rights of the dispossessed by the Ukrainian authorities is difficult in light of the fact that Ukrainian authorities have no control over any economic activity taking place in Donbass. The realities on the ground after the effective seizing of control of the Donbass region by the rebels, assisted by Russia, mean that life goes on and facts on the ground change outside any control of the Ukrainian authorities. This makes it unrealistic to expect a full reconstruction of the situation from before April 2014 once the conflict is resolved, however this may happen. This will necessitate some form of restorative justice focused on compensation, and that is likely to involve various forms of redistribution of wealth as part of the restorative process.

The economic aspect of peace versus justice dilemma in the case of the Donbass conflict is also reflected in the fact that, on 15 March 2017, Ukrainian authorities introduced an economic blockade of the occupied territories. As a result, the regions neighbouring Donbass witnessed a rise in contraband (Independent Defense Anti-Corruption Committee, 2017). The exact scale of this phenomenon remains unknown due to its obvious illegal nature. However, it is widely covered in the media (e.g., Polukhina, 2016). What is important from my perspective here is that, along with generating general economic injustices for the ordinary people and the legal economy, the conflict has created new illegal business opportunities. This includes smuggling, trading on an increasingly entrenched black market, and organised crime in the sense of organised criminal enterprise. Contrary to the difficulties in initiating any cooperation between the Ukrainian authorities and the leadership of the Donbass rebels, organised criminals throughout Ukraine have no qualms cooperating. There are thus actors on both sides of the conflict who are interested in maintaining the status quo of a low-intensity warfare rather than proceeding towards a resolution, much less towards exploring and revealing the truth about the conflict. For these actors, the reason for avoiding finding out of the truth is not a fear of the legal repercussions of committed war crimes, but the maintenance of illegal profits. Illegal trade with alienated territories has become exceptionally lucrative.

In summary, a political economy perspective on the Donbass conflict suggests serious challenges to any future process of transitional justice which would seek to address the injustices generated by the conflict, both because of the fear by certain leaders that they would be prosecuted for war crimes and due to reluctance by those who profit from illegal trade to end their illegal business. Any transitional justice strategy for Donbass would likely involve attempts, to establish responsibility for the crimes committed, a debate on the granting of amnesties and endeavours to involve international criminal justice in the process. None of these elements of transitional justice is in the interests of influential actors on both sides, who use the conflict for their own personal gain.

On the level of general strategy for resolving the conflict, the mentioned problem of hybridity is the main obstacle that prevents the Ukrainian state from developing a comprehensive approach to the conflict. Instead of developing such a consistent and logical approach on policy level, the Ukrainian authorities tend to resort to ad hoc reactions to particular problems. Such reactions might seem appropriate at particular points in time, however, if they do not translate into consistent policy, they start to create problems of their own. For example, the legal label of 'counterterrorist operation,' which seemed to be a good solution to allow the state to act against the Donbass rebels without at the same time introducing a martial law, legally entails an obligation for the state to provide compensation to the citizens for any losses or damages that occur as a result of the operation. Ukrainian citizens are now asking for such compensations. The Ukrainian state is unprepared for such requests, both financially (taking into account the difficult economic situation of Ukraine) and politically (questions are raised in public debate on 'why Ukraine should bear the costs of a de facto external aggression'). Thus, it seems that the label 'antiterrorist operation' has brought more problems to the state than it has solved. Perhaps more importantly, the resorting of ordinary Ukrainians to seeking compensation for financial and economic damages caused by the counterterrorist operation suggests that political economy is far more important in the Ukrainian perspective on the Donbass conflict than might seem at first sight. Clearly, the mentioned need for a redistribution of wealth, as well as the emergence of a new *systemic* problem of illegal trade — both basically missing from wider public debate — will almost certainly become important political issues in the future.

MUTUAL CONNECTIONS BETWEEN THE LEGACY OF CORRUPTION AND THE DONBASS CONFLICT

The two key dimensions of Ukrainian transitional justice project (systemic corruption and the war in Donbass) are not entirely separate processes — they overlap within the same political system. So far I have discussed them separately for the sake of clarity; it is now important to 'connect the dots' in order to present a more comprehensive picture.

Obviously, both problems exert a significant impact on the functioning of the Ukrainian state. Both constitute circumstances that give rise, or may be used to justify, the taking of extraordinary measures by the state within its overall policy of transitional justice. They are also intimately interrelated: the mass dissatisfaction with the economic, social and political situation generated by systemic corruption had led to Euromaidan, and Euromaidan, in turn, was used as a trigger for Russia to annex Crimea and destabilise the situation in the eastern regions of Ukraine, eventually resulting in the outbreak of the armed conflict.

The Donbass conflict became an important condition for extraordinary anticorruption measures, implemented immediately after Euromaidan, as it disrupted the popular definition of the most significant problems faced by the state. Prior to the conflict, corruption was the most important issue; with the development of the conflict, achieving peace became the top priority (Razumkov Centre, 2017). As a result of this shift in public perceptions, the decision makers have been able to dilute the implementation of anticorruption measures, and the conflict (which is without a doubt an extremely grave problem) has become a convenient justification for failing to achieve the proclaimed goals of 'cleansing the government.'

On the other hand, the Donbass conflict increased the dependence by Ukrainian government on support by their Western partners. In turn, these partners, who provided political, diplomatic, and economic support to the Ukrainian post-Euromaidan government, insisted (and to some extent conditioned their support) on Ukraine's implementation of reforms, and especially of anticorruption measures. Thus, despite a desire by some policy makers, reforms could not be abandoned. This may explain the complexity and sophistication of the anticorruption legislation on the vetting of public officials on the one hand, and the perceptible lack of its decisive implementation, on the other. The enactment of complex legislation, followed by a 'soft' implementation of these laws, was seen as a way for Ukrainian authorities to present a picture of doing something against corruption, while minimising the actual impact of the anticorruption policies in reality.

The lowering of the emphasis of what I have called 'extraordinary anticorruption measures' through complex legislation and soft implementation has allowed the Ukrainian authorities to gradually switch their attention to ordinary anticorruption policies, focused not on punishments for past abuses, but on the prevention of such crimes in the future. The obvious advantage of such an approach — from the perspective of a predominantly unchanged class of decision makers — is that a soft implementation policy can be stretched in time. This allows the new/old political class to adapt themselves to a changing legal environment without being prosecuted for their own actions.

This dialectic shows how the need to address the crisis in Donbass has reverberated through the failed anticorruption policy. The connection in the other direction, namely the impact of the failed anticorruption policy on the resolution of the Donbass conflict, is less clear and more hypothetical, partly because the transitional justice mechanisms designed to address the consequences of the Donbass conflict are still nascent. First, one of the (perhaps idealistic) ways of thinking about a possible peaceful resolution of the Donbass crisis is the idea that a dynamic economic and institutional development of the Ukrainian state will eventually attract the inhabitants of the self-proclaimed republics to seek a better life through resuming a full membership in the Ukrainian society as a whole, and thus lead to a kind of their natural return to the mainland. The failure by the Ukrainian state to effectively and aggressively address corruption in its own ranks militates against this idea, as Ukraine cannot rocket to a status of economic prosperity while it is being bled out of its resources and institutional efficiency through systemic corruption.

Second, the prospect of transitional justice in the repressive context requires the establishment of institutions and policies that will be able to mete out justice in a highly professional and impartial way. Such impeccable institutions require considerable state resources, which would need to be committed to transitional justice opulently, and at the same time transparently. Given that systemic corruption stifles economic development, it severely limits the resources necessary to implement any form of accountability in an impartial and credible way.

LESSONS LEARNED FROM UKRAINIAN TRANSITIONAL JUSTICE SO FAR

The variety of problems addressed by the discussed transitional justice policies implemented by Ukraine's post-Euromaidan authorities dictate fairly multifaceted conclusions.

The failure by the Ukrainian authorities to use the public thrill generated by announcements that the institutional system would be thoroughly 'cleansed' by using extraordinary, revolutionary anticorruption measures in full swing, and their resorting, instead, to lower-level systemic interventions that do not address the past crimes, has in fact been a way for the post-Euromaidan authorities to preserve the inherited political system, of which corruption have been an immanent element. Effectively turning a blind eye on misdeeds from the past and refocusing on 'prevention' of corruption in the future has allowed the political elites, many of whom have been continuously in power since Yanukovych's time, to avoid punishment for their past actions and adapt their *modus operandi* to a gradually changing legal environment in Ukraine.

As for the Donbass conflict itself, thinking in terms of the costs and benefits of any attempt to achieve justice reveals important challenges that are not present in the public debate so far. In particular, it is hard to imagine any modality of transitional justice that would be able to entirely avoid restorative justice. As restorative justice requires resources to compensate those who have been adversely affected by the conflict-related developments, this inevitably raises the question of who should bear the costs. In a country suffering from major economic hardships, such as Ukraine, the issue of costs will necessarily impact the peace negotiations.

The uniqueness of the Ukrainian case, defined by the intertwining of two different types of transitional justice, obviously limits the extent to which my conclusions here can be generalized. Nevertheless, at least two issues discussed here are generalisable. The first is that systemic corruption may trigger a public demand for some kind of extraordinary policy of justice, although the actual design and implementation of such policies may not of itself be sufficient to restore trust in the existing political order. The second is that a protracted low-intensity armed conflict creates new structural economic and social problems and a new structure of interests, which may militate against the very resolution of the conflict and certainly against an effective implementation of any kind of postconflict justice. Protracted situations of either systemic corruption or of internal (or hybrid internal and international) conflict tend to breed informal institutions that benefit increasingly broad sections of the stake holders. However improper and unjust they may seem from the perspective of a society's dominant system of values, any definitive break with them requires either a strong change in the 'normative anchor' of society through the transitional process. Alternatively, the key social norms can be changed through a more gradual procedure where the balance between continuity and change, if only slightly, is still in favour of change. In this latter strategy, which appears to be adopted by Ukrainian authorities, 'dealing with the past' will likely be limited, and justice will tend to be predominantly future-oriented.

NOTES

1. Preparation of the chapter was possible thanks to research grant no. 2016/23/D/HS5/02600, financed by the National Science Centre, Poland.

2. The notion of 'revolution' does not describe the Ukrainian transition phenomenon accurately. I will use the term 'revolution' in the chapter merely in order to describe the events that have triggered transitional justice in Ukraine.

3. The idea of Ukraine being 'not normal' and needing to be 'normalised' is part of the common rhetoric in many postcommunist countries. The attribute of 'normalcy' is usually ascribed to a typically Western society. The notion basically idealises the attributes of a fully functional state and society. At the same time, this type of rhetoric proves that there is a collective awareness among Ukrainians of what is lacking in their political system. Thus, the idea that Ukraine is not 'normal,' while Western democracies are 'normal' is merely an indication of the strength of the democratic striving by the Ukrainians, and not an actual description of Ukraine. In fact most postcommunist states were not nearly as 'abnormal' as might be concluded from the current rhetoric of the citizens striving for democracy and the rule of law.

4. This statement is not based on a blind belief in a systemic political and ideological authority. It only suggests that the political model of liberal democracy should be used as a reference point to assess the actual steps taken by Ukrainian authorities.

5. All laws cited within this text are retrieved from the official database of Ukrainian legislation, available at the website of the Verkhovna Rada of Ukraine (the parliament), http://zakon0.rada.gov.ua/laws.

6. In this particular case, by 'lustration' I mean the formal procedures introduced by the mentioned law, 'On the cleansing of government (lustration).' Vetting, in turn, is used as a broader concept, describing policies of limiting the right of representatives of the old regime to hold public office under a new regime. Lustration is thus an element of vetting.

7. This statement should not be regarded as suggesting a complete ineffectiveness of Ukrainian policy of assets recovery. The process is legally complex and may take

longer than expected. At the moment of writing, however, the policies have not significantly reduced corruption in Ukraine (Transparency International's Corruption Perception Index, World Bank's Control of Corruption Index).

8. Conflict resolution and transitional justice are processes that are often closely intertwined. Any conflict generates resentments, which last longer than the conflict itself. Hence the transitional justice policies that address such resentments should try to guarantee the sustainability of conflict resolution. In practise, however, the modality of postconflict justice may be strongly influenced by the modality of the peace-building process in a particular country. Specifically, when the solution to a conflict is negotiated, the system of meting out justice is often agreed upon by the former belligerents. On the other hand, when one side to the conflict prevails and eventually wins the war, victor's justice may ensue. In any case, postconflict justice is constrained by the principles of international law, such as the respect of human rights on the one hand, and the inadmissibility of amnesties in situations when the gravest international crimes are committed on the other.

9. This is not to say that violation of economic rights is the only problem generated by the conflict. Deaths, injuries and torture (among both servicemen and civilians) are certainly no less important. The violation of economic rights, however, affects a greater number of individuals overall.

REFERENCES

Addison, Tony. (2009). 'The Political Economy of the Transition from Authoritarianism.' In *Transitional Justice and Development: Making Connections*, edited by Pablo de Greiff and Roger Duthie, 110–41. New York: Social Science Research Council.

Anti Corruption Action Centre. (2016). Povernennya aktyviv koruptsioneriv: dva z polovynoyu roky bez rezzultatu. Retrieved from https://drive.google.com/file/d/0B4ui487xb0SpeGwzcFpSRUZGMU0/view.

Bachmann, Klaus, and Igor Lyubashenko, eds. (2014). *The Maidan Uprising, Separatism and Foreign Intervention: Ukraine's Complex Transition*. Frankfurt am Main: Peter Lang.

Beigbeder, Yves. (2011). *International Criminal Tribunals: Justice and Politics*. New York: Palgrave Macmillan.

De Greiff, Pablo. (2009). 'Articulating the Links between Transitional Justice and Development: Justice and Social Integration.' In *Transitional Justice and Development: Making Connections*, edited by Pablo de Greiff and Roger Duthie, 28–75. New York: Social Science Research Council.

Elster, Jon. (2004). *Closing the Books: Transitional Justice in Historical Perspective*. Cambridge: Cambridge University Press.

Freeman, Mark. (2009). *Necessary Evils: Amnesties and the Search for Justice.* New York: Cambridge University Press.

Galtung, Johan. (1969). 'Violence, Peace, and Peace Research.' *Journal of Peace Research* 6 (3): 167–91.

Independent Defence Anti-Corruption Committee. (2017). *Peretynayuchy mezhu: nelehalna torhivlya z okupovanym Donbasom, shcho pidryvaye oboronu.* Kyiv: Transparency International Ukraine.

Lyubashenko, Igor. (2017). *Transitional Justice in Post-Euromaidan Ukraine: Swimming Upstream.* Frankfurt am Main: Peter Lang.

McAuliffe, Padraig. (2017). *Transformative Transitional Justice and the Malleability of Post-Conflict States.* Cheltenham, Northampton: Edward Edgar.

Office of the United Nations High Commissioner for Human Rights. (2015). *Report on the Human Rights Situation in Ukraine 16 May to 15 August 2015.* Retrieved from http://www.ohchr.org/Documents/Countries/UA/11thOHCHRreportUkraine. pdf.

Olsen, Tricia D., Payne, Leigh A., and Reiter, Andrew G. (2010). *Transitional Justice in Balance: Comparing Processes, Weighing Efficacy.* Washington, DC: United States Institute of Peace.

Polukhina, Yuliya. (2016). Vlast' vzyala kontrabanda, *Novaya Gazeta.* Retrieved from https://www.novayagazeta.ru/articles/2016/10/24/70277-vlast-vzyala-kontrabanda.

Prosecutor General's Office of Ukraine. (2015). *Zlochyny proty Maydanu: rezultaty rozsliduvannya.* Retrieved from http://www.gp.gov.ua/ua/news. html?_m=publications&_c=view&_t=rec&id=165726.

Razumkov Centre. (2017). Sotsialno-politychna sytuatsiya v Ukrayini. Retrieved from: http://razumkov.org.ua/uploads/socio/2017_PRESS_Prezent_UA.pdf.

Sharp, Dustin N. (2015). 'Emancipating Transitional Justice from the Bonds of the Paradigmatic Transition.' *International Journal of Transitional Justice* 9(1): 150–69.

Yevseyev, Oleksandr. (2017). 'Pravosuddya na postkonfliktnyh terytoriyah (na prykladi Donetskoyi ta Luhanskoyi oblastey).' In *Bazove doslidzhennya iż zastosuvannya pravosuddya perehidnoho periodu v Ukrayini*, edited by Arkadiy Bushchenko and Mykola Hnatovskyy, 385–96. Kyiv: Rumes.

Chapter 7

Historical Justice, National Identity and Memory in Contemporary Ukraine

Adrian Mandzy

On the night of 21 November 2013, a small number of Ukrainians took to the capital and sought to express their dissatisfaction with the current president's refusal to sign a Treaty of Association with Europe. In the days and weeks that followed, the civil unrest grew and by 1 December eight hundred thousand people gathered (Bilash, 2016). Among the underlying demands put forth by the protestors was to end corruption and the restoration of justice. Justice for the individual, justice for the victims murdered by the current administration and justice for Ukraine. To emphasise the Ukrainian nature of the protests, activists carried the blue and yellow flag of Ukraine. Ruslana, a Ukrainian pop musician and winner of the 2004 Eurovision contest, joined the demonstrations and sang with the crowd the Ukrainian national anthem. In early December, unknown masked individuals attacked a still standing statute of Lenin in the capital. A few days later, the symbol of Ukraine's Soviet past crashed to the ground and in the place of the former effigy, a man waived a Ukrainian flag atop the now empty pedestal (Butenko and Gumuchian, 2013). On New Year's Eve 2013, hundreds of thousands of protestors, including the future president of Ukraine, Petro Poroshenko, joined Ruslana in singing the Ukrainian national anthem (Ruslana, 2013/2014). In the first seconds of 2014, upon the conclusion of the singing of the national anthem, Ruslana proclaimed the phrase 'Glory to Ukraine,' which was answered by the crowd with 'Glory to the Heroes.'

As the protests continued and the government's repressive measures failed to end the unrests, the violence continued to escalate. The protests moved beyond the capital and occurred throughout the country. Within the confines of the protests, which were now being shared via live posting on social media sites, the western media was trying to boil down the events into simple explanations. Russian and old Soviet-era 'experts' were often quoted, as were western correspondents stationed in Moscow. Although the Maijdan protests originally arose from about forty different groups coming together for their common good, the most radical and extreme activists gathered the most media attention (Shuster, 2014). Within the Russian media, the Right Sector, a small right-wing minority, was second most mentioned political group in 2014 (Kozlowska, 2014). To counter this perception, Ukrainians created the Babylon 13 project, a place where people could post films about the ongoing situation in Ukraine (#Babylon 13, 2013).

For millennia, Ukraine has been an area of conflict between people, ideas and geography. Outsiders who come into the region often misinterpreted what they see and seek to simplify their observations. As a result, much of what the popular western media presents about Ukraine is either outdated or simply wrong. Perhaps the greatest myth that continues to be popularised is that there are two Ukraines — a western and eastern one, a European and Soviet one, an Orthodox and a Greek Catholic one, a Polish/Austrian and a Russian one. Various historical maps with thick dividing lines or shaded areas are often attached to substantiate these claims.

Yet such an approach is too simplistic and does not take into account the evolution of the idea of Ukrainian-ness. After all, nations are constructs and the Ukrainian identity continues to evolve over both time and space. Such a process is not unique to Ukraine and has occurred in all national expressions of identity. For example, if one were to look at even well-established national frameworks, such as France, one would find significant differences in 1895, 1952 and 2015. Discussions of French national identity could include questions of religion (Protestants, Jews, atheists, and Muslims), territory (Alsace, Loraine, Algeria), race, and historical memory (Napoleon, the Paris Commune, Boulanger, and Petain). In this regard, Ukraine is no different. Unlike France, which has had a state structure to advocate for a national French identity, independent Ukrainian statehood in the modern world has been limited to a few years after the end of the First World War and the two and a half decades since 1991. Not surprisingly, the idea of what is Ukraine remains different, at times radically, to both the people who live in the Ukrainian state and those outside of its boundaries.

Following the events of 2014, which included Revolution of Dignity which toppled Victor Yanukovich, the former president of Ukraine, the Russian annexation of the Ukrainian Crimea and the subsequent war between the Ukrainian state and Russian nationalists in the Donbas and Luhansk *oblasts*, Ukraine entered a period of self-definition and reexamination. As independence occurred rather quickly in 1991, who or what defined Ukraine was never called into question by many of the republic's citizens. In 2014, that all changed and the citizens of Ukraine recognised that the survival of a Ukrainian state required their active participation. For the first time, hundreds of thousands volunteered in the cause of justice for Ukraine — first on the barricades protesting the government and later collecting supplies for the under-equipped Ukrainian army fighting against Russian nationalists. The self-realisation among the volunteers is best illustrated in the phrase 'Nobody but us' which later became a Ukrainian patriotic song performed by the band Tartak (Tartak, 2014). The song, dedicated to the Ukrainian defenders of the Donbass airport, has been viewed more than a million times and appears to encapsulate contemporary Ukraine. Yet, as with other national ideas, what constitutes Ukraine and Ukrainian continues to evolve.

One idea of Ukraine is the exclusive nationalistic approach. Beginning in the second half of the nineteenth century, in a climate of competition with other national movements, this idea of Ukraine for ethnically self-identified Ukrainians gained new momentum following the failure to defend the Ukrainian states that arose in the aftermath of the First World War. Both the Western Ukrainian National Republic (located in those provinces previously ruled by the Austrian-Hungarian Empire) and the Ukrainian National Republic (which originally included all the Ukrainian territories that were previously incorporated into the Russian Empire) were unable to survive repeated foreign invasions and internal challenges to their authority. The concept 'Ukraine for Ukrainians' gained favour with the Organisation of Ukrainian Nationalists (OUN) and expanded its ideological grounding through the writings of such authors as Dontsov (though the irony of having an ethnic Russian arguing for an exclusive Ukrainian state is not fully appreciated by some people) (Subtelny, 1991: 441–42). As Ukraine was torn between the Soviet and Nazi war machines, exclusive nationalists turned their frustrations of statelessness into the ethnic cleansing of Poles in Volhynia and were generally ambivalent to the plight of Jews during the Holocaust. Though by 1943 the OUN leadership began to move away from its totalitarian tendencies, many that see themselves as the inheritors of this historical legacy at times fall back upon an ethnically based definition.

For Ukrainian scholars working in the West during the Cold War, much attention was devoted towards proving that a Ukrainian nation existed. This underlying theme dominated both the academic activities of these scholars and their involvement with public education programmes. Perhaps one of the most enduring legacies of the political refugees and immigrants from Ukraine was the establishment of primary schools for Ukrainians living in the diasporas of western Europe, North America and Australia. Primarily the subjects taught in these institutions were Ukrainian language, geography, literature, culture and history. The history taught in these schools was based on Mykhailo Hrushevsky's model and followed a straight line — chronologically as well as thematically (Hrushevsky, 1952). Textbooks, such as *History of Ukraine: A Short Survey* published in 1971 by the Ukrainian Congress

Committee of America, continued Hrushevsky's scheme and added new materials to discuss events of the later twentieth century (K., 1971). The argument presented was that the indigenous people living in Ukraine built a state based in Kyiv, which was destroyed by the Mongols in 1240. A century later the Ukrainian Kingdom of Halych was captured by Poland. Since then Ukrainians sought to reestablish their statehood, first in the seventeenth century during the Cossack War of National Liberation, and then twice in the twentieth century during the Cossack War of Nagain in 1941. Though all of these attempts failed, the Ukrainian National Liberation struggle continued until 1991, when Ukraine became an independent state. The role of nonethnic Ukrainians living in Ukraine, as well as Ukrainian participation within the structures of other states, was not addressed in this narrative.

Yet this perception is not the only view of Ukraine. Ukrainians living within the Soviet Union were exposed to different ideas of what made Ukraine. At various times public displays of one's Ukrainian-ness could have serious consequences. Depending on the date of the display of Ukrainian nationalism, state authorities could and often did imprison or execute the nonconformists. State authorities were not the only means used to enforce the current views towards conscious ethnic minorities, as negative comments could be heard from neighbours, coworkers and shop workers about how individuals displayed their ethnic identity. Unlike visible minorities, who display physical characteristics different from the majority, the Soviet rhetoric stressed that ethnically conscious Ukrainians could become part of the Soviet majority if they simply stopped behaving as backwards country bumpkins.

The official policy of the Soviet Union was always to recognise the rights of ethnic groups within the USSR, but what was on paper did not always translate into policies. Unlike the previous Romanov monarchy, which denied the existence of the Ukrainian language, the Soviet Union continued to change its views of what made Ukraine depending on the political leadership in Moscow. In the 1920s, Ukrainian art, history, scholarship and literature were encouraged by the state and a cultural renaissance occurred (Shkandrij, 1992). By the 1930s this changed and being Ukrainian was perceived by the Soviet leadership to be a threat against its authority. The wide-scale destruction of Ukrainian intellectuals was followed by the *Holodomor*, an act of ideologically motivated mass murder during which four to six million Ukrainians were starved to death. Following the 1939 Soviet occupation of Poland, films like *Khmelnytsky* (1941) and the introduction of the *Order of Bohdan Khmelnytsky* (1943) acknowledged the existence of Ukrainian people. At that time, Ukrainians were understood to be in no way equal to Russians, but were relegated to the position of 'little people' within the 'great Russian' pantheon. By 1953, Soviet ideology officially interpreted the Treaty of Pereyalsav as 'the culmination of the Ukrainian aspirations for reunification with Moscow' (Basarb, 1982). By the 1960s, the political winds changed and new Ukrainian topics were explored. With the assent of Brezhnev the pendulum swung once more and being too ethnically Ukrainian carried serious negative repercussions. Though the scale of these repressions was significantly lower than in the 1930s, the memory of previous state-sponsored violence remained in the Ukrainian psyche. By the late 1980s, the winds of change allowed individuals to display signs of being ethnically Ukrainian without public censorship or imprisonment.

Many individuals embraced the change and accepted an elusive dream of a better future. Individuals involved with the struggle for independence could identify with the previous national liberation struggles and followed the Hrushevsky historical model of Ukrainian progression.[1] However, this was not a necessity. Unlike in the Baltic countries, where the renewed conflict between nationalists and Soviet authority became confrontational in the first few years of *perestroika*, the conflict in Ukraine was much less noticeable. Ukraine's *Rukh*, the largest opposition block, was still developing when the USSR imploded in 1991.[2]

Between 1989 and 1991, Ukrainian topics became extremely popular. Much attention was devoted to the 'white pages of history,' which were erased by the previous regime. Mass publications of repressed historians appeared, first in newspaper form and later in books. These works flooded kiosks and disappeared overnight. Many of the publications were simply reprints of older historical works, while others were written specifically to 'educate' the general population. One popular journal of the time, *Pam'iatky Ukrainy*, illustrates the interest in historical topics. Early issues of the journal focus on such benign subjects as Lenin monuments, but by 1989 previously forbidden topics, such as Ukrainian wooden churches in North America, appeared within the pages of the journal. Every new issue explored Ukrainian specific subjects and the journal sponsored expeditions searching for lost Cossack settlements. In 1990, *Pam'iatky Ukrainy* published an article on the commemoration of a World War I–era battlefield where a group of Ukrainian volunteer 'bourgeoisie nationalists' fought against Imperial Russia (Ratushnyj, 1991).

In the last years of the Soviet Union, different nationalities began to explore their historical heritage with increased vigour. For Ukraine, the Cossacks were always a source of identity, even during the most oppressive periods of Soviet rule, but by the late 1980s, a type of Cossack mania was sweeping the Republic. Cossack music, dress and folklore became the current fashion and popular cartoons like the 'Cossacks play Football' became a source of pride. For some, Cossacks came to symbolise the lost parts of Ukrainian history — the so-called white pages; others saw Cossacks as the embodiment for personal freedom and the ability to create something new. Much like long hair for the hippie and a punk's Mohawk, the Cossack *oseledets* hairstyle clearly identified the individual as someone who had rejected the establishment. For others, the Cossack Age reflected a simpler world, one yet unspoiled by the aftereffects of Chernobyl.

In August 1990, the first of many conferences/festivals were held to honour the five-hundred-year anniversary of the Cossack stronghold of the Zaporizhian Sich.[3] What had started as an academic debate quickly became a rally for future studies of the 'lost white pages of Ukrainian history.' Hundreds of people travelled to Zaporizhia for the three-day festival. In between the official events, people camped out along the banks of the Dnipro and the author personally witnessed how individuals from different towns first began to talk among themselves. Conversations began about the problems in their local communities and then came the realisation that they were not alone. When these individuals returned to their local communities, they were energised for further action.

By 1990, new monuments were constructed to Ukrainian national heroes throughout western Ukraine. In almost every village symbolic mounds began to appear that celebrated the armed struggle for independence. These often focused on conflicts from the twentieth century, but also included battles wage by the Cossacks against the Polish-Lithuanian Commonwealth. At the site of the 1649 Battle of Zboriv, for example, a small historical man-made knoll, which had been knocked down by the local Polish population in the 1930s, was rebuilt in a grand style. To make it difficult to knock down the new monument, both concrete and steel were used in the forty-meter high mound.

As new monuments were being constructed, older Soviet era monuments began to disappear throughout the more western provinces of Ukraine. So-called Liberator Tanks, which commemorated the Soviet liberation of settlements from the Nazis, dominated urban public spaces. These monuments included a piece of military hardware, such as a tank, tank destroyer or rocket launcher, which was placed on a pedestal at the entrance to a settlement. By the early 1990s, these objects were removed from their central locations, at times being sold for scrap or as in Ternopil,' repainted in pink and purple colours. Public images of Lenin also began to disappear in western and central Ukraine. Many offices that once prominently displayed bust or portraits of Lenin quickly replaced them with Taras Shevchenko.[4] Similarly, many statues of Lenin that dominated public spaces were replaced with Ukrainian figures, most often Shevchenko. The removal of the remaining Lenin statues occurred during and after the Revolution of 2014 and is commonly called 'Leninopad,' literally 'Lenin fall.'

Since the 1940s, Soviet Union had continued to preach about the brotherhood of three nations — Ukrainian, Russian and Belo-Russian, but in 1991 the Soviet Union had fragmented into fifteen independent states. Political independence brought new challenges for the population of the new Ukrainian state. The renewal of previously banned Ukrainian nationalist symbols as emblems of the new state, such as the trident and the blue and yellow flag, brought little satisfaction to many citizens — nationalists lamented that the attempts were rather feeble, while others reacted to the images as foreign and outside their intellectual context. For generations, Soviet citizens were taught by the Communist Party that these Ukrainian nationalist symbols were, in a word, 'evil.'

The elections of 1991 are rather telling about what people were thinking at the time. In December 1991, the citizens of former Ukrainian Soviet Socialist Republic overwhelmingly voted for independence. That same day, the same citizens who wanted independence voted in the first president of Ukraine — the former communist leader — and not the nationalist and democratic opponents. Unlike the Baltics, Moldova or the Caucasus states, where nationalists won the elections, the highest seat in the new country went to Leonid Kravchuk.

Kravchuk, who was once in charge of party ideology, was faced with almost insurmountable challenges — creating a new infrastructure necessary to administer a new state, shifting the economic foundations of the state from a command economy to capitalism and creating a new national identity. As a centrist, Kravchuk sought to 'use nationalism to build the state' and at the same time 'recognized Ukraine as a multinational country' (D'anieri et al., 1999: 60). Kravchuk's ratings plummeted as the economy collapsed and he was not reelected. His successor, President Kuchma, curtailed the state sponsored promotion of the Ukrainian language and historical national Ukrainian culture. In its place, the new president cultivated the idea that Ukraine was a 'bridge' between Russia and the West (Nahaylo, 1999: 474).

Though Kuchma was despised by many Ukrainians, his ideas did not translate into Ukraine becoming reintegrated into the Russian fold. Having Ukraine become a client state of Moscow would have diminished Kuchma's position as president, and as a result, the president's policies focused on playing off the United States and Russia. The resulting crony capitalism allowed government officials to acquire large amounts of capital, which they quickly converted for their own use (Yekelchyk, 2007: 200).

In 1999, Viacheslav Chornovil, one-time presidential candidate and the leader of the nationalist opposition was killed in a car crash under dubious circumstances. In 1991, Chornovil had stood for the post of president and placed second among the six candidates. Debates about the possibility that Chornovil's death was not an accident but a politically motivated liquidation of Rukh's candidate for president continued for some years, and many still believe he was assassinated (Harasymiw et al., 2015).

Chornovil was a political realist and continually argued that once Ukraine gained its independence and was able to maintain it for a few years, it would never become reunified with Moscow. His view was that once separation was complete, Ukraine's path would diverge from Russia and each would go their own separate way. Furthermore, according to Chornovil, children growing up in the new state would have little in common with their northern neighbour. Chornovil's views were considered to be both dangerous and treasonous by those who sought to bring the parochial Ukrainians into the Great Russian fold.

It was within the environment of the Kuchma presidency that a second concept of Ukraine began to take hold — that Ukraine is not Russia. Such a concept of Ukraine is not new and has been articulated by both outsiders, such as Voltaire, and local authors such as Kostomarov since the nineteenth century (Prymak, 2012; Sichynsky, 1953). Yet by the late twentieth century, such a statement was often encountered from even the most pro-Moscow Ukrainian citizens who felt disenchanted after spending time in Russia (Kuprianova, 2016). This concept that Ukraine is not like Russia is a well-established cornerstone of Ukrainian nationalist thought, but under Kuchma, this idea that 'we are not them' began to slowly emerge as a commonly accepted view. Kuchma later published a book with the title *Ukraine — Not Russia* (Kuchma, 2003). For the generation coming of age, traditional 'western' Ukrainian nationalism is still perceived as foreign, as demonstrated by the low percentage of votes gathered by the nationalist parties, but for the majority of the citizens, what defines Ukrainian remained unclear.

Although the 2004 Orange Revolution failed to achieve many of its goals, the overwhelming majority of its activists preached the inclusive nature of Ukraine during the winter demonstrations. This view of Ukraine as a home to all ethnic groups remained relatively untarnished, even as the politicians connected with the events of 2004 fell out of favour. In 2013, the inclusive nature of Ukraine was clearly evident by the first call for demonstrations on Maidan by an Afghan-born immigrant, Mustafa Nayyem. The tragic first death of the Heavenly Hundred, was an ethnic Georgian.[5] Unlike the 1991-era demonstrations for Ukrainian Independence, those marching for a regime change in 2013 and 2014 came from all over the Ukraine. Speeches were given in Ukrainian as well as in Russian and Facebook postings appeared in both languages. In the final hours of Yanukovych's presidency, demonstrations and barricades stood throughout the country, and not just its western or central regions. Indeed, demonstrations in Donbass against the regime, the central power base of Yanukovych's party, graphically illustrated the insolvency of this regime. In the euphoria immediately following the success of Revolution of Dignity, thousands of people in Donbass came out with blue and yellow flags to celebrate the unity of Ukraine.[6]

For many Russian speakers, the question of Ukraine was never perceived as a threat to their privileged status. After all, for generations people were taught of the Great Russian accomplishments and the legal recognition of Russian as equal to Ukrainian translated that one did not need to bother with Ukrainian. Many Ukrainians argued that language is the cornerstone of identity and to be a Ukrainian, one must not use a foreign tongue. In a recent article, which was reposted a multitude of times on social media, the well-known Ukrainian writer and poet Serhij Zhadan summarised the arguments of Russian speaking Ukrainian patriots (Zhdan, 2016). In his view, Russian speaking Ukrainian patriots have contributed highly to Ukrainian society and many have laid down their lives in the war with Russia. By rejecting Russian speakers, Zhadan argues, Ukrainians are doing themselves a disservice, and give 'our accomplishments to the Russians' (Zhdan, 2016). Other ethnic Russians have fled Putin's regime and have tried to settle in Ukraine (Frolov, 2015).

At the beginning of the twenty-first century, many individuals no longer argue for a culturally monolithic state. Such views were commonplace in the nineteenth century, but immigration, and the recognition of the evils committed in the name of cultural imperialism and ethnic cleansing has led to the de facto recognition of multiculturalism as a viable alternative. States no longer need to be culturally or linguistically homogenous to be different from each other. For example, Germany and Austria both use the same language, but are separate states. The same argument could be made from French-speaking Swiss.

Modern Ukraine is no different and many people see the country as a counter-balance to Russia. The idea of Kyiv as a counter-balance to Moscow is not new and resurfaces periodically throughout the twentieth century. The first manifestation became a political reality when the Bolsheviks seized power at the end of 1917. Ukrainian nationalists did not recognise the authority of Lenin and established their own state, the Ukrainian National Republic. Recognising that many different nationalities reside within the territory of the newly created Ukrainian state, an attempt was made to embrace all citizens. These ideas were strongly espoused in the writing and actions of Volodymyr Vynnychenko (Vynnychenko, 1920). In the 1920s, Ukraine's unique nature as a counter-weight to Moscow is commonly noted among both the Soviet party members and the intellectuals. After World War II, the idea of counter-balance was circulated among many members of the Ukrainian Human Rights Helsinki Group.

The historical interpretation of events plays a critical role in defining how nationalists and emerging nationally conscious citizens view themselves. This philosophy in part predates the common use of term Ukraine and anchors itself to the idea of the Kyivan State. The overwhelming majority of nationally conscious Ukrainians see the Kyiv state as the foundation of modern Ukraine. Moreover, Moscow, as is continually pointed out on various postings of social media, was a peripheral settlement that grew and developed under almost three hundred years of Mongol patronage. The cornerstone to this theory is that the Muscovites are a Mongolian civilisation that acquired some outward trappings of the Kyivan State, such as the Orthodox Church, but they are not really European. Often the term used to describe the Russians is Eurasian. 'Eurasianism, the idea that Russia was neither Europe nor Asia but a world unto itself' is found in much of the writings of the Russian-born American historian George Vernadsky (Halperin, 1982; 1987). This Eurasian idea is also currently promoted in the early twenty-first century by the Russian neofascist Alexandr Dugin (Dugin, 2017). The majority of Ukrainian historians argue that Rus' Ukraine, based on its eleventh- and twelfth-century ties to Central and Western Europe, is part of Europe.

The radical Ukrainian nationalist argument takes this perception and advances it a step further. Based on social media posting, many nationalists recognise the Mongolian influence in Moscow and call into question the use of the term Russia. Nationalists argue on social media that 'Moscow stole the name Rus' from us and we need to call them by their correct name — Muscovite Mongols' (Dashkevych, 2014). Ukraine, as is argued by various radical nationalists on social media pages, is the true inheritor of the Kyivan tradition and is in the fight against the Asian Mongols. Ukrainian nationalist volunteers fighting in the east have often adopted signs and symbols of the Kyivan state. Both the eleventh and the twenty-fifth Territorial Defense Battalions are referred to as Kyivan Rus' (Dunnett, 2014).

Yet what these two views of 'Ukrainian-ness' have in common is that Ukraine is a unique country with its own culture, heritage, traditions and language. As such, both perceptions would argue that Ukraine is the homeland that needs to be loved and protected. Self-identifying Ukrainians also recognise that there are those people who Ukraine as nothing more than a means to an end. The claim is often levelled that these individuals recognise the existence of Ukraine but exploit it for personal benefit. This idea that some individuals use the idea of 'Ukraine for personal profit' was periodically levelled at various leaders of the Ukrainian diaspora throughout the twentieth century, but it became a much wider spread concept when the Ukrainian state was being reestablished in the 1990s. At that time, former Soviet elites, who for years had attacked 'bourgeoisie Ukrainian nationalism' began to 'wrap themselves in Ukrainian national symbols and shout how Ukrainian they were' (Pravocud, 2017). This perception is still commonly encountered on social media. One commonly repeated image shows a number of political opponents of President Poroshenko wearing embroidered shirts under the heading of 'Not everyone, who wears an embroidered shirt, loves Ukraine. Very often — it's camouflage.'

Throughout the 1990s, as monumental fortunes were being made in the privatisation of former state industries, it was commonly believed that many of the newly rich exploited the system for personal enhancement, rather than use their position in authority to the benefit of society as a whole. As the rise of this new class of rich Ukrainians occurred at a time when the rest of the population could barely make ends meet, it resurrected the well-rehearsed Soviet-era ideological claims of 'bourgeoisie Ukrainian nationalist class exploitation,' as well as drew the ire of older Ukrainian nationalists who had previously worked in poverty and suffered for the cause of building a better future. This perception of 'fake patriots,' who capitalising on their Ukrainian authority to increase their wealth, legally or more often than not, illegally, gained further traction when it became clear that being elected as a deputy of the National Parliament provided immunity from prosecution. Often this type of behaviour is referred to by nationalists as 'pseudo-nationalism' (Illienko, 2009). Similarly, this perception was applied to individuals sought to become judges, as those within this position were also immune from prosecution. Whether elected representative, businessman or bureaucrat, the perception was that such flag waving individuals use their authority to increase their wealth by whatever means possible at the expense of the nation. For the last twenty years, this view of Ukraine has been applied not only to the former President Yanukovych, but also to most nationally well-known politicians. Such claims continue to be levelled at the equally powerful oligarchs, as well as the thousands of corrupt judges, bureaucrats, military officers, elective officials, taxmen and policemen who made their fortunes from the backs of the Ukrainian people. Such activity often is reported in the press (Holovh'ov, 2012). The idea of the state existing for the personal benefit of an individual is not a new concept nor is it limited to a specific political state, but it is a commonly held belief in Ukraine.

The fourth concept of Ukraine is that it is not a sovereign state and Ukrainians are not a nation. This idea was prominent in the dreams of various imperialistic powers over the course of the last few centuries, but many will argue that the only external threat the Ukrainian state is currently facing comes from Moscow. This point of view appears to be expressed in the actions of President Putin, who as commander in chief of the Russian military, is on record ordering the 'little green men' to capture of the Crimean Peninsula (Kondrachev, 2014). This ongoing violation Ukraine's sovereignty and territorial integrity is understood by the Ukrainian president that 'Putin hates Ukraine' (Bonner, 2017).

As a point of clarification, this view of Ukraine does not deny the existence of a unique Ukrainian ethnicity. Unlike the argument put forward in the nineteenth century by those ruling territories inhabited by ethnic Ukrainians, which stated quite clearly that Ukrainians were not a separate ethnicity and no Ukrainian language existed, this new perception of Ukraine clearly recognises Ukrainians as an ethnic group. This view of Ukraine can trace its origins to Lenin's Soviet ideology, who, according to Ivan Dzyuba, argued for Ukrainian culture not to be submerged in Russian (Dzyuba, 1974). Beginning in the 1930s and continuing in the decades that followed, the Soviet Union continuously highlighted the idea of 'brotherly' nations. Ukrainians, Belo-Russians and Russians were brothers, but with Russians clearly being the most senior. This myth, which can trace its origins to the 1930s and continued to be proclaimed through the end of the USSR, was propagated in academia, political parades, public monuments and television. Mr. Putin is on record stating that Russians and Ukrainians are in fact brothers, a claim that many Ukrainians now reject (*Russia Today*, 2015).

What is critical to this view is that Ukraine is and has never been a real political system. According to this perception, attempts to establish a Ukrainian state are always facilitated by foreign powers and occur in times of Russian weakness. Thus, Hetman Mazeppa's 'betrayal' of the Russian Tsar during the Great Northern War and the German creation and recognition of a Ukrainian Republic at the 1918 Treaty of Brest-Litovsk were both failed attempts to destabilise 'Great Russia.' Lenin's reaction to Ukrainian independence in the aftermath of World War I was to launch numerous invasions of Ukraine to forcefully bring this territory within his sphere of control (Subtelny, 1991: 376). Ukraine's independence in 1991, which occurred during what Mr. Putin referred to as the 'the greatest geopolitical catastrophe of the century' is nothing more than yet another attempt to take away from Russia (Associated Press, 2005). Not surprisingly, for Mr. Putin, the Russian capture of the Crimea is looked at as a 'restoration of historical justice' (Sekretarev and Isachenkov, 2014).

Much of the support for this idea comes from individuals who feel a loss of 'Russian privilege.' Like the 'white privilege' noted in Western societies, 'Russian privilege' refers to the perceived innumerable advantages awarded to individuals who adopted the Russian language and began to view themselves as Russians. During the eighteenth century, for example, Cossacks elites could join the Russian nobility if they left behind their local customs and embraced Great Russian society. In the late nineteenth and twentieth centuries, Ukrainian peasants who moved to the cities often began to speak Russian to separate themselves from rural populations. These new urban dwellers often spoke Russian very poorly and often the resulting system of communication was a hybrid between the two languages. Though all education was free in the Soviet Union, Russian language schools dominated, and pupils were encouraged to read, write and think in Russian. Russian was perceived to be the language of science and international discourse and academic success depended mastery of the Russian language.

The unexpected Soviet collapse in 1991 and the half-hearted Ukrainianisation policies enacted in the early 1990s did little to change popular attitudes of the people who benefited from 'Russian privilege' and, if anything, resulted in a knee-jerk reaction against expressions of ethnic Ukrainian culture. Anti-Ukrainian hate literature published in Russia and imported into Ukraine, usually in the form of cheap novels, continued to reinforce Soviet-era perceptions of Russian dominance. One such series, *Ukraine — Field of Battle*, first appeared in 2009 and depicted the rise of NovoRossia (Tsenzor, 2009).

Though the *Ukraine — Field of Battle* series was initially perceived by many Ukrainians as the ravings of small minority, a perception of the loss of 'Russian privilege' played a significant role in Ukrainian politics since 1991. After Independence, the old elite adopted the symbols of Ukraine — the blue and yellow flag, trident, anthem, but no effort was made to ensure the prominence of Ukrainian language or culture. Kravchuk's half-hearted attempts to Ukrainise the country centred on constructing a national myth and establishing Ukrainian as the state language. His policies failed to impress those who envisioned a Ukrainisation policy on the level implemented by Shelest in the 1920s and petrified the revived Moscow-centred Communist Party. According to Vasyl' Kreman, the deputy head of the presidential administration under Kuchma, Kravchyk's linguistic Ukrainianisation policies 'resulted in considerable alienation' and were 'responsible . . . for the abrupt decline in the prestige of the idea of the nation-state' (D'anieri et al., 1999: 61). Similarly, Yanukovych exploited the feelings of the loss of Russian privilege and alienated many Ukrainians when he instigated laws to protect the Russian language. Since Ukrainian language television, radio and publications were always overshadowed by works in the Russian language, many Ukrainian speakers believed that the policies of Yanukovych signalled a state-sponsored measure that would reduce even further the presence of the Ukrainian language in their daily lives.

What is noteworthy is that these four concepts of Ukraine are not geographically determinant. There are some, even within the western-most city of L'viv, that treat Ukraine as nothing more than an entity from which to fill their overflowing pockets. The economic breakdown of the early 1990s made many people take bribes to feed their families but now some judges own more property in the city than did the most wealthy of noblemen at the height of their power. Similarly, the radical nationalist view espoused by Svoboda and Right Sector is now found throughout Ukraine. The ranks of the volunteer battalions, such as the ultra-right wing nationalist Azov battalion, are filled by people born in the eastern part of the country and not the western part. The overwhelming majority of these volunteers speak Russian, not Ukrainian.

They often use the image of Stepan Bandera and have universally adopted the black and red flag of the OUN as their own banner.[7] Yet as stated by Oleh Leliakyn, a Russian-speaking active member of the 18th Self Defense Company, before he came to Maidan, 'To my embarrassment, I didn't really know that much about Shukhevych (the Supreme Military Commander of the Ukrainian Partisan Army, which was the military wing of the OUN) or Bandera was or what he stood. So calling me a Banderite is ridiculous at least' (#Babylon 13, 2014).

The more Russian news media referred to the people demonstrating on the Maidan as 'Banderites,' the more positively acceptable the term became. Nationalists from the Svoboda Party and the Right Sector vehemently challenged claims of anti-Semitism, and given that the oligarch, Ihor Kolomoiski, who supported the Right Sector himself was Jewish, the term 'Zhydobandera' became popular a term on social media (Esch, 2015: 12). Red and black t-shirts appeared with the same phrase and interwove the Jewish Star of David with the Ukrainian trident.

As witnessed in the events of 2014, a great majority of Ukrainian citizens actively participated in creating a new Ukrainian future. This new Ukraine arose to challenge the existing political corruption and along the way is creating a new inclusive historical identity. Like many postcolonial states, the idea of historical justice has gained a new following in Ukraine. Since the events of 2014, the majority of Ukrainians now believe that previous Soviet state intentionally downplayed the accomplishments of the local inhabitants and sought to erase acts of violence and genocide perpetuated by the ruling authorities.

In 2014, Volodymyr Viatrovych became the Director of the Ukrainian Institute of National Memory. Upon his appointment, Viatrovych stated that recent events in Ukraine, in particular the criminal use of arms against peaceful protesters, is a result of the fact that in the past twenty-three years Ukraine did not analyse its history (Press Center, 2014). Further, he continues to say that 'We will show people what happens in societies where the regime neglects human rights. I am convinced that a proactive position of civil society will prevent the repetition of crimes in the future.' Though many have called Viatrovych an extreme nationalist, in 2016, Viatrovych stated in a television debate that the Jewish Holocaust is Ukrainian History (Shuster Live, 2016).

The calls for historical justice continue to be echoed on the local level as well. In the western city of L'viv, for example, 'Dolia' (Fate), focuses on the excavation, identification and public reburial of those killed in the twentieth century (Dolia, 2016). The process of providing a public space for the previously marginalised victims does more than just gives them a physical presence in the current landscape — it destroys the veil of silence that has shrouded them for decades and to a degree, delivers a small measure of justice. Not everyone supports the attempts to readdress historical injustices and in the east central city of Poltava, vandals have repeatedly attacked the newly constructed monument to the Ukrainian Hetman Ivan Mazepa (Ukrinform, 2016). In the southern Ukrainian city of Odesa, social justice activists, who recently restored a forgotten Cossack cemetery, seek to rebalance the historical narrative by demonstrating that Ukrainians lived in this location before Russian troops came to Odesa (*Ukrainian Times*, 2016).

A recently published work, *Historical Justice and Memory*, underscores the current global trend in acknowledging and readdressing historical wrongs (Neumann and Thompson, 2015). For the citizens of Ukraine, there is a critical need to embrace this process for the country has endured much wrongdoing over the last century. The recognition of such crimes as genocide, the systematic persecutions of religious and ethnic groups by one or more states, colonisation and the oppression of and the discrimination against minorities is currently ongoing in Ukraine, as the social preconditions for this occurrence were set in motion by the 2014 Revolution of Dignity. Indeed, justice for the victims — including those who were killed, tortured, raped, forced from their homes, and persecuted by the various previous regimes — is now a major point of consciousness among the general population.

NOTES

1. Mykhailo Hrushevsky argued that Kyivan state 'did no pass into the Volodimir-Moscow Period but passed into the Galician-Volhynian Period of the 13th century and later to the Lithuanian-Polish Period of the 14th–16th centuries.' The resulting model of Ukrainian history that emerges is Kyiv-Halych-Lithuania—Polish-Lithuanian Commonwealth—the Cossack Hetmanate—Ukrainian National Republic. M. Hrushevsky, *The Traditional Scheme of 'Russian' History and the Problem of a Rational Organization of the History of the Eastern Slavs. The Annals of the Ukrainian Academy of Arts and Sciences in the United States*, 2, 1952, p. 357; see also M. Hrushevsky, *A History of Ukraine*, New Haven, CT: Yale University Press, 1941.

2. *Rukh* was a popular front that brought together intellectuals, blue-collar workers, environmentalists, and Ukrainian patriots. Formed in 1989 as the People's Movement of Ukraine for Reconstruction, the movement transformed into a political party in 1990. After independence, *Rukh* served as an umbrella organisation. By the beginning of the twenty-first century, changes in leadership and continuous fragmentation of the party resulted in it being eclipsed by other organisations.

3. The Zaporizhian *Sich* was the cradle of the Ukrainian Cossack movement. Located on the remote but strategically placed island of Mala Khortytsia below the Dnipro rapids, the early Cossack leader Baida Vyshnevetsky, *starosta* of Kaniv, built

a fort to reduce Tatar raids and used it as a base from which to attack the Ottomans. The *Sich* was self-governing and did not recognise any foreign authority.

4. Taras Shevchenko (1812–1861) is perhaps the best-known Ukrainian author and artist. Born a serf, he spent most of his life in exile for his political commentary about the exploitation of Ukraine by the Russian ruling classes. His works romanticise the Cossacks and underline the unique nature of Ukraine.

5. The term Heavenly Hundred refers to the people killed by Ukrainian state security services in the fall of 2013 and the winter of 2014. Included in the Heavenly Hundred are both the individuals who were actively protesting the government and those who disappeared during the night.

6. The Revolution of Dignity refers to the street protests, both in the capital and regional centres, that led to the collapse of Yanukovych's presidency.

7. Stepan Bandera (1909–1959) remains a controversial figure in Ukrainian history. An active nationalist, he joined the Organization of Ukrainian Nationalists (OUN) in 1929 and quickly rose within its ranks. Sentenced to life imprisonment in 1934 for terrorism against the Polish state, he was released from prison in 1939. Following a split with the OUN, he headed his faction, commonly known as the OUN-B, or Banderites. Like many radical nationalists of the time, Bandera had strong dictatorial leanings. After his release from Polish prison, he began working with German authorities and in 1941 was involved the 30 June 1941 Proclamation of Ukrainian Independence. For his refusal to rescind the 30 June Proclamation, he was arrested by the Nazi and spent his time in prisons and concentration camps. While Bandera was in prison, the OUN carried out the ethnic cleansing of Poles in Volhynia. After 1945, he was in Germany and was assassinated by a Soviet agent.

While a growing number of people in Ukraine look to Bandera as an uncorrupted symbol of those who stood up to Soviet aggression, the Soviet official policy was that Bandera, much like Symon Petlura or Ivan Mazepa earlier, personified the ultimate evil—subjects that rebelled against Moscow. Unlike many Poles, who hold Bandera personally responsible for the wide scale murder of Polish citizens, the Russian perspective focuses not on his cooperation with the Nazis, but rather that Bandera fought against Soviet authority.

REFERENCES

Associated Press. (2005). 'Putin: Soviet Collapse a "Genuine Tragedy."' 25 April. Retrieved from http://www.nbcnews.com/id/7632057/ns/world_news/t/putin-soviet-collapse-genuine-tragedy/.

#Babylon 13. (2013). 'Cinema of Civil Society.' Retrieved from https://www.youtube.com/user/babylon13ua.

#Babylon 13. (2014). *Heaven's Hundred: The Winter That Changed Us All.* 1+1 Studio, Babylon 13 Film Project. Retrieved from https://www.youtube.com/watch?v=G_OlqRn2Eug.

Basarb, John. (1982). *Pereiaslav 1654: A Historiographical Study.* Edmonton: Canadian Institute of Ukrainian Studies.

Bilash, Borislaw. (2016). 'Euromaidan Protests — The Revolution of Dignity.' Retrieved from http://euromaidanpress.com/2016/02/20/the-story-of-ukraine-starting-from-euromaidan/2/#arvlbdata.

Bonner, Brian. (2017). 'Poroshenko: "Putin Hates Ukraine Deeply and Sincerely."' *Kyiv Post*, 17 February. Retrieved from https://www.kyivpost.com/ukraine-politics/poroshenko-putin-hates-ukraine-deeply-sincerely.html.

Butenko, Victoria, and Gumuchian, Marie-Louise. (2013). 'Lenin Statue Toppled.' Retrieved from http://www.cnn.com/2013/12/08/world/europe/ukraine-protests/.

Dashkevych, Iaroslav. (2014). 'Kak Moskoviya ukrala istoriyu Kievskoy Rusi Ukrainy.' 20 September. Retrieved from http://uainfo.org/blognews/398664-kak-moskoviya-ukrala-istoriyu-kievskoy-rusi-ukrainy-doklad-doktora-istoricheskih-nauk.html.

D'anieri, Pail, Kravchuk, Robert, and Kuzio, Taras, (1999). *Politics and Society in Ukraine*, Boulder, CO: Westview Press.

Dolia. (2016). 'Napriamky diial'nosti KP LOR "Dolia."' Retrieved from http://dolya.lviv.ua/napryamky-diyalnosti-kr-lor-dolya/.

Dugin, Alexander. (2017). *Foundations of Geopolitics: The Geopolitical Future of Russia.* English translation. Independent publisher.

Dunnett, Chris. (2014). 'Ukraine's "Battalions" Armies, Explained.' *Hromadske International.* Retrieved from https://medium.com/@Hromadske/ukraines-shadow-army-b04d7a683493#.2ixv2ysmu.

Dzyuba, Ivan. (1974). *Internationalism or Russification?* New York: Pathfinder Press.

Esch, Christian. (2015). '"Banderites" vs. "New Russia": The Battle Field of History in the Ukraine Conflict.' Reuters Institute Fellowship Paper, University of Oxford. Retrieved from http://reutersinstitute.politics.ox.ac.uk/sites/default/files/research/files/Banderites%2520vs%2520New%2520Russia%2520The%2520Battlefield%2520of%2520History%2520in%2520the%2520Ukraine%2520Conflict.pdf

Frolov, Grigory. (2015). 'Russian Refugees in Ukraine: The Broken Hopes.' *Huffington Post.* Retrieved from http://www.huffingtonpost.com/grigory-frolov/russian-refugees-in-ukraine_b_9243032.html.

Halperin, Charles. (1982). 'George Vernadsky, Eurasianism, the Mongols, and Russia.' *Slavic Review* 41(3): 477–93.

Halperin, Charles. (1987). *Russian and the Golden Horde: The Mongol Impact on Medieval Russian History.* Bloomington: Indiana University Press.

Harasymiw, Bohdan, Koshelivets, Ivan and Senkus, Roman. (2015). *Chornovil, Viacheslav.* Internet Encyclopedia of Ukraine, Canadian Institute of Ukrainian Studies at the University of Alberta. Retrieved from http://www.encyclopediaofukraine.com/display.asp?linkpath=pages%5CC%5CH%5CChornovilViacheslav.htm.

Holovh'ov, Serhiy. (2012). 'Havishcho idut' v mery?' *Ukrains'ka Pravda.* 24 February 2012. Retrieved from https://www.pravda.com.ua/articles/2012/02/24/6959405/.

Hrushevsky, Mykhailo. (1941). *A History of Ukraine.* New Haven, CT: Yale University Press.

Hrushevsky, Mykhailo (1952). 'The Traditional Scheme of "Russian" History and the Problem of a Rational Organization of the Eastern Slavs.' *Annals of the Ukrainian Academy of Arts and Sciences in the United States* 2: 355–64.

Illienko, Andrij. (2009). Nationalism and Pseudo-Nationalism. *Svoboda.* 24 December 2009. Retrieved from http://svoboda.org.ua/news/articles/00083141/.

K., I. (1971). *Istoria Ukrainy; Korotkyj Ohliad.* New York: Ukrainian Congressional Committee of America, Shkil'na Rada.

Kondrachev, Andrey. (2014). 'Crimea: The Way Home.' Retrieved from https://www.youtube.com/watch?v=c8nMhCMphYU.

Kozlowska, Hanna. (2014). 'The Fascists Are Coming, the Fascists Are Coming.' *Foreign Policy.* Retrieved from https://foreignpolicy.com/2014/06/02/the-fascists-are-coming-the-fascists-are-coming/.

Kuchma, Leonid. (2003). *Ukraina—ne Roccya.* Moscow: Vremya.

Kuprianova, Inna. (2016). 'Donbass Refugees Leave Russia for Home.' *Deutsche Welle.* Retrieved from http://www.dw.com/en/donbass-refugees-leave-russia-for-home/a-18996846.

Nahaylo, Bohdan. (1999). *The Ukrainian Resurgence.* Toronto: University of Toronto Press.

Neumann, Klaus, and Thompson, Janna. (2015). *Historical Justice and Memory.* Madison: University of Wisconsin Press.

Pravocud, Volodymyr. (2017). Author's interview of Volodymyr Pravocud (Shturm), Commander of the 19th Self-Defense Company of Maidan during the Revolution of Dignity, 26 June 2017.

Press Center. (2014). 'The New Director of the Ukrainian National Memory Institute: Historical Memory Policy Is a Safeguard against Repeating the Crimes of the Past. Tsentr Doslidzhen' Vyzvol'noho Rukhu.' Retrieved from http://www.cdvr.org.ua/content/new-director-ukrainian-national-memory-institute-historical-memory-policy-safeguard-against-repeating-crimes-past.

Prymak, Thomas M. (2012). 'Voltaire on Mazepa and Early Eighteenth-Century Ukraine,' *Canadian Journal of History* 47: 259–83.

Ruslana. (2013/2014). 'EuroMaidan Ukrainian National Anthem — New Year's Eve 2013/2014.' Retrieved from https://www.youtube.com/watch?v=0GZgjrp23t4.

Russia Today. (2015). 'Russians and Ukrainians not brothers,' Ukrainian President claims. *RT.* Retrieved from https://www.rt.com/news/313017-ukrainians-russians-brothers-poroshenko/.

Ratushnyj, Roman. (1991). 'My neznyshchenni.' *Pam'iatky Ukrainy* (2) April: 42–44.

Sekretarev, Ivan, and Isachenkov, Vladimir. (2014). 'Putin Hails "Return" of Crimea in Sevastopol.' *The Times of Israel.* 9 May. Retrieved from https://www.timesofisrael.com/putin-hails-return-of-crimea-in-sevastopol/.

Shkandrij, Myroslav. (1992). *Modernists, Marxists, and the Nation: The Ukrainian Literary Discussion of the 1920s.* Edmonton: Canadian Institute of Ukrainian Studies Press.

Shuster Live. (2016). 'Kyiv, 30 September.' Retrieved from https://www.youtube.com/watch?v=-wXU6IXpBxQ

Shuster, Simon. (2014). 'Exclusive: Leader of Far-Right Ukrainian Militant Group Talks Revolution with TIME.' Retrieved from http://time.com/4493/ukraine-dmitri-yarosh-kiev/.

Sichynsky, Volodymyr, ed. (1953). *Ukraine in Foreign Comments and Descriptions from the 6th to the 20th Centuries.* New York: Ukrainian Congress Committee.

Subtelny, Orest. (1991). *Ukraine, A History.* Toronto: University of Toronto Press.

Tartak. (2014). Retrieved from https://www.youtube.com/watch?v=dVDq9uQaVLY.

Tsenzor. (2009). 'Zakony voyny': rossiyanye opublikovali plan 'navyedyeniya poryadka i podderzhaniya demokratiy' v Ukrainye. Retrieved from http://censor.net.ua/photo_news/156370/zakony_voyiny_rossiyane_opublikovali_plan_navedeniya_poryadka_i_podderjaniya_demokratii_v_ukraine.

Ukrainian Times. (2016). 'Cossak Graveyard: Cossack cemetery restored in Odesa.' Retrieved from https://www.youtube.com/watch?v=mAKt3onf9k4.

Ukrinform. (2016). 'Monument of Hetman Ivan Mazepa Vandalized in Poltava Today.' *Ukrinform*, 2 June. Retrieved from https://www.ukrinform.net/rubric-crime/2027676-monument-to-hetman-ivan-mazepa-vandalized-in-poltava-today.html.

Vynnychenko, Volodymyr. (1920). *Vidrodzhennia natsii.* Kyiv-Vienna: Dzvin.

Yekelchyk, Serhy. (2007). *Ukraine, Birth of a Modern Nation.* Oxford: Oxford University Press.

Zhdan, Sergiy. (2016). 'Ia vylitav z donetskoho aeroportu 3 travnia.' *Tsenzor.net.* Retrieved from https://m.censor.net.ua/resonance/378396/sergyi_jadan_ya_viltav_z_donetskogo_aeroportu_3_travnya_ltak_na_kiv_buv_zabitiyi_jurnalstami_ta_bznesmenami.

Chapter 8

Romanian Transitional Criminal Justice: The Story of Four Trials and a Failure

Cătălin-Nicolae Constantinescu

PRELIMINARY REMARKS CONCERNING THE CONCEPT OF TRANSITIONAL JUSTICE

Transitional justice has developed to be an interdisciplinary field of study, as a result of the appearance of more efficient means of violence during the twentieth and twenty-first centuries (Brewer, Mitchell and Leavey, 2013). Even though it is still connected to the traditional legal definitions of justice, it has grown beyond them in order to encompass various postconflict or post-totalitarian means of *reconciliation*. To properly understand transitional justice, it is, then, crucial to bear in mind the aspect of it which requires the achievement of reconciliation. This aspect is not present, or considered relevant, in most traditional conceptualisations of criminal justice (retribution, deterrence, reformation of the offender, etc.). It is only characteristic of the most recent philosophical view of criminal justice, which is often called 'restorative justice.' The enlargement of the notions included in the concept of transitional justice arose from a need, recognised by twentieth century societies, to deal with abuses and injustices committed by state agents or various official, semi-official, or entirely unofficial 'regime structures' in the recent past.

The Romanian communist regime lasted from 30 December 1947 until 22 December 1989, when Nicolae and Elena Ceauşescu were arrested by the new regime after an attempt to flee the country. Between 1947 and 1964, the political opponents, identified by the agents of *Securitate* (Romanian political police) and condemned in court during showtrials, had been imprisoned in political prisons and labour camps (Stan, 2010). During this period, there were 318 centres in Romania that made up a Romanian Gulag (Rusan, 2007). At this book's publication, there is still no official statistic in Romania of all the former political prisoners and deportees. As many important files have been lost forever due to the revolution, or were destroyed by the Securitate or other state agents, there is a good chance that might never be a chance to compile such statistics.

During the communist regime human rights were routinely trampled on. Apart from political prisoners (people who opposed the government and the ruling ideology), three more categories of victims were systematically victimised by the regime: the deportees (about 120,000 victims, including Germans and Serbs), women who had had abortions and were subsequently refused medical treatment (about 9,700) and people killed or wounded while attempting to illegally leave the country (unknown number).[1] As Beccaria remarked two centuries ago, the savagery of the political violence used by the state may serve as cause for those who want to revolutionise the established social and political order (Ruggiero 2006).

With a view of the nature of the Ceauşescu regime and the fact that it was removed through a revolution, with the Ceauşescu couple being executed in the process, Romanian transitional justice is at the same time post-totalitarian[2] and postconflict justice.[3]

On 17 December 1989, the revolution started in Timişoara and spread throughout the country. By 22 December 1989, when Nicolae and Elena Ceauşescu attempted to flee from Bucharest in a helicopter and were arrested, hundreds of revolutionaries had already been killed or wounded. The same day, after Ion Iliescu was already the de facto head of state, unknown shooters began firing at the crowds. Hundreds more died until 25 December 1989, when Nicolae and Elena Ceauşescu were swiftly executed after a fifty-five-minute trial.

In Romania, any initiative of organising transitional criminal trials met three problems: the presidential amnesty decrees dating back to the end of the Ceauşescu period and the early 1990s, the limitation periods, and the difficult legal framing of the acts which could fall under the category of imprescriptible crimes, according to the provisions of the Romanian Criminal Code of 1968 (Fijalkowski, 2014).

Regarding the first problem, one of the most important relevant decrees is the *January 1988 Decree 11 on the amnesty of some crimes and reduction of punishments*. According to the provisions of article 1, all the crimes punishable by up to 10 years of imprisonment were amnestied. Also, the *Decree-law no. 3 of 4 January 1990 on the amnesty of some crimes and the pardon of some punishments*, published in *Monitorul Oficial* no. 2 of 5 January 1990, all crimes punishable by up to three years of imprisonment or by a fine were pardoned. The Romanian civil society was the first to ask for the abrogation of those decrees in 2006. The decrees have, however, never been abrogated.

The second problem was generated by the statutory limitations as per the 1968 Romanian Criminal Code. According to Article 122 of that Code, the statutory limitation for homicide was fifteen years, for torture it was eight years and for inhumane treatment it was three years. As the longest statute of limitation for a crime in Romania was fifteen years, in 1990 it was already impossible to prosecute the persons who had committed a homicide before 1975 (Fijalkowski, 2014).

It should be noted that during the 1990s, the prosecutors managed to find a legal means in the 1968 Criminal Code which allowed them to prosecute various perpetrators who would have otherwise been exempted by the statutory limitations. According to the provisions of Article 128 of the Criminal Code of 1968, the statutory limitation is suspended 'while there is a legal provision or unforeseeable or unavoidable circumstance which prevents the formalisation of an indictment or the continuation of a criminal trial.' The prosecutors argued that the communist regime was such an *unavoidable circumstance*, as the judiciary was under the complete control of the Romanian Communist Party. They thus argued that for abuses committed by the former regime the term of prosecutability should resume on 22 December 1989 (Fijalkowski, 2014). The judges agreed with the prosecution, but paradoxically the argument was used in only four indictments.[4] Overall, there were only four major trials until the mid-2000s.

Starting with 2005, the only legal possibility of prosecuting persons suspected of having committed crimes during and in the name of the communist regime was the framing of those acts under the provisions of crimes with no statute of limitation: crimes against peace and mankind.[5] However, it was thought that the specificity of the acts committed by the leaders and agents of the Romanian communist regime turned this possibility into a legal impossibility. Crimes against peace and mankind meant at the time war propaganda, genocide, inhumane treatments, destruction of property and destruction of monuments and culturally valuable constructions. The Vişinescu and Ficior cases, which I discuss in what follows, radically changed this legal presumption.

The situation was finally solved in 2012, when Article 121 of the 1968 Criminal Code was modified, introducing the nonapplicability of the statutory limitations to certain crimes, including murder. The introduction of crimes against humanity in the 2014 Criminal Code provided the Romanian justice system with legal means to prosecute former agents of the communist regime. In what follows I discuss the evolution of the postrevolutionary criminal justice in Romania and present five key trials that have marked that transition in the country's criminal justice.

CRIMINAL TRIALS WHICH HAVE MADE UP
ROMANIAN TRANSITIONAL CRIMINAL JUSTICE

As was previously mentioned, the Romanian transitional justice could be considered at the same time as postconflict and post-totalitarian criminal justice. However, the criminal trials which form the substance of Romanian transitional criminal justice only deal with the crimes committed during the events of December 1989 and a few of the human rights abuses committed in political prisons between 1947 and 1964. In what follows I use a chronological order of presentation, as this reflects the exact way in which the Romanian transitional criminal justice has evolved. I use five important criminal trials in a twenty-five-year-long history of transitional criminal trials to illustrate various aspects of the process. The analysis will begin with the Nicolae and Elena Ceauşescu trial; it will continue with the trials of members of the Executive Political Committee or CPEx ('the trial of the four') and of Army personnel or law enforcement agents ('the Timisoara group'). The case study ends with an overview of the revolution and the Alexandru Visinescu files. These trials reflect what the author considers the three stages of the Romanian criminal transitional justice: the revolutionary phase (Nicolae and Elena Ceauşescu trial), the witch hunt for the top collaborators of the Ceauşescus (CPEx and the Timişoara Group trials) and the rule of law phase (Alexandru Vişinescu trial).

THE NICOLAE AND ELENA CEAUŞESCU TRIAL

On the 24 December 1989, the Council of the National Salvation Front passed a decree stablishing an Extraordinary Military Tribunal in Târgovişte. On the basis of this decree, the trial of Nicolae and Elena Ceauşescu took place on 25 December. It lasted fifty-five minutes and the defendants were condemned and executed promptly afterwards.

The indictment was two pages long, handwritten by Prosecutor Dan Voinea, with no evidence attached. The prosecutor accused the defendants of committing the crimes of genocide, undermining the state, acts of diversion and undermining state economy (Grosescu and Ursachi, 2009). During the trials, the judges accepted only the evidence submitted by the prosecution: The Program for Rational Nourishment, approved by Nicolae and Elena Ceuaşescu, the public policy of rural systematisation (the urbanisation process Nicolae Ceauşescu wanted for Romania: every peasant was supposed to live in an apartment building), the embezzlement of public funds, etc. (Grosescu and Ursachi, 2009). All these accusations were considered notoriously well known and were therefore not considered as allegations that needed to be proven.[6] However, to better present the lack of legal basis for the accusations, an analysis of the specific charges is in place here.

The definition of the crime of genocide in the 1968 Romanian Criminal Code specified *expressis verbis* that any of the specific ways of committing the crime had to be based on the *intent* of the perpetrator 'to destroy partially or in whole a national, racial, ethnic or religious community or group.'[7] The prosecution claimed, and the tribunal agreed, that Nicolae Ceaușescu had the intention to 'slowly destroy the Romanian national group.' The prosecution also claimed that the 'slow genocide,' organised by Nicolae and Elena Ceaușescu during their reign, was to be completed during the events of December 1989, when the defendants ordered the law enforcement agents to use deadly force against the revolutionaries. The prosecution never submitted an actual number of the victims; one of the judges stated, without indicating a source, that the Revolution alone produced sixty-four thousand victims and the *defence attorney* actually *accused* the defendants of committing the 'crime of deprivation of heat, food and electricity' against the entire population (Grosescu and Ursachi, 2009). Although such public policies had indeed been implemented by the Romanian state under the orders of the defendants, the conviction for committing the crime of genocide had no legal basis, given the fact that neither the requirements of *mens rea*, nor the *dolus specialis* were satisfied by the prosecution's argument. The fact that the policies were well-known facts did not justify, under Romanian law, the absence of a proof with regard to the subjective elements of the crime (the intent). This problem was also encountered during the proceedings of the International Criminal Tribunal for Rwanda and during those of the International Criminal Tribunal for the former Yugoslavia.

Undermining the state was the second crime allegedly committed by the defendants. The 1968 Romanian Criminal Code included this crime and the crimes of undermining the state economy in the first title of the Special Part, 'Crimes Against State Security.'[8] As this crime could only be committed through violent and armed actions, the prosecution accused the defendants of committing this crime during the events of December 1989, before and after 22 December.[9] Again, no evidence was submitted for the charge. Nicolae and Elena Ceaușescu had repeatedly ordered the Securitate and the military to use deadly force against the revolutionaries, both in Timișoara and Bucharest, and this was subsequently proven during the CPEx trials. However, the lack of evidence or legal proof at the time of the 'conviction,' even if the facts were considered notorious enough and were proven so later, deprived the trial of its proper legal basis, and made the conviction illegal.

Contrary to the accusation of undermining state power, which referred to the period of the revolution, the charge of undermining the state economy referred to the defendant's entire reign.[10] The prosecution used the same arguments as for genocide, stating that Nicolae and Elena Ceaușescu had slowly degraded the national economy by unjustified depletion of the national resources in order to destroy the Romanian people. The prosecution claimed that the defendants had done so by 'unreasonable' use of public funds for 'megalomaniac' or 'snobbish' goals (the actual words used by the prosecutors) and by the embezzlement of over one billion dollars, which had been moved into foreign accounts for the sole benefit of the ruling couple (Grosescu and Ursachi, 2009). The fact that Elena was considered a coperpetrator of the crimes, alongside Nicolae Ceaușescu, was a consequence of another presumption based on the general public consensus, namely that of Elena Ceaușescu being as powerful as Nicolae in most domains. The prosecution argued that these kinds of actions were a direct cause of the lack of medical supplies in the country and for the starvation of many Romanian citizens. Both the depletion of national resources and the unjustified use of public funds may have been considered notorious realities of socialist Romania under the defendants' rule (e.g., the changes made in the architecture and urban planning of Bucharest and the construction of the House of Parliament (House of People in 1989), both 'megalomaniac' and 'snobbish' projects). However, in the Ceaușescu trial, the Exceptional Military Tribunal did not prove either that these actions had resulted in undermining the national economy, or that they had caused the starvation of Romanians or a shortage of medical supplies. The allegations had not been properly investigated, nor had there been a proper legal analysis, both of which would have been necessary in order to prove that the defendants had actually committed the crimes. This alone is sufficient grounds for considering the conviction illegal.

Last, but not least, the accusation of committing acts of diversion was introduced into the indictment as a logical link between the crimes of genocide, undermining the state and undermining the state economy. The judges *and the defence attorneys* argued that the defendants had committed diversion after 22 December 1989, when they had organised the shooting into the crowds, in order to destabilise the new regime, led by the Council of the National Salvation Front (Grosescu and Ursachi 2009). In short, the prosecution (represented by Dan Voinea), the judges (col. Gică Popa and col. Ioan Nistor) and the defence attorneys (Constantin Lucescu and Nicolae Teodorescu) argued that Nicolae and Elena Ceaușescu were guilty of all the charges.

From previous remarks it is clear that the trial of Nicolae and Elena Ceaușescu was severely flawed by procedural and substantial irregularities. There was no criminal investigation conducted by a body formed by prosecutors. The defendants had no real defence attorney and were not allowed to produce any evidence in their defence. The judges, the prosecutor, the defence attorney — actually, the entire staff of the tribunal — were handpicked by the de facto head of state at the moment, Ion Iliescu. The defendants were not allowed to appeal the verdict, which was never published, and disappeared immediately after the trial.[11] The actual verdict was replaced with a vague official statement by the Council of the National Salvation Front (*Frontul Salvării Naționale* FSN) (Stoenescu, 2009). When confronted with the realities of the aftermath of the revolution, Romanians should acknowledge publicly that the country's transitional criminal justice started in 1989, and it started with an injustice.

THE CPEX TRIALS

At the very top of the structure of the Romanian Communist Party was the Executive Political Committee (*Comitetul Politic Executiv al Partidului Comunist Român*, CPEx). It was the most important ruling organ of the party. From 1967 to 1989 it was led by Nicolae Ceaușescu, the Secretary General of the Party and Elena Ceaușescu, his wife. In December 1989, the members of the Permanent Bureau of CPEx were: Nicolae Ceaușescu (Secretary General), Elena Ceaușescu, Emil Bobu, Constantin Dăscălescu, Ion Dincă, Manea Mănescu, Gheorghe Oprea and Constantin Rădulescu.

During the events of the December 1989 revolution, most orders by Nicolae Ceaușescu were conveyed by members of the Permanent Bureau of the CPEx to various agents of the state involved in repression of the revolutionaries: officers of the Securitate, the military, the police and other law enforcement agencies. Therefore, after the revolution, the Romanian public opinion believed that the members of CPEx were the most culpable for the crimes committed against the revolutionaries. The new 'democratic' regime, led by Ion Iliescu, used this opportunity to legitimise its political role and at the same time to get rid of some very important former collaborators of Nicolae and Elena Ceaușescu.

The CPEx trials started on 27 January 1990 with the trial of four close political 'yes-men' of Nicolae and Elena Ceaușescu: Tudor Postelnicu, Emil Bobu, Ion Dinca and Manea Manescu.[12] The Romanian press often referred to it as 'the trial of the four.' The defendants were charged with complicity to genocide that they had allegedly committed by failing to oppose the orders to use deadly force against the revolutionaries issued by the dictator and his wife, and by supporting the violent actions against the revolutionaries between 22 and 31 December (firing at the crowd by snipers). The prosecution argued that Nicolae and Elena Ceaușescu and their allies were guilty of all the crimes committed by state and by private persons during the revolution and in its aftermath (Grosescu and Ursachi, 2009).

The prosecution only produced two pieces of evidence, namely the transcripts of two meetings of CPEx members on 17 December and 22 December 1989. As in the Ceauşescu trial, the first CPEx trial was riddled with procedural and substantive irregularities (Grosescu and Ursachi, 2009). The judges opened the first session by declaring that the defendants were guilty as charged. The prosecution had virtually no evidence to support its allegations. The defendants were constantly insulted and they were not allowed to speak, except to incriminate themselves. However, in the CPEx case, the defendants were too afraid that they would be executed, so they pleaded guilty, apologised for their inaction, and even acknowledged that they had acted 'in an asshole manner' (Grosescu and Ursachi, 2009).

All four were initially sentenced to life imprisonment for the crime of genocide during December 1989. Their trial was followed by twenty-six more trials of various members of CPEx or other prominent members of the Romanian Communist Party, including General Andruţa Ceausescu, the brother of the dictator.[13] The charges revolved around the claim that Nicolae and Elena Ceauşescu had committed genocide, with the prosecution calling on the judges to convict all of these defendants of genocide on the basis of their connections to the Ceausescu couple. The Bucharest Military Tribunal, however, changed the charges and convicted most of the defendants for ordinary crimes, including negligence, manslaughter, and aiding and abetting.[14] In 1994 and later in 1996, Ion Iliescu, acting in his capacity as president of Romania, passed two presidential decrees that pardoned all the convicted defendants.[15]

A particularly interesting perspective on the above trials looks at how the figures depicting the victims of the revolution 'evolved' during the trials. At 'the trial of the four' the prosecution argued that the defendants were guilty of allowing Nicolae and Elena Ceauşescu to order the violence which resulted in the killing of 689 people and the wounding of over 1,200 in Timişoara and Bucharest. Later on, during the rest of the trials, the figures increased, with the prosecution mentioning 1,033 dead and 2,198 wounded. Some of this confusion might be due to the fact that the first CPEx trial had started only a month after the revolution, when the prosecution did not have all the data, which was subsequently compiled by the Ministry of the Interior. However, the first four defendants were accused of committing a crime against a still unknown number of victims. There appears to have been no real concern about working with accurate figures in the trial. This suspicion is further supported by the fact that not a single victim was allowed to take the stand during the trials, and the courts never even considered awarding any financial or other types of compensation for wrongful detainment or public defamation.

TRIALS OF THE MILITARY

The trials of army and law enforcement officials who had actively engaged in the violent repression against the revolutionaries started in 1990 and lasted until 2007. Like the CPEx trials, the military trials only took into account the crimes committed during the revolution of 1989 by various agents of the state who had been a part of, or had been controlled by, the military. Most Romanian historians and political scientists now consider these trials to have been the means for legitimising the new regime in the public eye by shifting the blame from political leaders to the army (Grosescu and Ursachi, 2009). At the time, most of the political leaders, including President Ion Iliescu, were former second- or third-tier members of the Romanian Communist Party.

The first trials occurred during the presidency of Ion Iliescu, from 1990 until 1996. By the end of 1996, multiple agents of Securitate (Romanian secret police under Ceauşescu), the police and the army had already been convicted or under investigation. In Timişoara, the most publicised trial was the "Timişoara Group" case, involving twenty-five defendants. However, only eight were convicted for first-degree murder. The rest were acquitted or protected by the Presidential Decree on Amnesty no. 3/4, of January 1990, also passed by Ion Iliescu. In total, in Timişoara, forty-eight people had been investigated for various political crimes during the events of December 1989. In other Romania's cities the situation was much less tense: in Sibiu, for example, only sixteen people were put on trial, with only one, Nicu Ceauşescu,[16] being convicted of illegally carrying a weapon.[17] In Alba Iulia, only four Securitate officers had been convicted for attempted murder of protesters from Cugir.[18] However, all were quickly released on appeal. In Bucharest, 534 people were killed and 1,879 wounded during the events of 1989. Between 1990 and 1996, with the exception of the CPEx trials, only a single major trial was conducted regarding the events of December 1989: the Otopeni group file. Three Securitate and Army officers were put on trial for the murder of forty soldiers and eight civilians, who had been killed in an ambush while in transport to Otopeni airport on the 23 December 1989. The file was sent back to the prosecutors for lack of evidence in 1995, and it was reopened in 1998, when the defendants were convicted.

In 1996, Emil Constantinescu won the presidential election against Ion Iliescu, thus reorienting the interests of the political scene regarding the involvement of the army in the events of December 1989. During the Constantinescu administration, the prosecutors launched numerous investigations against former or active military officers, as well as against numerous former Securitate and police officers. However, I should like to emphasise here that most of the investigations from this period were only concerned with the events from December 1989, while mostly ignoring the human rights abuses committed after that time (Grosescu and Ursachi, 2009). However, Raluca Grosescu and Raluca Ursachi believe that the most important merit of the 1997–2000 trials is that they established, beyond a reasonable doubt, that both the political elite of the Romanian Communist Party and the leadership of the Romanian army were responsible for the crimes committed against the 1989 revolutionaries.

The described criminal trials were developing simultaneously with the idea of 'lustration' in Europe. On 10 July 2003 the Parliamentary Assembly of the Council of Europe passed Resolution no. 9,875, which obliged all members, including Romania, to facilitate public access to all the archives of the political police. On 7 July 2004 the Resolution was modified in order to ban all former collaborators of political police from holding public office. However, it is notable that the Romanian political elites completely ignored the Resolution (Stan, 2010). Even now, former members of the Communist Party continue to hold positions of Members of Parliament or those in the executive government.

The trials against the army, police and Securitate officers continued until 2007. Over two hundred people were put on trial and many more were investigated. The political nature of the trials, their legal shortcomings and the apparent injustices committed by revolutionary justice, along with the seeming absence of substantial effects of such trials on the Romanian society demonstrate that in a post-totalitarian society, the justice system may fail to promote the accountability of former human rights abusers even when hundreds of trials are conducted by various courts. In my opinion, this paradox is a direct result of the vast corruption that ruled the judicial system in the 1990s and early 2000s.

THE ALEXANDRU VIȘINESCU CASE

On 30 July 2013 (before the coming into effect of the current Romanian Criminal Code), the Institute for the Investigation of Communist Crimes and Memory of the Romanian Exile (IICCMER) forwarded a denunciation to the Prosecutor's Office attached to Territorial Military Tribunal Bucharest against Lieutenant-Colonel Alexandru Vișinescu for the commission of genocide by organising and coordinating a regime of extermination of political prisoners in the Prison of Râmnicu Sărat, while he was the commander of that institution. It should be noted here that the Râmnicu Sărat prison was not a large prison; it only had a limited number of inmates at the time. The criminal complaint was accompanied by voluminous evidence, including the testimonies of former political dissidents, death certificates, documents from the state investigation of the detention regime for political dissidents between 1952 and 1964 conducted under orders by the Romanian Communist Party in 1968 and the like. The complaint was elaborated so it would serve two purposes. First, the authors tried to prove that, between 1956 and 1963, a detention regime had been introduced in the Romanian penitentiaries and labour camps whose purpose was to degrade the health of the imprisoned dissidents and ultimately exterminate them. The system had been designed and implemented by the political leaders of the Communist Party. Second, the authors highlighted it that Alexandru Vișinescu had deliberately applied and endorsed this detention regime as the commander in charge of the Râmnicu Sărat Penitentiary.

The analysis by IICCMER researchers underlined it that the objective of exterminating the political prisoners was the essence of the Romanian Gulag system, although it was never *expressis verbis* mentioned in any legal documents. In fact, the detention regime was specifically designed to include insufficient food rations, an isolation regime, forbidding any relations between the prisoners and their respective families, lack of medicine, lack of medical treatment, lack of heating, torture, inhumane treatment and so on. All this information was used in the crimin
al complaint and it was released to the general public only during the trial.

Based on the testimonies in the criminal complaint, Alexandru Vișinescu was indicted for coordinating a regime meant to physically exterminate political prisoners by direct and indirect means. In total, with the help of the Ministry of Internal Affairs, 138 former political prisoners in the Râmnicu Sărat Penitentiary during the time of Alexandru Vișinescu were identified. IICCMER researchers were able to reconstruct only six deaths where the causes of death were ordinary, including cancer, cardiovascular illness, cerebral stroke, cerebral haemorrhage or digestive system problems. It can be assumed that the other deaths were avoidable, and most likely deliberately inflicted by a regime of deprivation and violence which had been coordinated by the penitentiary's commander.

The adoption of a new Criminal Code in 2014 and the introduction of crimes against humanity allowed the prosecutor to indict Mr. Vișinescu for crimes against humanity, a more correct approach in comparison with genocide or murder. The trial started on 18 June 2014 in the Bucharest Court of Appeal. It lasted for about a year and ended with a conviction and a twenty-year prison sentence for crimes against humanity. The ruling was upheld by the High Court in 2016. Vișinescu was found culpable for six deaths and for imposing what was in effect an almost unimaginable suffering on all survivors of the prison, as a part of a systematic attack on political prisoners under the supervision of the Securitate and Ministry of Internal Affairs.

The Vişinescu trial was a milestone from the jurisprudential point of view. For the first time in the history of postsocialist Romanian jurisprudence a court ruling acknowledged a regime of extermination in Romanian political prisons, thus confirming the historical studies and testimonies by thousands of former political prisoners. The sentence installed a sense of justice being served in the minds of many ex-political prisoners.

On 18 September 2013, IICCMER forwarded a criminal complaint against Ion Ficior for committing crimes against humanity between 1953 and 1954. Ficior had been the commander of the Poarta Albă political prison. In May 2016 he was found culpable for the deaths of 106 people and for coordinating a regime intended to exterminate the political prisoners in his care. He was sentenced to twenty years in prison for crimes against humanity, but he appealed the sentence. Like in the Alexandru Vişinescu trial, the High Court of Cassation and Justice upheld the decision of the Bucharest Court of Appeal.

The Ion Ficior trial is very similar to the Vişinescu trial. Its importance resides in the fact that it established a clear line of Romanian jurisprudence: crimes against humanity were committed in the Romanian political prisons between 1947 and 1964. However, both trials were also conducted in a manner intended to reinforce the credibility of the justice system by ensuring a strict conformity with the standards of the European Convention of Human Rights and those of the Romanian criminal procedure.

THE OUTCOMES

When Alexandru Vişinescu was sentenced to twenty years in prison for crimes against humanity, the Romanian public opinion was neither happy, nor sad. Some thought that the punishment was too harsh and too late, and some (including the former political prisoners) thought that the punishment was too light and that condemning just one individual was not enough to right the wrongdoings of the past. As previously stated, hundreds of criminal investigations of events during the communist regime have been conducted in Romania, and still people in this country do not trust the transitional efforts. It is an apparent paradox with very reasonable explanations. The Romanian reality proves that transitional justice is a delicate and complex process which must be closely managed in order to be successful. Especially when criminal investigations are involved, the image of a justice system which establishes clear accountability for the perpetrators from the ranks of the previous government and institutions is mandatory. The political elites must be seen as willing to support the justice system without an own agenda in play. In other words, political and legal elites must collaborate in order to serve justice without tainting the independence of the criminal justice system. Last, but not least, the transitional criminal justice mechanisms employed in a post-totalitarian society must conform with the ideals of a rule of law and human rights-oriented democracy; they must not in any way resemble the tools for the repression of political opponents which were used by the former government in Romania. These goals have not been achieved, because in the first twenty years of criminal investigations of the crimes of the past the new political regime, even though formally 'democratic,' has continued to use the justice system as a tool for removing political opponents from positions of power. The corruption, the visible political agendas, an absence of real reformative effects, a failure to systematically promote democratic values, represent only a few of the factors that are now infamous in transitional studies for their harmful effects on transitional societies. All of them, reunited in one gangrenous mélange, are ingredients of the failure of the Romanian transitional criminal justice. Who is responsible? The political elites for being too corrupt. The legal elites for abandoning their democratic values. The civil society for being so passive and so trusting of the government. Maybe even the international community, for not involving itself more.

George Orwell once said that the man who controls the past controls the future. In theory, transitional criminal justice should be about uncovering the truth about the past, be it individual or collective. Romanian transitional criminal justice has mostly been a struggle to control the past.

NOTES

1. More information on the subject may be found on the website of the Institute for the Investigation of Communist Crimes and Memory of the Romanian Exile (IICCMER), www.iiccmer.ro.

2. The extreme right military dictatorship of Marshall Ion Antonescu lasted between 4 September 1940 and 23 August 1944.

3. This was due to the Second World War and the Romanian revolution. However, I would argue that acts committed by the Romanian army in 1956 in Hungary should also be taken into account.

4. Case no. 15/P/1999 in the archives of the Bucharest Military Court of Appeal. The argument was validated by the High Court of Cassation and Justice, Criminal Section, in its Decision no. 2579 of 7 July 2009.

5. Articles 356 (war propaganda), 357 (genocide), 358 (inhumane treatment), 359 (destruction or appropriation of goods) and 160 (destruction, robbery or appropriation of cultural values) of the 1968 Romanian Criminal Code.

6. According Article 63 of the Romanian Code of Criminal Procedure, which was in effect at the time of the Revolution, in December 1989, the judges were free to

210 *Cătălin-Nicolae Constantinescu*

examine any kind of useful and conclusive evidence 'according to their own socialist legal conscience.'

7. This definition, including the instrumental *dolus specialis*, is consistent with the definition of the crime of genocide used in the UN Convention on the Prevention and Punishment of the Crime of Genocide from 1948.

8. The definition of the crime of undermining state power is given in Article 162 of the 1968 Romanian Criminal Code. In 1989, the same crime was defined by the Romanian law any armed action (or any violent action committed by two or more persons together) which might weaken the state's power.

9. As previously stated, Nicolae and Elena Ceauşescu were arrested by the new political and military leadership of the Romanian state on 22 December 1989.

10. According 1968 Romanian Criminal Code, the crime of undermining the economy of the state was defined as using a public institution or preventing it from its normal activity, in a way which might undermine the national economy.

11. Some of the files and documents used during the trial were reconstructed years later, in 2003, by General Ion Panaitescu. Those documents may be found in the Archive of the Territorial Military Tribunal, file no. 417/2003.

12. All four were members of the Council of the Political Executive Committee and took part in the last two meetings, on 17 and 22 December 1989, when Nicolae and Elena Ceuaşescu ordered the violent repression of the revolutionaries.

13. General Andruţa Ceauşescu (1924–2000) was the brother of Nicolae Ceauşescu.

14. Six of the defendants were acquitted and one died during trial.

15. Presidential Decree no. 41/1994 and Presidential Decree no. 579/1996. For extensive data about the trials and a very interesting analysis of their social effects see Grosescu and Ursachi, 138–53.

16. Nicu Ceauşescu (1951–1996) was one of the two sons of Nicolae and Elena Ceauşescu. In 1989, he was the head of the Sibiu branch of the Romanian Communist Party. Paradoxically, he was well liked by the citizens of Sibiu. During his trial, people would bring him flowers, protest, and demand his acquittal. During the 1980s, Sibiu was one of the places that offered the best living conditions in Romania.

17. Ninety-nine people died and almost two hundred were wounded in Sibiu during the revolution of December 1989.

18. Twenty-three people and 111 were wounded in Alba Iulia and Cugir during the 1989 revolution. Most of the casualties arose from the revolutionaries attacking the police Cugir headquarters, when the police opened fire. The police headquarters was then set on fire by the protesters.

REFERENCES

Brewer, John, Mitchell, David, and Leavey, Gerard. (2013). *Ex-Combatants, Religion, and Peace in Northern Ireland: The Role of Religion in Transitional Justice.* New York: Palgrave Macmillan.
Fijalkowski, Agata. (2014). 'The Criminalization of Symbols of the Past: Expression, Law and Memory.' *International Journal of Law in Context 10*(3): 295–314.

Grosescu, Raluca, and Ursachi, Raluca. (2009). Justiția Penală de Tranziție. De la Nurnberg la postcomunismul românesc, Iași: Polirom.

Ruggiero, Vincenzo. (2006). *Understanding Political Violence: A Criminological Analysis*. Maidenhead: Open University Press.

Rusan, Romulus. (2007). Cronologia și geografia represiunii comuniste în România. Recensământul populației concentraționare (1945–1989). București: Fund. Academia Civică, 80–94.

Stan, Lavinia. (2010). Prezentul trecutului recent. Lustrație și decomunizare în postcomunism Bucharest: Curtea Veche.

Chapter 9

A Theory of National Reconciliation: Some Insights from Africa (Revised Edition)[1]

Thaddeus Metz

UNIFYING JUDGEMENTS ABOUT RECONCILIATION

In this chapter, I consider how best to construe the essential nature of an attractive sort of national reconciliation. Supposing that national, or political, reconciliation is something to be sought consequent to a period of intense social conflict, what are its necessary and sufficient conditions, or at least its salient recurrent properties, and how do they account for a variety of widely and firmly held views about the subject? An answer to this question is a theory of national reconciliation, something I aim to articulate and defend here.

In advancing a theory of *national reconciliation*, I focus strictly on that concept, considering related ideals such as restorative justice and transitional justice merely in passing. In addition, I am not out to capture just anything that might be fairly called 'national reconciliation,' but rather a desirable instance of it, one that particularly merits pursuit. Still more, I am interested in what a good form of national reconciliation is, not what is likely to bring it about or how it can be done so permissibly; my question is strictly about what constitutes national reconciliation, though I will address other issues when necessary.

In seeking a *theory* of national reconciliation, I do not spend much time reflecting on imprecise definitions of it that one commonly finds in the litera-ture. For instance, I pass over, or rather intend to surpass, not only vague, first pass definitions, such as that national reconciliation is a matter of 'rebuilding damaged relationships,' 'establishing improved relationships,' or 'achieving stable peace,' but also metaphorical characterisations about coming to 'share the same symbolic and political space' (Moosa, 2000: 119), to 'build bridges' (de Gruchy, 2002: 184), or to 'renew damaged social capital' (Huyse, 2008b: 188; Quinn, 2009: 183). In addition, taking a theoretical approach to the topic means considering neither one or two examples of it in detail, which already pepper the literature, nor one or two piecemeal facets of it, say, insofar as it bears on forgiveness (Helmick and Petersen, 2001), apology (Barkan and Karn, 2006) or acknowledgement (Govier, 2009b).

In contrast, my aim in this chapter is to be clear and comprehensive; I propose a basic principle capturing the 'underlying structure' of an attractive sort of national reconciliation that entails and plausibly explains a wide array of disparate judgements about the subject. Such a theory would provide specific and systematic guidance about the myriad things that states, institutions and individuals should aim for when seeking to promote national reconciliation, and it would, one hopes, provide strong evidence that the category of reconciliation is a useful one for normative and descriptive analyses, and is not merely 'little more than a buzzword, an amenable but loose framework for different contents, depending on the user' (Hermann, 2004: 41).

There are extant theories of national reconciliation in the literature, most of which are informed by Kantian, liberal-democratic and similar perspectives (e.g., Crocker, 2002; Gutmann and Thompson, 2000; Moellendorf, 2007).[2] In contrast to those accounts, I spell out one grounded on a comparatively underexplored sub-Saharan ethic. As I and others have been working to show recently (Ikuenobe, 2006; Metz and Gaie, 2010; Metz, 2017a; 2017b), there are communal approaches to morality prominent in sub-Saharan worldviews that should be taken no less seriously than Kantianism, utilitarianism, contractualism and the like. My foremost aim here is to demonstrate how African ideals about communion, still largely unfamiliar to an international audience, do a promising job of providing a unified foundation for the roles of truth-telling, apology, forgiveness, compensation, amnesty, and related practises often associated with national reconciliation. A systematic comparison and defence of the Afro-communal principle with competitors must wait for another occasion.

I begin by spelling out what nearly all those who have reflected on national reconciliation would agree is inherent to it, my aim being to articulate an uncontested core that clarifies the subject of enquiry and debate as something distinct from, say, national unity. Next, I articulate a conception of communion that lies at the heart of much African thought about morality and, in the following section, present an account of national reconciliation that is grounded on an Afro-communal moral ideal. I then apply the principle to several facets of national reconciliation, demonstrating its explanatory breadth and depth, often in the context of South Africa to illustrate. I conclude by suggesting that it would be worth critically comparing the theory of national reconciliation that I advance with rival theories in future work.

NATIONAL RECONCILIATION: SOME
UNCONTROVERSIAL ELEMENTS

My overarching aim in this chapter is to provide a theory of national reconciliation, and, so, to provide clarity about the subject of this theory, I start by differentiating it from related topics and point out some definitional facets of it that virtually all theorists would accept. I here bring out what competing theories of national reconciliation are *about*. Although I do not intend to be presenting anything particularly controversial in this section, it should be revealing to see what the uncontested facets of the concept include.

First off, national reconciliation, of the sort I theorise about in this chapter, is a kind of relationship between people. One group is thought to reconcile with another group, which differs from a kind of reconciliation that I do not address, one in which people come to terms with their past and seek to 'get on with life' (much of the focus in Dwyer, 1999; Hughes, 2001; cf. Murphy, 2013: 4451–53; Villa-Vicencio, 2000). The latter sort of reconciliation often does require relating to other people in a particular way in order to eventually 'move forward.' However, it need not; imagine the culprits have all died, leaving the victims on their own to adjust and to accept. The key point is that being reconciled *to the fact of one's having been mistreated or harmed* differs from being reconciled *with other people who mistreated or harmed one*, where I am interested strictly in the latter, essentially relational condition.

In addition, national reconciliation is an interpersonal relationship that necessarily follows a period of serious societal conflict, characteristically one in which there was grave injustice between at least two groups. This is one major respect in which the concept of national reconciliation differs from ones such as national cohesion (*contra* Quinn, 2009: 183). Seeking the latter condition does not imply a prior condition of civil war, large-scale oppression, moral atrocity or the like.

Although the 're' in the word 'reconciliation' might be thought to imply that there must have been an absence of conflict at some point in the past (Krog, 1998: 109), few mean something so literal by the term. Instead, nearly all academics, activists and policy makers would agree, upon reflection, that it is conceivable for something they call 'reconciliation' to emerge from groups that have always been deeply antagonistic towards each other (as per Dwyer, 1999: 83; de Gruchy, 2002: 14–15; Hamber and Kelly, 2009: 294). Hence, 'reunification' is also not an exact synonym of "reconciliation" (*contra* Alie, 2008: 133; Hughes, 2001: 130).

Another fairly uncontroversial element of national reconciliation is that it is not a sociopolitical ideal, in the sense of an unsurpassable condition, let alone the 'Holy Grail' (as per Gerwel, 2000). Achieving a state of national reconciliation hardly implies utopia, or even a somewhat lower standard such as, say, the absence of injustice. Instead, nearly all agree that reconciliation is a way station or a stepping stone towards an even more desirable condition for a nation.

Now, the fact that national reconciliation is not an ultimate end-state for a society does not mean that it is necessarily to be valued merely as a means. Some do emphasise the instrumental nature of reconciliation as a path towards a better sociopolitical condition, while others suggest that it is *also* something good for its own sake. Although I think that the sort of national reconciliation most worth pursuing is one the value of which is not merely instrumental, I doubt that this is part of the mere concept of national reconciliation. For instance, I balk at the suggestion that reconciliation is analytically a matter of justice, whether distributive, transitional, restorative or something else. A desirable sort of reconciliation might well be a form of justice (de Gruchy, 2002; Philpott, 2009), but, if so, it is not the case by definition. It is an open question whether reconciliation is just (see, e.g., Dwyer, 1999), and, indeed, some radicals in South Africa are currently calling for doing away with reconciliation as a hindrance to the realisation of distributive justice (not the usual suspect of retributive justice).[3] Hence, I simply point out that national reconciliation is by definition neither of merely instrumental worth, nor of inherently final value. It may or may not merit pursuit in itself to some degree, and, if it does, it may or may not be a matter of justice.

For yet another relatively uncontested idea, most would readily say that national reconciliation is the sort of thing reasonably expected to be promoted to some degree by a Truth and Reconciliation Commission (TRC) (or some similarly named body) doing things such as making informed judgements of political wrongdoings, hearing out victims, assisting them with compensation for their losses, and facilitating ceremonies between them and their oppressors in which the latter express remorse or at least accept responsibility for what they have done. Almost no one believes that the workings of a TRC can be sufficient for national reconciliation, but most believe that the former can, under certain conditions, noticeably help to realise the latter.

Finally, national reconciliation is often captured with phrases such as 'reestablishing broken relationships' and 'healing deep wounds,' which are meant to convey something more richly interactive than merely a truce or peaceful coexistence. These characterisations are not inaccurate, but I maintain that it would be intellectually and practically useful not to rest content with them; it would be of interest to articulate a theory of national reconciliation, a principle that articulates the core of a desirable instance of reconciliation at the political level, and then to show how that core accounts for topics such as listening to victims, dealing with emotional trauma, accepting responsibility for misdeeds, offering amnesty, and many other, related practises.

In the rest of this chapter, I provide such a theoretical account, one that is informed by characteristic sub-Saharan prizing of communion.

AN AFRICAN ETHIC

As is well known, precolonial sub-Saharan societies often resolved conflict with an eye towards neither deterrence nor retribution in the first instance, but rather reconciliation or harmony of some kind (Aja, 1997; Krog, 2008). The aim when responding to wrongdoing was by and large to resolve conflict between the offender and his victims, or, more precisely, between his family and the families of those whom he had wronged. It has been no accident that reconciliation has figured prominently (even if with varying degrees of success) in responses to widespread conflict taken by countries such as Zimbabwe, South Africa, Rwanda, and Sierra Leone.

In the following, I appeal to salient values in the sub-Saharan tradition to articulate an ethic that is distinct from the dominant ones in the West and that grounds a promising conception of national reconciliation. In doing so, note that I am neither recounting traditional African ethics as they may have been understood *in toto* by a particular people, nor seeking to defend any specific reconciliatory practises that a given sub-Saharan society employed. My aims are instead constructive; I spell out a way of understanding African morality that is philosophically refined and will appeal to an analytical temperament, and then use that to spell out a novel theory of national reconciliation that is revealing. Although I draw on elements of traditional African culture, I am not seeking to describe or mirror the past, but rather to develop something out of it that will be of theoretical use now for sub-Saharan societies, although not only them.

According to one large swathe of sub-Saharan thought about morality, one's basic goal in life should be to realise one's humanness ('*ubuntu*,' as it is famously known among many southern Africans), which one can do if and only if one enters into community with others. One should strive to live a genuinely human way of life, something that is largely, if not solely, a function of prizing communal relationships with other human persons.

As for what is meant by 'communion' or the relationships constitutive of it, consider the following statements from a variety of African thinkers. According to the Ghanaian Kwame Gyekye (2004), the most influential African political philosopher of the past twenty-five years, '(t)he fundamental meaning of community is the sharing of an overall way of life, inspired by the notion of the common good' (p. 16); Pantaleon Iroegbu (2005), a Nigerian theologian, remarks that 'the purpose of our life is community-service and community-belongingness' (p. 442); the Kenyan historian of African philosophy Dismas Masolo (2010) highlights what he calls the 'communitarian values' of 'living a life of mutual concern for the welfare of others, such as in a cooperative creation and distribution of wealth. . . . Feeling integrated with as well as willing to integrate others into a web of relations free of friction and conflict' (p. 240); and, finally, the South African public intellectual Muxe Nkondo (2007) notes that if you asked adherents to an African ethic what they live for, '(t)he answers would express commitment to the good of the community in which their identities were formed, and a need to experience their lives as bound up in that of their community' (p. 91).

As I have spelled out in detail elsewhere (Metz, 2011b; 2017b), implicit in these and other analyses of how to develop one's humanness or what communion consists of in the African tradition are two distinct relationships, what I call 'identity' and 'solidarity.' Identity is a matter of sharing a way of life, belonging, feeling integrated, and experiencing oneself as bound up with others, while solidarity consists of working for the common good, serving, expressing concern for people's welfare, and being committed to the good of others.

More carefully, identifying with another is the combination of exhibiting certain psychological attitudes of 'we-ness' and cooperative behaviour. The psychological attitudes include a tendency to think of oneself as a member of a group with the other and to refer to oneself as a 'we' (rather than an 'I'), a disposition to feel pride or shame in what the other or one's group does, and, at a higher level of intensity, an emotional appreciation of the other's nature and value. The cooperative behaviours include being transparent about the terms of interaction, allowing others to make voluntary choices, acting on the basis of trust, adopting common goals, and, at the extreme end, choosing for the reason that 'this is who we are.'

Exhibiting solidarity with another is also the combination of exhibiting certain psychological attitudes and engaging in helpful behaviour. Here, the attitudes are ones positively oriented towards the other's good and include a belief that the other merits aid for her own sake, an empathetic awareness of the other's condition, and a sympathetic emotional reaction to the empathetic awareness. And the actions are not merely those likely to be beneficial — that is, to improve the other's state, but also, in the ideal case, are ones done for that reason and for the sake of making the other a better person or for the sake of communal relationship itself.

Notice that communion, understood as the combination of identity and solidarity, is more or less what English-speakers mean by the word 'friendliness' or even a broad sense of 'love.' To be friendly with another is pretty much a matter of identifying with him, engaging in joint activities, and acting for his sake, giving oneself and one's resources. As Desmond Tutu (1999) has remarked of characteristically African approaches to morality,

We say, 'a person is a person through other people.' It is not 'I think therefore I am.' It says rather: 'I am human because I belong.' I participate, I share. . . . Harmony, friendliness, community are great goods. Social harmony is for us the *summum bonum* — the greatest good. (p. 35)

Perhaps at this point one can begin to see why I have argued in recent work that a prescription to prize communion *qua* sharing a way of life and caring for others' quality of life forms the basis of a promising ethic, one that differs from Kantianism, utilitarianism, contractualism, egoism, divine command theory, and the other moral theories that are at the forefront of Euro-American debate (e.g., Metz and Gaie, 2010; Metz, 2017a). From the present Afro-communal perspective, what makes a person bad or an action wrong is, roughly, that one is not being friendly or is being unloving, as opposed to that one causes harm in the long run, degrades autonomy, violates a social agreement, does what has been forbidden by God, and so on.

Notice, too, that this African ethic differs from salient forms of Western communitarianism, which tend to be relativistic, defining wrongness as what flouts a group's norms and sensibilities (e.g., Sandel, 1984; Walzer, 1983). In contrast, the opposite of developing humanness from a characteristically sub-Saharan standpoint consists of honouring the contraries of identity and solidarity through relationships of division and ill-will. To engage in crimes against humanity and other gross forms of injustice — that is, the sorts of wrongful behaviour that call for national reconciliation — is basically to prize enmity.

It is not my concern in this chapter to defend a new moral theory, but instead a new theory of reconciliation. One readily sees how a concern for reconciliation consequent to conflict would be recurrent in societies that prize communion understood as the combination of identity and solidarity or something akin to that. If what is of utmost importance is relating communally or prizing people's capacity for friendly relationships, then one who acts in an unfriendly manner should be responded to in ways that are likely to counteract his unfriendliness and to foster friendliness between him and others. Imposing retribution in the manner of an eye for an eye, with no essential expectation of good to come from the imposition of harm, would be out of place.

A THEORY OF NATIONAL RECONCILIATION AS PARTIAL COMMUNION

In this section, I appeal to elements of the African ideal of communion to articulate the essentials of a desirable kind of national reconciliation.[4] It is only in the following section that I apply it to a variety of topics, in order both to shed light on them and to illustrate and motivate the view.

Above I contended that national reconciliation, generally construed, is a relationship consequent to serious social conflict between people tighter than mere peaceful coexistence that is desirable but not an ideal and that is typically fostered to some degree by a TRC, a body which, for example, makes public characterisations of the conflict upon careful historical inquiry, pays special attention to victims, and facilitates encounters between them and those who wronged them in egregious ways. There are a variety of different ways that such a general idea could be realised in practise. My present aim is to proffer a particular version of reconciliation that is attractive, rich and informed by the African ideal of communion sketched in the previous section.

If one major proper aim of the state were to promote communal relationships in its territory, and if national reconciliation were a stepping stone towards such an end-state, then it would be sensible to think of national reconciliation as constituted by only *some* of the elements of communion. Reconciliation should be seen as a substantial step on the path towards realising a society that fully respects communal relationships, ones of identity and solidarity. Specifically, then, a promising conception of national reconciliation would be based primarily on the *behavioural* facets of a characteristically African conception of communion, or at least not so much the attitudinal ones. As a first approximation, consider the view that to reconcile is for two parties to engage in cooperative behaviour oriented towards mutual aid, and that it need not involve mental states such as thinking of oneself as a 'we,' taking pride in others' accomplishments, exhibiting sympathetic emotions, and the like.

Including the latter, attitudinal aspects would be expecting 'too much' from the concept of reconciliation, veering it too closely to a social ideal. After a period of great conflict between groups, one cannot expect people's attitudes to change quickly, whereas their behaviour can. Although immediately after World War II many Germans continued to favour Hitler's policies, they nonetheless conformed to a constitutional order that sought to repair some of the damage done to the Jewish population. What (desirable) changes to mind-set there were came later. Similarly, at a small-scale level of just two people reconciliation intuitively is possible despite an absence of shared pride, altruistic motivation, and the like.

Hence, if reconciliation were a stepping stone towards a society of full-blown communion, then it would be plausible to think of it as consisting mainly of the behavioural facets of identity and solidarity, and not requiring all the emotional and motivational ones. Of course, people's hearts and minds would need to change to *some* degree in order to move from a conflict-ridden society — that is, one of division and ill-will, or enmity — to one with the core, behavioural components of identity and solidarity as noted previously.

However, they would need to do so to a much lesser degree than they would in order, say, to be motivated by altruism or compassion or to feel a sense of togetherness with former opponents.

Now, since prizing or honouring a final value such as communion is not merely a matter of promoting it, but also expressing certain positive attitudes towards it, reconciliation will plausibly involve *something* attitudinal. Specifically, if agents are to prize communal relationships, then an attractive notion of reconciliation would be one that acknowledges when they have been flouted. That will involve at least public institutions, if not offenders in the first instance, expressing disapproval of the grave injustice, the love of enmity, as it were.

Although sometimes people who have fought and who have been treated wrongly are able to come together and repair the relationship without thinking in terms of wrongdoing, or at least not expressing themselves in those terms, my suggestion is that, in cases of gross and large-scale wrongdoing, such so-called reconciliation is not particularly desirable. To honour communion means acknowledging when it has been seriously undermined in impermissible ways, and to treat people as special in virtue of their capacity for communion means responding to them in the light of the way they have greatly misused this capacity.

Putting these two ideas together, I proffer the following principled statement of what national reconciliation is:

> *a condition consequent to serious social conflict in which a country's residents interact on a largely voluntary, transparent, and trustworthy basis for the sake of compossible ends largely oriented towards doing what will help one another and in which at least public institutions, if not also substantial numbers of the public and the offenders themselves, disavow grave wrongdoing that had been a part of the conflict.*

This account should seem *prima facie* attractive, but in the following section I work to bring out its explanatory power.

APPLYING THE THEORY

In this section, my aims are to shed light on several aspects of national reconciliation and to demonstrate the ability of the principle advanced in the previous section to provide compelling accounts of them. I explore eight different facets of discourse about reconciliation, arguing that the Afro-communal view provides a unified and plausible explanation of them. By the end of the section, a powerful theory of national reconciliation will have emerged.[5]

Peace, Order, Rule of Law

It is a given that reconciliation requires, and is even by definition constituted by, the cessation of serious conflict. It is interaction that comes after civil war and related forms of enmity. It therefore is instantiated by the presence of peace, law, and order, and, some would add, democratic institutions.

By the Afro-communal conception, national reconciliation includes such conditions, but is far from exhausted in them; reconciliation merely as the achievement of institutional stability is 'too little.' Since social conflict is well understood in terms of people seeking to undermine one another's goal-seeking and to harm each other — that is, the opposites of the behavioural facets of community in the African tradition — the centrality of peace is easily accounted for by the present principle prescribing cooperation and mutual aid. However, the way that the Constitutional Court of South Africa (2009) has sometimes thinly understood reconciliation, as more or less a matter of establishing the 'proper rule of law' and 'strengthening peace, democracy and justice' (para. 21; but cf. para. 56), fails to capture much of what counts as reconciliation, in at least two respects.

First, reconciliation plausibly involves peace not merely in the sense of the absence of conflict, but also in Thomas Hobbes's (1651: ch. 13) understanding of it as the absence of a tendency towards it. To have reconciled means that the public by and large has a reasonable expectation that conflict will not arise again, and does not significantly act out of fear of such.

Second, if reconciliation were merely the achievement of peace, order, the rule of law, and even related conditions such as democracy, then South Africa, for instance, would be a fully reconciled society, or at least nearly so. However, most in South Africa would deny that claim; there is still much reconciliation to be achieved among different racial groups. It is common, here, to point to stark economic inequalities (e.g., de Gruchy, 2002: 195, 200–201; Mgxashe, 2000) as glaring evidence of a lack of reconciliation. One could also add, among other things, the clannishness of various groups, by which I mean the tendency not to trust others not of one's race and instead to favour one's own when making appointments, exchanges, friends, and the like.

One proper task of a TRC is to help 'normalise' dealings between groups so that they are willing, say, to make economic exchanges, to deliberate together in the media about legislation, and to engage in academic study with one another. A commission can and should promote such relationships by expressing the state's intention that from now on things will be done differently, exhorting members of the populace to go out of their way to engage with one another, and encouraging by example, for instance, by showing leaders of conflicting groups speaking to one another and expressing a commitment to work to build something new.

Emotions[6]

Some might suggest that another salient respect in which South Africa, for instance, is not fully reconciled is that people's emotions are still negative; they are often ones of anger, resentment, bitterness and disappointment. According to some, 'the essence of reconciliation is a psychological process, which consists of changes of the motivations, goals, beliefs, attitudes, and emotions of the majority of society members' (Bar-Tal and Bennink, 2004: 17). In particular, some would suggest that reconciliation consists of replacing negative emotions with 'positive attitudes' towards others (Bar-Tal and Bennink, 2004: 15; see also Govier, 2009a), perhaps ones in which one 'feels a sense of belonging' with others, 'embracing . . . those who are different' (Hamber and Kelly, 2009: 292), or in which 'others are not seen in merely instrumental terms' (du Bois and du Bois-Pedain, 2008: 302). These are of course desirable conditions, and, indeed, are part of the sub-Saharan ideal of communion. But are they essential to national reconciliation?

I view reconciliation as a mere stepping stone to the realisation of fully communal relationships, and, so, as I have indicated previously, I suspect that conceiving of reconciliation as *requiring*, let alone *consisting of*, positive emotions (and related attitudes) is expecting 'too much' of this category. Recall the example of two individuals who have had a fight, talked openly about what happened, and are now engaging in joint projects and doing what they expect will be good for one another. Even if they continued to have lingering negative emotions, my intuition is that they can be said to have reconciled if they are 'going about their business' in ways that are cooperative and involve mutual aid. If these two also took pride in one another's activities and felt compassion for each other, these would be manifestations of a new category of value, such as full-blown friendship or communion, and not mere reconciliation. (Or, at most, I suggest they would be instances of a much *better* or *thicker* instance of reconciliation, but not necessary for reconciliation *simpliciter*.) Similar remarks apply at the political level.

Although some dissipation of anger, achievement of closure, and the like are *usually instrumental* for reconciliation to occur, what I deny is that they are essential to it. I accept that it is often the case that one could not have reconciliation without some emotional change, and yet I deny that reconciliation is well understood as *consisting* of it.

Forgiveness

One might still reasonably suspect that my account of reconciliation leaves out too much when it comes to people's mental states. In particular, forgiveness lies at the heart of national reconciliation not only for many whose views are grounded on the Christian tradition (e.g., de Gruchy, 2002: 170, 178–79; Helmick and Petersen, 2001; Tutu, 1999; 2009), but also for a notable number of those who do not appeal to any religious perspective (e.g., Bar-Tal and Bennink, 2004: 19; May, 2011: 589–90; Philpott, 2009; cf. Auerbach, 2004). I therefore devote a separate subsection to accounting for the exact relationship between the two ideas, advancing what I suspect are some underrecognised reasons to believe that forgiveness is not essential to reconciliation (but cf. Govier, 2009a: 14).[7]

I want, as much as I can, to avoid the tricky issue of how forgiveness is to be understood; I do not thoroughly address what it precisely is.[8] However, if it is plausibly construed, it is reasonable to think it has some kind of close tie to reconciliation. I here provide additional reason to think that it is not constitutive of reconciliation, and instead related insofar as it can be a reliable cause of it.

Now, the most straightforward way of trying to show that reconciliation does not require forgiveness would be to show that it can instead come consequent to mere forgetfulness. Suppose that among two people who had been fighting, the victim elects simply to forget, as opposed to forgive. That is, imagine that he simply succeeds in putting out of mind what had happened, instead of continuing to be aware of the wrongdoing and evincing a forgiving disposition towards the wrongdoer. Having removed the offending events from his awareness, he then engages in cooperative projects involving mutual aid with the offender. It seems that one could fairly conclude that reconciliation without forgiveness is possible, even somewhat common.

Although this is a tempting manoeuvre, it is not one that I can dialectically invoke since, as I discuss next, the Afro-communal principle of reconciliation implies that it is a process that includes knowing the truth about the past. A proper form of reconciliation, informed by the sub-Saharan conception of communion, is one in which people come together consequent to an awareness of the wrongdoing that has occurred between them.

At this point, I could suggest that a desirable form of reconciliation would be possible if the victim and offender first became clear about what had transpired between them, the victim then elected to forget about it all rather than forgive, and then both engaged in the relevant behavioural changes. Perhaps that works to establish my point.

Here, though, is another rationale for thinking that forgiveness is not necessary for reconciliation, one that does not appeal to the idea that reconciliation could come upon the victim forgetting the wrong done to him. I accept that *part of* forgiveness is essential to reconciliation to the extent that forgiveness by definition involves the absence of an inclination to inflict harm or to rebut another's end-seeking. Since reconciliation by the African view is roughly a matter of cooperation and mutual aid, there must not be a behavioural tendency to engage in the opposites on the part of the victim. However, I maintain that forgiveness *as such* is not necessary for reconciliation since forgiveness is invariably understood to be more than merely a change in behaviour. Forgiveness plausibly also involves an emotional element such as 'a changed view of the wrongdoer as a person in which you cease to have towards her the personal retributive reactive attitudes that her wrongdoing supports, without a change in judgement about her responsibility for the wrong' (Allais, 2008: 57). Whatever extra element that forgiveness includes beyond the letting go of conflict, it is something that is not essential to reconciliation. To see this, return once again to a case of two persons. Imagine that the victim remains fully aware of the wrong done to him (instead of forgets), that the victim and wrongdoer have had it out about what transpired, perhaps with the latter apologizing, that the victim and wrongdoer then successfully embark on cooperative projects involving mutual aid, but that the victim continues to harbour negative emotions towards the wrongdoer. He just cannot shake a feeling of resentment, at least for a long while. To the extent there is the latter condition, there is an absence of forgiveness. However, I submit that the two parties are plausibly described as having reconciled; for there is at least the *commitment* to (more fully) commune (cf. Villa-Vicencio, 2009: 154). What applies to a case of two individuals would seem to apply to a case involving two large groups.

Of course, it will sometimes be the case that the change in behaviour could not come about without a prior or accompanying change of mind. Many times, then, forgiveness will be a particularly fruitful means to reconciliation — but not always, not necessarily. And it is of course also true that the offender might well want more than merely a change in behaviour on the part of the victim, and in addition to be viewed in a positive light. However, emotional change is usually hard to come by in the short to medium term after conflict and therefore is not so clearly a matter of reconciliation, a basic form of which can, in contrast, often be expected in that timeframe.

Listening to Victims

Central to most people's thoughts about national reconciliation is the hearing out of victims. It is not enough that, say, a scholar interviews victims and reports on what they said in a professional journal. Instead, a crucial part of reconciliation is a process by which, in the ideal case, offenders listen to their victims, and, failing that, some kind of public body does so. A satisfactory theory of national reconciliation must entail and plausibly explain why this is so.

Notice that it will not do to appeal to the value of truth here. Of course, one way to access the truth about the nature of the social conflict would be to listen to victims. However, it appears that the historical facts could also be ascertained behind the scenes by academic interviews that are then published in scholarly forums and newspapers as well. While an interest in truth supports the idea of listening to victims, it does not uniquely do so.

To make sense of why it is important that victims address specific people, such as their offenders or the public in general, one must appeal to something beyond the content of what victims have to recount. For instance, in South Africa, a common explanation given of why victims needed to be heard, by offenders or by the TRC, has been that it would help them to achieve catharsis and obtain closure, which, in turn would enable them to move forward to create a peaceful and democratic order (see, e.g., Constitutional Court of South Africa, 2010). In short, it is not just what victims have to say, but the fact that they say it to a certain audience, that promises to produce a desirable outcome.

Such a rationale might be part of the reason to hear out victims, but it cannot be all of it. Suppose, for instance, that such an order could have been created without listening to victims, as basically happened in Chile and Argentina. Or consider a case in which it has already been created, but not all victims have yet been heard; there would be reason to continue to listen to the remaining victims, despite large-scale nation building proceeding on track. Similar remarks apply even if the broader sociobehavioural facets of reconciliation — that is, cooperation and mutual aid — are considered.

Another reason that reconciliation plausibly requires victims to be heard, beyond the content of what they have to say, is that it is a way for the public, and in the ideal case offenders, to disavow the injustice that was done. Recall that honouring communion means expressing disapproval of when it is egregiously undermined. For offenders to take responsibility for their misdeeds and to express contrition for what they have done requires being willing to undergo the discomfort of hearing how one has wrongfully harmed others. And for a public institution such as a TRC, to disavow injustice means coming closer to victims, while tending to distance itself from offenders, where coming closer to victims naturally involves listening to the way they were mistreated and, as I now discuss, offering assistance.

Compensation

Another core element of national reconciliation is the attempt to help victims overcome their plight. Offenders themselves should offer restitution to their victims, or at least express an apology with the aim of easing psychological burdens. And where offenders are unwilling to do that, or unable to cover the extent of victim suffering, it is common to hold that the state ought to step in and use public funds to help compensate victims.

The Afro-communal conception of reconciliation naturally accounts for these judgements. If hearing out victims is a way for offenders to disavow their misdeeds, then so is offering victims resources to help make up for their losses. When considering what it is that should be offered to victims, it is natural to consider what was taken away in the first place. If land was stolen, then there is strong *prima facie* reason to think that land should be returned. However, there can be considerations favouring the offer of something other than repayment in kind for what was unjustly taken. National reconciliation is a process that takes time, and the kind of compensation offered should ideally be one that supports an ongoing improvement in the extent to which there is cooperation and mutual aid between formerly antagonistic groups.

For instance, in South Africa, an interest in national reconciliation probably did not, all things considered, prescribe an *immediate* large-scale transfer of farmland and mineral wealth from whites to blacks in the mid-1990s.[9] The reason is that whites have primarily been the ones with the skills and knowledge to run farms and mines, and it is well known in South Africa that a very large majority of what little transfers of farmland have been made so far had (at least until recently) become unproductive. Those who suffered under apartheid, and their descendants, would be unlikely to be better off were South Africa to be no longer able to feed itself or to extract the minerals in an efficient manner. In this context, the right sort of compensation was not merely the return of land, but also the transfer of the ability to make use of it, which would have taken some time (had it been attempted systematically). Or it might have been to provide resources that would enable black people to flourish in urban areas, should they prefer that kind of support.

A commission can help to facilitate compensation for those who have been particularly wrongfully harmed by the conflict. It can identify the latter, for one, and it can make sensible recommendations about who precisely should take responsibility for working to make up for their losses. Sometimes it should recommend that specific wrongdoers be the ones to do so, a particularly welcome form of reconciliation in which wrongdoers would also be disavowing their wrongdoing by working to make restitution to their victims. However, national reconciliation would also be fostered if those not responsible for wrongful harm pitched in to improve the lot of victims, something a commission is in a position to recommend, as South Africa's TRC did when it advised the government to pay a certain amount of public tax money to some individual victims of political crimes.

Truth

Another key facet of national reconciliation, or at least a desirable form of it, is the search for, and dissemination of, truth about the social conflict that occurred. As I now point out, salient accounts of how truth relates to reconciliation conceive of it instrumentally, as something that fosters reconciliation in the long run. In contrast, the theory I support entails that reconciliation is partially constituted by obtaining the truth about the past. From this perspective, to speak of 'truth and reconciliation,' as per some influential commissions, is ultimately redundant, as the right sort of reconciliation itself includes truth.

Why think that reconciliation, properly conceived, requires digging up the truth about the past? Why not just 'move forward,' rather than stir up negative memories and emotions, as many white people in South Africa have favoured? The standard answer to these questions in the South African context has been that victims can move forward only upon expressing themselves, being heard and releasing negative feelings.

However, while this might be a plausible rationale for listening to victims, it is not a particularly good one for a mandate to get at the truth, which would require much more than obtaining the perspectives of victims. Offenders' stories, too, would add to the truth, as would more impersonal and dry enquiries such as forensic investigations into gravesites and academic scholarship about the negative influences of social conflict on institutions, relationships and opportunities. While the latter kinds of information might help to foster solace and closure on the part of victims, including ones who were not direct victims of political crimes, they might not. Even if victims had already obtained solace, or even if they never would obtain it, reconciliation intuitively would demand obtaining clarity about what transpired between conflicting groups. This is one way to grasp a recurrent criticism of South Africa's TRC, that it focused mainly on crimes done to individuals, and did not also highlight evidence of more collective wrongdoing and its foreseeable effects.

According to the theory of national reconciliation that I favour, accurate and comprehensive historical awareness is partially constitutive of national reconciliation. Part of genuinely *sharing* a way of life among formerly antagonistic groups, which includes the idea of cooperative behaviour between them, is acting consequent to knowledge of what has happened between them. That means not merely the absence of deception, but also the revelation of truth.

If one has a serious fight with one's spouse, reconciliation of a desirable sort would involve clearing the air. It would mean that both parties listen to one another, and that they move forward in the light of a clear understanding of what happened, or at least of the various perspectives about what did. A genuine sort of reconciliation would not sweep the fight under the rug. Analogous remarks apply at the political level.

One might question the analogy in that it appears merely to require both parties to the conflict to be heard, and not to support the more academic and scientific enquiries that I maintain are central to national reconciliation. However, upon reflection, the analogy is strong. Couples rarely have access to a third party who has the time, resources, and interest to comment on what happened between them. However, sometimes they do, and when they do, a welcome form of reconciliation would involve taking such a perspective into account. For instance, if a couple has been seeing a counsellor, one would expect the pair to bring up the issue of the fight with her, and to be open to her opinion about what caused the conflict and how it has likely affected a given party. An ideal kind of reconciliation is one in which those who for a time exhibited enmity towards each other seek to get to the bottom of things. To the extent that one party attempts to hide things, or one party fails to acknowledge things, or both parties close their eyes to the input of a sympathetic and informed observer, there is less of a shared way of life, less reconciliation, than there could and should have been.

Orientation towards the Guilty

A possible sort of reconciliation is one in which there is no thought of wrongdoing, or at least no talk of it, or no censure for it. However, it would not be a plausible sort, at least by the Afro-communal account, which includes the requirement of disavowing injustice, ideally on the part of offenders, and at least on the part of public institutions.[10]

Here is one respect in which I believe the South African Constitutional Court (2009) has judged correctly about national reconciliation, when it says the latter must not be understood as permitting the guilty to receive 'the lion's share of benefits' or as requiring the state 'to ameliorate hardship for the perpetrators of human rights abuses' (pp. 53, 55). If reconciliation did not include judgements of culpable wrongdoing, then guilty parties would have no less of a claim to the receipt of benefits and the lifting of burdens as their victims. For instance, it would apparently mean that, say, a state should allow neither a newspaper to call a perpetrator of an atrocity a 'murderer' (see Constitutional Court of South Africa, 2011), nor an organisation, such as the police force, to take into account a person's political-criminal past when deciding to hire or fire (Constitutional Court of South Africa, 2009).

Although such a neutral approach would of course provide the utmost encouragement to the guilty to participate in so-called reconciliatory processes, it would come at the expense of a failure to adequately respect the value of communion, which, as per above, requires taking account of when this value has been seriously undermined. A better sort of reconciliation is surely one in which offenders themselves acknowledge their wrongdoing, apologise for it, and contribute to making victims better off because of what they have done, and in which, at least if offenders are unwilling to do these things, public institutions step in to stand by victims.

A commission would be well positioned to assist with the public disavowal element. It would have become accurately and comprehensively informed about the wrongdoing, and might itself express disapproval of it on behalf of the government or the new society more generally. In addition, it could furnish other public institutions, particularly the executive branch of government, but also, for instance, universities and accrediting bodies, the grounds for further expressions of disapproval.

Amnesty

In the previous two subsections, I indicated that the Afro-communal conception of national reconciliation implies that the truth about the past as well as disavowal of injustice are both inherent to it. However, as is well known, one cannot expect these two desiderata to be maximally jointly fulfilled. In order to get substantial truth from offenders about their unjust behaviour, a state often must reduce the extent to which it otherwise would have responded negatively to them.

This point must not be taken to be a strike against the present understanding of national reconciliation; in fact, I submit just the opposite is true. It is a plus for the Afro-communal view that it plausibly accounts in a new way for a widely recognised tension in reflection about national reconciliation. It explains the tension not in terms of any conditions external to reconciliation, as, say, between truth and justice, but rather as intrinsic to reconciliation itself. A *fully* reconciled society would be one in which there is *both* a completely accurate picture of the nature of the conflict *and* a systematic disavowal of the extent to which that conflict was unjust. Although such a state of affairs is possible, it is not likely to obtain, and achieving the most reconciliation that a given society can along the two dimensions requires careful judgement about how much to trade off disavowal for the sake of truth.

One salient strategy by which to balance these two elements of reconciliation has been to offer amnesties to offenders in exchange for full disclosure about their misdeeds, as was done by South Africa's TRC. Sensitivity to context will determine whether amnesty, and which sort, is necessary to obtain an adequate amount of truth from offenders.

I have sought here to unify several concepts routinely associated with thought about national reconciliation by providing a principle that purports to capture its essential nature. According to this view, reconciliation is a condition consequent to serious social conflict in which a country's residents interact on a largely voluntary, transparent, and trustworthy basis for the sake of compossible ends largely oriented towards doing what will help one another and in which at least public institutions, if not also substantial numbers of the public and the offenders themselves, disavow grave wrongdoing that had been a part of the conflict. I have spelled out this principle, demonstrated that it follows from a *prima facie* attractive communal ethic informed by sub-Saharan values, and argued that it plausibly accounts for myriad practises such as truth-telling, forgiving, listening to victims, offering amnesty, and the like.

I have lacked the space to defend this theory of national reconciliation systematically against those who would question it. On the one hand, there will be those who doubt the theory because they reject one of its implications, say, that forgiveness is not essential to reconciliation. On the other hand, there will be critics who favour alternate theories (see esp. Murphy, 2010; Philpott, 2012). I have hoped in this chapter merely to articulate a new theory grounded on Afro-communal values and to show that it is attractive enough to merit rigorous comparison with rival perspectives in future work.[11]

NOTES

1. A revision version of what originally appeared in *Theorizing Transitional Justice* (2015), edited by Claudio Corradetti, Nir Eisikovits, and Jack Rotondi, 119–35. Farnham: Ashgate. Reprinted with permission from Ashgate.

2. There are of course also those who reject reconciliation as something illiberal, too (e.g., Ash, 1997), or as otherwise asking way too much of a state or its people (Gerwel, 2000).

3. This is an explicit element of the manifesto of Julius Malema's new party intended to rival the African National Congress (Economic Freedom Fighters, 2013: para. 29, 35).

4. I first articulated this conception of national reconciliation in Metz (2011a) and applied it to the issue of amnesty for political crimes; I did not there analyse the concept of reconciliation in general or apply my favoured conception of it to a wide array of issues beyond amnesty.

5. In the following I do not address what Murphy (2010) maintains is a core desideratum for a theory of national reconciliation, namely, the ability to plausibly explain

when and why it is called for. However, appealing to the African ethic, my explanation would be founded on the idea that national reconciliation is apt in response to systematic, extreme unfriendliness or enmity between social groups, an account that readily captures the routine description of those in need of reconciliation as 'enemies.'

6. In this chapter I do not address the relationship between belief change and reconciliation (beyond apprehension of facts about the past), though acknowledge that it merits addressing in a fuller statement (cf. de Gruchy, 2002: 152–53; Bar-Tal and Bennink, 2004: 21–22; du Bois and du Bois-Pedain, 2008; Eisikovits, 2010).

7. Often those who reject forgiveness as essential to national reconciliation have worries about whether it is a realistic and permissible goal for a state to pursue.

8. I am sympathetic to the account in Allais (2008).

9. Here I draw on ideas first published in Metz (2011b: 551–54).

10. While Bashir (2008) is good about highlighting the idea that reconciliation centrally involves the revelation of truth about misdeeds and the censure of them, I am afraid that he appears to reduce reconciliation to these conditions alone.

11. I am thankful that Lucy Allais, Alex Broadbent and Nir Eisikovits took the time to read an earlier draft and to offer supportive comments. This chapter has also benefited from the input of audiences at a colloquium sponsored by the University of Johannesburg Philosophy Department and at a workshop to honour the jurisprudence of former Constitutional Court of South Africa Chief Justice Sandile Ngcobo organised by Drucilla Cornell's Ubuntu Project at the University of Pretoria School of Law.

REFERENCES

Aja, Egbeke. (1997). 'Crime and Punishment: An Indigenous African Experience.' *Journal of Value Inquiry* 31: 353–68.

Alie, Joe (2008). 'Reconciliation and Traditional Justice.' In *Traditional Justice and Reconciliation after Violent Conflict: Learning from African Experiences*, edited by Luc Huyse and Mark Salter, 123–45. Stockholm: International Institute for Democracy and Electoral Assistance.

Allais, Lucy. (2008). 'Wiping the Slate Clean.' *Philosophy and Public Affairs* 36: 33–68.

Ash, Timothy Garton. (1997). 'True Confessions.' *New York Review of Books* 17 July: 33–38.

Auerbach, Yehudith (2004). 'The Role of Forgiveness in Reconciliation.' In *From Conflict Resolution to Reconciliation*, edited by Yaacov Bar-Siman-Tov, 149–75. Oxford: Oxford University Press.

Barkan, Elazar, and Karn, Alexander, eds. (2006). *Taking Wrongs Seriously: Apologies and Reconciliation.* Stanford, CA: Stanford University Press.

Bar-Tal, Daniel, and Bennink, Gemma. (2004). 'The Nature of Reconciliation as an Outcome and as a Process.' In *From Conflict Resolution to Reconciliation*, edited by Yaacov Bar-Siman-Tov, 11–38. Oxford: Oxford University Press.

Bashir, Bashir. (2008). 'Accommodating History Oppressed Groups: Deliberative Democracy and the Politics of Reconciliation.' In *The Politics of Reconciliation in Multicultural Societies*, edited by Bashir Bashir and Will Kymlicka, 48–69. Oxford: Oxford University Press.

Constitutional Court of South Africa. (2009). *Du Toit v Minister for Safety and Security and Another* (CCT91/08) 2009 ZACC 22.

Constitutional Court of South Africa. (2010). *Albutt v Centre for the Study of Violence and Reconciliation and Others* (CCT 54/09) 2010 ZACC 4.

Constitutional Court of South Africa. (2011). *The Citizen (1978) (Pty) Ltd & Others v Robert John McBride* (CCT 23/10) 2011 ZACC 11.

Crocker, David. (2002). 'Punishment, Reconciliation, and Democratic Deliberation.' *Buffalo Criminal Law Review* 5: 509–49.

de Gruchy, John (2002). *Reconciliation: Restoring Justice.* Minneapolis: Fortress Press.

du Bois, François, and du Bois-Pedain, Antje. (2008). 'Post-Conflict Justice and the Reconciliation Paradigm.' In *Justice and Reconciliation in Post-Apartheid South Africa*, edited by François du Bois and Antje du Bois-Pedain, 289–311. Cambridge: Cambridge University Press.

Dwyer, Susan. (1999). 'Reconciliation for Realists.' *Ethics and International Affairs* 13: 81–98.

Economic Freedom Fighters. (2013). *Founding Manifesto of the Economic Freedom Fighters.* Available at http://www.politicsweb.co.za/politicsweb/view/politicsweb/en/page71619?oid=393903&sn=Detail.

Eisikovits, Nir. (2010). *Sympathizing with the Enemy: Reconciliation, Transitional Justice, Negotiation.* Dordrecht: Martinus Nijhoff Publishers.

Gerwel, Jakes. (2000). 'National Reconciliation.' In *Looking Back Reaching Forward: Reflections on the Truth and Reconciliation Commission of South Africa*, edited by Charles Villa-Vicencio and Wilhelm Verwoerd, 277–86. Cape Town: University of Cape Town Press.

Govier, Trudy. (2009a). 'The Concept of Reconciliation.' In *Taking Wrongs Seriously: Apologies and Reconciliation*, edited by Elazar Barkan and Alexander Karn, 9–25. Amherst, NY: Humanity Books.

Govier, Trudy. (2009b). 'A Dialectic of Acknowledgment.' In *Reconciliation(s)*, edited by Joanna Quinn, 36–50. Montreal: McGill-Queen's University Press.

Gutmann, Amy, and Thompson, Dennis. (2000). 'The Moral Foundations of Truth Commissions.' In *Truth v. Justice: The Morality of Truth Commissions*, edited by Robert Rotberg and Dennis Thompson, 22–44. Princeton, NJ: Princeton University Press.

Gyekye, Kwame (2004). *Beyond Cultures*. Washington, DC: Council for Research in Values and Philosophy.

Hamber, Brandon, and Kelly, Gráinne. (2009). 'Beyond Coexistence: Towards a Working Definition of Reconciliation.' In *Reconciliation(s)*, edited by Joanna Quinn, 286–310. Montreal: McGill-Queen's University Press.

Helmick, Raymond, and Petersen, Rodney, eds. (2001). *Forgiveness and Reconciliation.* London: Templeton Foundation Press.

234

Thaddeus Metz

Hermann, Tamar. (2004). 'Reconciliation: Reflections on the Theoretical and Practical Utility of the Term.' In *From Conflict Resolution to Reconciliation*, edited by Yaacov Bar-Siman-Tov, 39–60. Oxford: Oxford University Press.

Hobbes, Thomas. (1651). *Leviathan*. Available at: http://archive.org/details/hobbessleviathan00hobbuoft.

Hughes, Paul. (2001). 'Moral Atrocity and Political Reconciliation.' *International Journal of Applied Philosophy* 15: 123–33.

Huyse, Luc. (2008a). 'Introduction: Tradition-based Approaches in Peace-making, Transitional Justice and Reconciliation Policies.' In *Traditional Justice and Reconciliation after Violent Conflict: Learning from African Experiences*, edited by Luc Huyse and Mark Salter, 1–20. Stockholm: International Institute for Democracy and Electoral Assistance.

Huyse, Luc (2008b). 'Conclusions and Recommendations.' In *Traditional Justice and Reconciliation after Violent Conflict: Learning from African Experiences*, edited by Luc Huyse and Mark Salter, 181–98. Stockholm: International Institute for Democracy and Electoral Assistance.

Ikuenobe, Polycarp. (2006). *Philosophical Perspectives on Communalism and Morality in African Traditions*. Lanham, MD: Lexington Books.

Iroegbu, Pantaleon. (2005). 'Beginning, Purpose and End of Life.' In *Kpim of Morality Ethics*, edited by Pantaleon Iroegbu and Anthony Echekwube, 440–45. Ibadan: Heinemann Educational Books.

Krog, Antjie. (1998). *Country of My Skull*. Johannesburg: Random House.

Krog, Antjie. (2008). ' "This Thing Called Reconciliation . . ."; Forgiveness as Part of an Interconnectedness-towards-Wholeness.' *South African Journal of Philosophy* 27: 353–66.

Masolo, Dismas. (2010). *Self and Community in a Changing World*. Bloomington: Indiana University Press.

May, Simon Cabulea. (2011). 'Moral Compromise, Civic Friendship, and Political Reconciliation.' *Critical Review of International Social and Political Philosophy* 14: 581–602.

Metz, Thaddeus. (2011a). 'Limiting the Reach of Amnesty for Political Crimes.' *Constitutional Court Review* 3: 243–70.

Metz, Thaddeus. (2011b). '*Ubuntu* as a Moral Theory and Human Rights in South Africa.' *African Human Rights Law Journal* 11: 532–559.

Metz, Thaddeus. (2017a). 'An Overview of African Ethics.' In *Themes, Issues and Problems in African Philosophy*, edited by Isaac Ukpokolo, 61–75. London: Palgrave Macmillan.

Metz, Thaddeus. (2017b). 'Toward an African Moral Theory, Revised Edition.' In *Themes, Issues and Problems in African Philosophy*, edited by Isaac Ukpokolo, 97–119. London: Palgrave Macmillan.

Metz, Thaddeus, and Gaie, Joseph. (2010). 'The African Ethic of *Ubuntu/Botho*: Implications for Research on Morality.' *Journal of Moral Education* 39: 273–90.

Mgxashe, Mxolisi (2000). 'Reconciliation: A Call to Action.' In *Looking Back Reaching Forward: Reflections on the Truth and Reconciliation Commission of*

South Africa, edited by Charles Villa-Vicencio and Wilhelm Verwoerd, 210–218. Cape Town: University of Cape Town Press.

Moellendorf, Darrel. (2007). 'Reconciliation as a Political Value.' *Journal of Social Philosophy* 38: 205–21.

Moosa, Ebrahim. (2000). 'Truth and Reconciliation as Performance.' In *Looking Back Reaching Forward: Reflections on the Truth and Reconciliation Commission of South Africa*, edited by Charles Villa-Vicencio and Wilhelm Verwoerd, 113–122. Cape Town: University of Cape Town Press.

Murphy, Colleen. (2010). *A Moral Theory of Political Reconciliation.* Cambridge: Cambridge University Press.

Murphy, Colleen. (2013). 'Reconciliation.' In *The International Encyclopedia of Ethics*, edited by Hugh LaFollette, 4451–59. Malden, MA: Blackwell.

Nkondo, Gessler Muxe. (2007). 'Ubuntu as a Public Policy in South Africa.' *International Journal of African Renaissance Studies* 2: 88–100.

Philpott, Daniel. (2009). 'An Ethic of Political Reconciliation.' *Ethics and International Affairs* 23: 389–407.

Philpott, Daniel. (2012). *Just and Unjust Peace: An Ethic of Political Reconciliation.* New York: Oxford University Press.

Sandel, Michael. (1984). 'The Procedural Republic and the Unencumbered Self.' *Political Theory* 12: 81–96.

Quinn, Joanna. (2009). 'What of Reconciliation?' In *Reconciliation(s)*, edited by Joanna Quinn, 174–206. Montreal: McGill-Queen's University Press.

Tutu, Desmond. (1999). *No Future without Forgiveness*. New York: Random House.

Tutu, Desmond. (2009). 'Foreword.' In *Walk with Us and Listen: Political Reconciliation in Africa*, edited by Charles Villa-Vicencio, ix–xii. Cape Town: University of Cape Town Press.

Villa-Vicencio, Charles. (2000). 'Getting On with Life: A Move towards Reconciliation.' In *Looking Back Reaching Forward: Reflections on the Truth and Reconciliation Commission of South Africa*, edited by Charles Villa-Vicencio and Wilhelm Verwoerd, 199–209. Cape Town: University of Cape Town Press.

Villa-Vicencio, Charles. (2009). *Walk with Us and Listen: Political Reconciliation in Africa*. Cape Town: University of Cape Town Press.

Walzer, Michael. (1983). *Spheres of Justice*. New York: Basic Books.

Index

About the Contributors

Klaus Bachmann is professor of political science at the University of Social Sciences and Humanities in Warsaw, Poland. Formerly, he was affiliated to the University of Vienna, Bordeaux, Stellenbosch and Wroclaw, as well as to Renmin University, Beijing, and Johns Hopkins University (at the American Center for Contemporary German Studies in Washington, D.C.). He concentrates on transitional justice, international criminal law and EU Treaty reform. He recently published, with Aleksandar Fatić, *The UN International Criminal Tribunals: Transition without Justice* (2015) and *Genocidal Empires: German Colonialism in Africa and the Third Reich* (2018).

Cătălin-Nicolae Constantinescu works as a legal adviser for the Institute for the Investigation of Communist Crimes and Memory of the Romanian Exile. He is a PhD candidate in criminal law at the University of Bucharest, where he is also a teaching assistant in General Theory of the Law. Prior to that he worked for the Centre for the Investigation of Communist Crimes in Romania and volunteered for or coordinated various projects on similar topics. His domains of interest include domestic and international criminal law, human rights and transitional justice.

Aleksandar Fatić is professor of philosophy at the Institute for Philosophy and Social Theory, University of Belgrade, Serbia. Aleksandar leads a project on Collective Memory and Identity and is president of the Serbian Association of Philosophical Practitioners. He specialises in applied ethics and philosophy of conflict. His most recent monographs include *Virtue and Identity: Emotions and the Moral Personality* (2016) and, with Klaus Bachmann, *The UN International Criminal Tribunals: Transition without Justice?* (2015).

Thomas Hancocks is a teaching fellow based at the IDEA CETL at the University of Leeds. He was recently awarded his PhD from the University of Leeds for his thesis *Transitional Justice, Punishment and Security*, which explored the moral issues surrounding periods of transitional justice and democratisation. At present, his research is concerned with core problems at the intersection of ethics and the law. This includes the problem of political legitimacy and the legitimacy of law-making, the concept of the rule of law and the ethics of legal punishment.

Igor Lyubashenko is assistant professor at the University of Social Sciences and Humanities in Warsaw, Poland. He holds a PhD in political science from the Maria Curie-Sklodowska University in Lublin. His current academic interests focus on different aspects of transition to democracy in postcommunist states (in particular Poland and Ukraine). His latest research is devoted to transitional justice. He is the author of the monograph *Transitional Justice in Post-Euromaidan Ukraine: Swimming Upstream*, and principal investigator in the research project "Application of Transitional Justice Mechanisms in Ongoing Armed Conflict."

Adrian Mandzy is associate professor of History at Morehead State University (Morehead, Kentucky). A Fulbright Scholar, Professor Mandzy has spent the last twenty years studying former fields of conflict in Ukraine and the United States. His body of work includes studies of the Siege of Zbarazh (1649) and the Battles of Zboriv (1649), Poltava (1709), Blue Licks (1782), the Crater at Petersburg (1864), Makivka (1915), Lysonia (1916), and Kosmach (1945). His most recent monograph, cowritten with Bo Knarrstrom and J. P. Nilsson, is *Poltava, Karl XII:s karoliner och stormaktens undergang* (2017).

Thaddeus Metz is currently distinguished professor at the University of Johannesburg (2015–2019), where he is affiliated with the Department of Philosophy. Author of more than two hundred published works, he is particularly known for having analytically articulated an African moral theory, applied it to a variety of ethical and political controversies, compared it to East Asian and Western moral perspectives and defended it as preferable to them. His book, *A Relational Moral Theory: African Contributions to Global Ethics*, is expected to appear in 2019.

Mrdjan Mladjan is assistant professor of financial economics at EBS Business School in Wiesbaden, Germany. He received his PhD in economics at the Universitat Pompeu Fabra (Spain) and holds a BSc in economics from the Massachusetts Institute of Technology. He teaches and researches at the intersection of finance, economics, history and philosophy, and in particular in the areas of the economics of financial crises, corporate finance and philosophy of economics.

Nataša Radovanović is senior police inspector, Serbian Police Directorate. A lawyer by training, she specialises in anti-organised crime methodology, especially criminal intelligence. She is a pioneer in criminal profiling and an expert in interpolice cooperation with a focus on organised crime as a transitional issue in Southeastern Europe.

Axelle Reiter is lecturer in Public International Law at the University of Verona in Vicenza, Italy. She is a lawyer working in the contested region of Kosovo, Serbia, and she is mainly interested in the application and limitations of the general principles of criminal law to issues of transitional criminal justice and war crimes.